TRADING SECRETS

3rd edition

Killer trading
strategies to beat
the markets and finally
achieve the success
you deserve

LOUISE BEDFORD

Wrightbooks

D1224600

Also by Louise Bedford

Charting Secrets
The Secret of Candlestick Charting
The Secret of Writing Options

This third edition first published in 2012 by Wrightbooks
an imprint of John Wiley & Sons Australia, Ltd
42 McDougall St, Milton Qld 4064

Office also in Melbourne

Typeset in Perpetua Std Regular 12.5/14pt

First edition published by Wrightbooks 2001

Second edition published by Wrightbooks 2005

© Louise Bedford 2012

The moral rights of the author have been asserted

National Library of Australia Cataloguing-in-Publication data:

Author:	Bedford, Louise.
Title:	Trading Secrets: Killer Trading Strategies to Beat the Markets and Finally Achieve the Success You Deserve/Louise Bedford.
Edition:	3rd ed.
ISBN:	9781118319260 (pbk.)
Notes:	Includes index.
Subjects:	Stocks—Australia.
	Speculation—Australia.
	Stock exchanges—Australia.
	Investments—Australia.
Dewey Number:	332.632280994

Cover design by David Riedy

SuperCharts version 4 © TradeStation Technologies, Inc. Reproduced with permission. All rights reserved.

Printed in China by Printplus Limited

10 9 8 7 6 5 4 3 2 1

Disclaimer

The material in this publication is of the nature of general comment only, and does not represent professional advice. It is not intended to provide specific guidance for particular circumstances and it should not be relied on as the basis for any decision to take action or not take action on any matter which it covers. Readers should obtain professional advice where appropriate, before making any such decision. To the maximum extent permitted by law, the author and publisher disclaim all responsibility and liability to any person, arising directly or indirectly from any person taking or not taking action based on the information in this publication.

Contents

Preface

Many years have passed since I wrote the first edition of *Trading Secrets*. When it came time to review the information I'd written all those years ago, I realised the old adage, 'Markets stay the same more than they change,' is still as true today as it has ever been. Sure, there are a few whiz-bang new tools, such as CFDs, and some new ways that I've learned to approach trading psychology, but, in essence, very little has changed since I first wrote *Trading Secrets*.

If you've read the previous editions, you'll notice the differences I'm sure. I've added extra information in several chapters to bring you the latest and greatest concepts and tools that the share trading world has to offer. I have also interwoven relevant concepts into the very fabric of each chapter to update and refresh the information previously presented. The structure of this book reflects the way I believe you should approach the market to maximise your chances of success. Setting your enterprise up as a professional business and understanding the role of trading psychology are two of the most important things you can do. For this reason, I have placed these topics at the very beginning of the book.

This book is separated into six separate parts, as detailed below.

Part I — Business secrets
This introduces you to some of the most important aspects of establishing your trading career. It discusses data and software requirements, some techniques to help you handle trading pressure and the more functional issue of when to quit your day job.

Part II — It takes all sorts

This section shows you that all types of people can succeed at the trading game. The market does not discriminate. It rewards people who have skill, regardless of their gender, age or experience.

Part III — Trading tools

You'll get into the meat of trading in this part of the book. By the end of this section, you'll be comfortable with charts, indicators and trend analysis.

Part IV — Trade management secrets

This is a major key to trading profitably. Trade management includes setting stop losses, position sizing so that you buy the correct number of shares, and measuring your performance.

Part V — Recession-smashing strategies

Knowing how to handle a downtrending bear market is incredibly useful. This part of the book aims to help you feel comfortable with tools such as CFDs, foreign exchange (FX), options and short selling so you know how to profit in any market condition.

Part VI — Words of wisdom

This part of the book focuses on showing you how to write a trading plan based on your own individual requirements.

If you are serious about learning how to trade effectively, this is the book for you. *Trading Secrets* is designed to work as a companion to my book *Charting Secrets*, which also provides practical exercises on technical analysis to give you an edge in recognising chart patterns and using indicators. These two books work well when read as a pair, providing enough information to safely get you started trading or investing.

Acknowledgements

My website staff at Trading Game <www.tradinggame.com.au> and Trading Secrets <www.tradingsecrets.com.au> have enthusiastically and professionally organised my seminars and ongoing product development.

Thanks to Chris Tate <www.artoftrading.com.au> for providing the opportunity to interview him about CFD trading and FX trading.

Finally, my husband, Chris Bedford, edited and reviewed many of the finer details of this book. His patience is greatly appreciated.

Introduction

It all started for me over 20 years ago. I went to a seminar about the sharemarket and I thought to myself, 'It's about time I took control'. Back then I was a manager for a large multinational company and I was flying high. My professional ambitions had finally begun to come true. I started to trade alongside my job and then, just a few short years later, the unexpected happened.

Over the course of a few months, I progressively lost the use of my arms through an unexplained tendon condition. I found that even simple tasks, such as opening doors, had become a day-to-day, painful struggle. Dressing, driving and feeding myself became daily challenges. Because of this, I had to quit my terrific job.

Life was looking bleak indeed.

Actually, I'm completely understating the situation. I felt black most of the time, unable to picture my future, and certain that the loss of the use of my arms meant that my hopes of becoming a mother had to be put aside.

I felt like my guts had been ripped out.

I kept fast-forwarding the images of what my life could have been before my arms stopped working, and everywhere I turned all I could see was despair. The little self-respect I had left was eradicated one day when I got trapped in my own bathroom, unable to escape because I couldn't get the door open. By the time my husband found me, I was howling with frustration on the floor and shaking all over with fury at my situation.

I found comfort under my doona and spent long hours with my head buried in the covers, sleeping or miserably contemplating my future. Every public toilet with a handle became my enemy. Putting on a pair of tight jeans was a thing of the past as I just couldn't get my hands to coordinate to pull up the zip. If I was itchy, I'd find a wall to act as a scratching post. If I needed my seatbelt on, I might as well have tried to run up Mount Everest.

As I did my endless physiotherapy sessions at the public pool, I found myself surrounded by people in much worse conditions than I was. Amputees, people with brain tumours, and people suffering the ravages of cancer—they all became my friends. We inspired each other and didn't allow excuses as we struggled for freedom from our bodies that had let us down.

I dug deep and was able to access a core of strength that I had always known was there—it's just that it had seemed to desert me when I needed it most.

Then one day, I told my accountant that I couldn't work and that I was going to trade full-time. Well, you know how some people just want to kick you when you're down? I'm guessing he was just that sort of guy because then I heard him try to smother a cackle. Yes, a cackle!

He said, 'You can't be serious! Barely anyone makes it as a full-time trader. Barely anyone! Especially NOT YOU! Look at you—you can't even type in your orders into the computer.'

Bam! That's all it took. I got angry. Really angry. Here he was sitting across his desk from me … laughing at me! How dare he!

So, I got angry and I got even.

I learned how to type with a pen in my mouth. It opened up a whole new world for me. I could share trade online and email my friends. It meant freedom!

Trading was a terrific diversion to the continual physiotherapist visits. Instead of being stuck at home and bored, trading allowed me to gain control over a major aspect of my life and provided a reason for getting out of bed in the morning. Eventually I made my living out of trading the markets and I've never looked back.

Oh yeah, and that accountant? I dropped him shortly after I made more money than I guessed he was making per year! ...I kept him as my accountant long enough so I could watch him eat his words. Ha! ... Now I've got a friendly accountant who applauds my efforts, instead of dragging me down.

Years later, even though I regained the use of my arms, trading had become such a way of life I would never give it up.

It occurred to me that there must be many other people who have found themselves in a situation where they would like to create a regular part-time or full-time income from their own home. Maybe they have fallen victim to company downsizing or are finding that they would just like to scale back the hours they work on someone else's goals and dreams.

This book is for you if:

- you've got a sneaking suspicion that there are other people creating a great lifestyle for themselves that doesn't require dollars for hours and a nine to five slog

- you're sick of treading water or slipping backwards in your sharemarket returns

- you've been on the wrong side of the trend before and it's hurt you financially — heaps of people caught in the GFC crush are with you on that one!

- you want to transform your open mind into trading cash that sticks in your account and can never be taken away from you

- you can taste trading success but you just don't know how you're going to achieve it.

If this sounds like you then you have to read this entire book, because the basis for your escape is buried within it.

When I first started trading, I didn't realise that the primary goal of trading was to survive long enough so that the sharemarket could reveal its secrets to me. Money is made as a by-product of following a sound trading plan, and adhering to the principles of money management. If you end up losing a significant proportion of your trading capital due to greed and ignorance, you can no longer trade, so you are out of the game.

Over time, I came to realise that some inherent trading skills are essential to master. There are some undeniable commonalities between traders who succeed, and those who do not. In essence, throughout this book I have sought to encapsulate the key secrets I believe separate profitable traders from those poor, miserable creatures who never quite get their act together.

Contrary to popular opinion, trading can be difficult, frustrating, and incredibly exasperating from time to time. There will be occasions when you will question your own judgement and wonder if you really have made a wise decision in trading the markets. I have written this book with the assumption that you are willing to persist beyond these obstacles.

Surprisingly, a number of traders will never actually put money into the sharemarket, but prefer the intellectual thrill of learning about the intricacies of indicators. Others trade for the feeling they experience when they make a win. If you are trading for these reasons, then put this book back on the shelf and look for the one entitled *Amateur Crocodile Wrestling*. That should get the adrenaline pumping. This book is designed to show you how to survive in the sharemarket, and ultimately derive profits: it is not designed to fulfil a misguided sense of adventure.

One of the differences between novice traders and those who trade for a living is the number of mistakes that they have made. I can bet that I've made more than you if you're starting your trading career. I still make trading mistakes, even though I have been doing this for years. In any endeavour, if you're not making mistakes, then you've probably stopped learning. I would like to help you to navigate this proverbial minefield by showing you where I have made errors and pointing you in the right direction.

In effect, I'd like you to think of me as your trading coach. Like any coach, I will give you a quick clip over the ear if you need one, but also encourage you to continue your education in a particular area if this is required.

I cannot promise that you will make money by simply reading this book. Trading is a form of self-directed learning. It will depend how you apply the knowledge that I am seeking to relay. Trading excellence will take time and practice to develop. Your own individual mindset and the application of the techniques discussed will determine your level of success.

People who say that trading is easy, or that it will take nanoseconds to perfect, are either kidding themselves or desperately trying to sell you something. This book will provide you with the necessary tools to succeed, and perhaps encourage you to continue your quest for information. I will show you techniques that are effective and point out the methods that are not, but it will be up to you to practise and apply the information presented. When it comes to trading, profitability is disguised as hard work.

Reading guide

You are welcome to read this book in chapter order, as you would with any other publication. If you are starting out in the markets, then this is exactly what I suggest you do. However, each chapter of this book can be read as a stand-alone topic. Much like a show bag, you can pick and choose the areas that you like the most, and would like to access first. In years to come, when you require a quick reference about a particular topic, you'll be able to read about this issue without re-reading the entire book.

Some of the issues discussed throughout this book are quite advanced, while others are much more basic in nature. Wherever possible, I have aimed to make the complex appear simple, so that you don't drown in a sea of technical detail. Trading excellence comes through mastering the basics. However, if at any stage you begin to feel a little daunted, grasp what you can, but feel free to move on to the next topic. When you're ready, you can return to any area that you initially found a little beyond you. Alternatively, if you find that a particular area is a trifle elementary for your level of experience, skip forward a chapter, and you're bound to discover something more to your liking. Whenever I have described a beginner's issue (that could be glossed over by experienced traders) or an advanced issue (with the potential to unnecessarily complicate a beginner's life), I've specifically pointed this out.

Please note that throughout this book you should assume that an uptrend is necessary to make money from the markets. For example, to understand the full implications of the chapters that cover stops, pyramiding and money management, it is important to take the view that an uptrend is required to profit. This view is taken for the purpose of clarity only. There are a few chapters that discuss making money from a downtrend via short selling and options and I am careful to define when this is necessary. With knowledge regarding appropriate strategies to suit a downtrend, you need never fear a bear market again.

I've mainly used Australian charts in this book; however, the principles I discuss hold true regardless of where you are based and which instrument you're trading. In fact, if you're trading from a country other than Australia, you have a huge advantage. You are less likely to be swayed by preconceived ideas about the charts I use as examples because you may not be familiar with their names. Bias is the hidden enemy of the technical analyst.

Many of the chapters have review sections at the end. Other chapters are completely devoted to testing your knowledge and are designed to help you to personalise the presented information. These sections are critical. Adults learn most effectively by doing. These sections will ensure that you have a chance to practise your newfound skills, as quickly as possible, in a safe environment. It is in your own best interests to complete these exercises, so I challenge you to pick up a pencil and write down your ideas. In fact, run over to your desk and pick up a pencil now so that you'll be ready.

I am even more enthusiastic about trading now than I ever have been. In the time between writing this book initially and writing this edition, so many things have happened in the world, and to my own life circumstances. Having now had my own children, I can really relate to people trying to establish financial stability and a legacy for their family. I am convinced that there is simply no better time than now to begin your trading career. You owe it to yourself, your family and your future to develop the skills necessary. In five years from now, if you make the right choices, your life could look very different from the way that it does today. What decisions are you currently making that will affect the shape of your life in the years to come? If you really focus on developing and practising your trading skills, what will this mean to you in the future? What are you prepared to do today so that you can achieve your future goals?

If the thought creeps into your head that freedom can't really be possible, remember that countless others just like you are already doing it. Don't believe me? Have a look at <www.tradingsecrets.com.au> and <www.tradinggame.com.au> and you'll see heaps of web pages of rave reviews of traders just like you, many who are already living your ideal lifestyle, all because of the decisions that they made in the past. Don't just take my word for it — there are hundreds of traders there for you to read about and listen to.

These aren't traders who made their fortune a decade ago. These people are in the trenches right now, bringing money into their trading accounts. Some have stuck like glue to my methods for 15 years or more, and some are just kicking off. Many have a special place in my heart because they know that I know they started with very, very little, and they've made huge changes to their lives as a result of the training I've provided for them.

Trading has the potential to supplement your income or, over time, replace your income altogether. Your levels of discipline and application of the lessons I am about to present will bring you a step closer to fulfilling your individual trading goals. Allow me to be your guide and I will help you to fast-track your journey to trading success.

Louise Bedford
Melbourne
May 2012
<www.tradingsecrets.com.au>

Part I
Business secrets

1

Stop trading, start thinking

In this chapter, you will learn that:

- Most traders dive into the markets before they even plan for success. If you're ready to stop whingeing and start making money, don't shirk the work.

- Fundamental analysis involves making evaluations regarding the future share price direction based on company balance sheets, profit/loss details and announcements.

- Technical analysis and charting take into consideration share price and volume action to establish whether share prices are likely to go up or down in the future.

- Good traders come from both schools of analysis. The key is to find a method that resonates with your way of thinking and to use strategies suitable to your level of trading development.

- Trading on tips and gossip will never lead to consistent results.

- It's best to avoid applying leverage too early in your trading career. Learn how to trade effectively using shares first before you move into trading options, CFDs or futures.

IF THIS IS THE FIRST BOOK ABOUT investing and trading that you've ever looked at, you may find the jargon involved in this field a little tricky to understand. The first part of this book is designed to get you into the swing of how traders approach the market, and to broaden your foundation of knowledge. You may find that you are unfamiliar with quite a few trading and financial terms, so give yourself some time to come to grips with all of the weird terminology. Instead of trying to single-handedly work out what certain words and phrases mean, and perhaps in the process missing the lessons that the chapter is trying to convey, turn to the glossary on page 301 before reading on. Unfortunately, there is no simple way to fill your mind with the necessary information unless you put in an effort to learn some of the jargon. You've got to start somewhere — all traders have at some stage felt exactly the way you are feeling.

I've been able to help a vast number of ordinary people trade all sorts of different instruments all around the world. I'm dedicated to helping individuals become successful traders, so that they can live life on their own terms. It's within your power to make this your richest year ever. All you need is the correct training.

Once you grasp the basics, you'll feel much more comfortable with the whole process. Successful trading involves applying basic principles over and over again. So let's dive in!

Tug of war

In the investment field there is often a tug of war between those with a fundamental viewpoint and those with a technical perspective. Just what are these forms of analysis and how can they help you make a profit from the sharemarket?

Fundamental analysis

Fundamental analysis seeks to detect shares that have a probability of increasing or decreasing in value based on announcements, company balance sheets and profit/loss details. If you are used to reviewing figures, ratios and interpreting data, then this type of analysis may suit you.

Considered traditional, but tried and true, the big issue is whether fundamentals have a direct effect on the share price. Many times I've seen a company release a great profit result, and the share price turns down the next day. Even a surprisingly good track record does not necessarily ensure sharemarket success. It is perception that drives share price action. The emotions of the players in the market will ultimately create an uptrend or a downtrend. Positive announcements that are released to the press are often already factored into the share price, so even a strong profit result will not necessarily lead to a bullish reaction.

Technical analysis

The majority of brokers tend to be fundamentalists at heart, so they may discourage you from exploring the field of technical analysis. Luckily, you are in charge of your own financial future, so it is your responsibility to fully explore all avenues before making a decision. I encourage you to persist in the field of technical analysis and develop your skills in the sharemarket. Technical analysis has helped many traders increase their profitability and proficiency. It may provide a whole new career for you, or allow you to develop a valuable source of additional income. At a minimum, with a bit of study in this field, you'll definitely be able to impress your friends at dinner parties with amazing terms such as 'trendlines', 'Stochastic Indicators' and 'going short'!

Technical analysis is a method used by an increasing number of traders to determine the points at which they will enter and exit the market. Some misinformed investors feel that this method is somewhat akin to reading tea leaves or tarot cards because it involves a degree of subjective interpretation. However, even fundamental analysts differ in their interpretation and projections; so let me assure you that this is definitely an area worth investigating.

Technical analysis involves reviewing actual price and volume action on share price charts to reach conclusions about the likely future direction of the price. In general terms, I'm the type of girl who doesn't care *why* a pair of shoes is on sale...I am just in seventh heaven to see them at 50 per cent off! That's why I focus on technical analysis and share charts. I have tried using fundamental analysis to trade but, for me, the true indication of market sentiment is gleaned from looking at charts, rather than analysing reams of ratios. The benefit of this method is that it crystallises the market sentiment by displaying information in a visual format. Many people think in pictures and so relate to the pattern recognition inherent in technical analysis. Rather than number-crunching figures, ratios and prices, technical analysis enables you to look at a chart that displays all the information you need to trade proficiently.

Technical analysts believe that everything known and unknown about the share is already factored into the share price. Often, by the time a media announcement is made, the share price has already displayed signs of reaction. It is this share price action that a technical analyst uses to detect buy and sell signals. Technical analysts often don't know the reasons behind the share price increase, but they are willing to buy the share based on the charting patterns that it presents.

This type of analysis is a way that you can access an early source of inside information. If company insiders know a pertinent piece of information about the company, they are likely to act on it prior to releasing it to the public. Their actions will show up on the share chart as either buying or selling pressure. You don't need to know why the share price is going up, you only need to observe that it is going up. The actual reason for the price increase is of little consequence—it should not make any difference to your ultimate purchase decision.

The majority of technical analysts tend to be trend followers. They wait for a share price to display a trend in a particular direction, prior to taking action. For trend followers, there are a few simple rules. The first rule is that if a share is trending up, buy it. The second rule is if it's going down, sell it. Many people overcomplicate trading but, in essence, if you become adept at identifying the direction of a trend, you are well on your way to trading like a professional. Technical analysis is part art and part science. The more you use it, the better you will be able to interpret the signals.

Over time, people who trade against the trend will ultimately run out of money and self-destruct.

There are some traders who continually try to trade against the prevailing trend. Over time, people who trade against the trend will ultimately run out of money and self-destruct.

Some traders seem intent on getting in at the bottom of a trend, and out at the top of a trend. Your friends may be impressed if you tell them that you rode the entire trend, but in all likelihood, the pursuit of this 'perfect trade' will leave you penniless. This has more to do with ego than with any objective form of technical analysis. It is practically impossible to repeat this activity with a high degree of probability ad infinitum.

When I started trading, it really was a case of learning by my own mistakes and banging my head against a lot of brick walls. Not only was this horribly expensive and time consuming, but I felt terribly alone and scared for a lot of the time. I didn't realise that it was really important to draw on the support of people who had already achieved what I was looking to achieve.

You see, successful technical traders have a defined set of rules to enter a trade, and to promptly exit from the market at the first sign of a downtrend, or to preserve their capital after the share has retraced in value. They maximise their profit potential through dedication to the principles of managing money and risk. Later chapters will explore these concepts.

Another method of analysis

The other type of analysis you could try is to read newspapers and listen to rumours, opinion and hearsay. Your neighbours, friends and favourite journalist may mean well, but it is unlikely that they will suffer any consequences if you act on the strength of their opinions. This popular, but exceptionally unproductive, technique is the way most people buy and sell shares. Headlines in newspapers directly feed our greed and fear. Unless you would like to create a small fortune — after starting with a large fortune — do not be tempted to take advice from these sources.

Many journalists who are expecting an announcement from a company will write two stories—one bullish story and the other bearish. Depending on the market's reaction to the news item, the journalist will run with the corresponding story that he or she has compiled to explain why the share price increased or decreased. This hardly sounds like you're getting the inside scoop, does it? You're receiving a jaded explanation of an event that has already occurred. Newspapers report on what has happened, not what is about to happen.

Amateurs react emotionally whereas professionals consider carefully the implications of their actions prior to responding.

Personally, I never give tips and I never listen to tips. I have found trading on information received in the form of a 'hot tip' to be unpredictable and foolhardy. Amateurs react emotionally whereas professionals consider carefully the implications of their actions prior to responding. The next time someone rushes up to tell you about the latest 'sure thing' — even if that person happens to be your broker — take time to review a share chart to see whether the recommendation makes technical sense.

Fundamental analysis may help to provide an indication regarding which shares are likely to increase in value, but it will not provide a timing tool. Technical analysis will help to pinpoint when to enter and exit a trade, but it won't provide any information regarding whether the company is financially sound. Many traders use a combination of both methods. You will need to make your own decision about how to engage the market.

This book will focus on technical analysis, as this is the method that I use to trade. I have tried using fundamental analysis to trade but for me the true indication of market sentiment is gleaned through looking at charts rather than analysing potentially subjective company reports. Charts show whether people are willing to put their money where their mouth is. Technical analysis puts you on the cutting edge and allows you to make money without becoming buried in a mountain of paperwork.

Strategy

Your analytical skills are your ammunition. Your skill in determining a share's direction is something that can be put to use in any market around the world. Wherever the forces of supply and demand provide a market, you will be equipped with the correct tools to make money. If there is more demand for a share, the price will be driven upward. If there is a predominance of emotional sellers, the share price will drop like a stone. This concept holds true whether you are trading soybeans in Brazil or gold stocks in Australia.

After you have completed your analysis, work out the appropriate strategy to use in order to profit from your findings. You will need to decide which type of vehicle is appropriate to make money from your observations; that is, shares, derivatives (including options, warrants and CFDs) or futures. Each strategy needs to be firmly based on the findings of your analysis or you will be destined to lose money. Some markets will move more slowly, and thus are easier to trade, because you have more time to consider your actions. The returns to be expected from these markets are lower compared with those of more leveraged areas. Other markets are incredibly volatile and require a different method of monitoring in order to protect your capital, but the returns can be very impressive. There is no reward without risk. To obtain exceptional rewards you must be prepared to accept a higher level of risk.

I see many novice traders, full of enthusiasm, borrowing funds to embark on margin lending, or moving into leveraged or volatile areas too early in their trading careers.

Learn how to analyse bullish and bearish market forces before plunging into a highly leveraged area. Some even take out a margin loan before they know how to profit consistently in the sharemarket. They become responsible for interest repayments when they don't even understand how to trade effectively. This is often a catastrophic decision, as the majority will destroy their hard-earned capital before they have a chance to learn the tricks of the trade.

Learn how to analyse bullish and bearish market forces before plunging into a highly leveraged area. Begin your sharemarket career by trading shares, preferably without a margin loan, while you have your training wheels on. Start with the bigger shares that have a significant market capitalisation, such as those in the Top 100 or at least the Top 300. Once you have cut your teeth in this generally less volatile arena, then consider moving into speculative shares, options, warrants, CFDs, foreign exchange (FX), futures or overseas markets. Only trade with leverage if you have a track record of success with non-leveraged items. The skills that you will have picked up during your time share trading will serve you well.

Novices who move into areas that contain greater inherent risk may learn the lessons more quickly, but they are much more likely to run out of money before they approach any level of proficiency. Usually for the inexperienced the only thing that improves with leverage is the speed at which their bank balances are destroyed!

For more information about how to begin your trading career effectively, I suggest you grab your free trading pack from <www.tradingsecrets.com.au>. I've put this pack together especially for you because I want you to get to the quickest possible start in your new career as a trader. When you listen to the five-part e-course in that trading pack, you'll find the lessons from this book are reinforced, and I know it will be just what you need.

There will be times as you read this book that you'll feel a bit confused, and feel that trading may be beyond you. I want to assure you that I'll do my best to give you everything I'd give my mum if my mum wanted to get started trading the markets. Stick with me and I'll show you where the money is.

Trading is more like running a marathon than a sprint. The first goal of trading is to preserve your capital. If you're out for the glamour of the quick dollar, your capital will quickly be redistributed into the hands of the professional traders.

Now, don't back away from this with a manic look in your eye and some urgent excuse about needing to examine the inside of your eyelids. Good traders are action takers. They test their skills and focus on their own education. Complete this review section right now and you'll be ahead of the rest. You'll be glad you did.

Review

1   Define fundamental analysis and technical analysis.

    . . . .

    . . . .

    . . . .

    . . . .

    . . . .

    . . . .

    . . . .

2 It is important to apply leverage as soon as possible in your trading career by trading the futures market or the options market.

a) True   b) False

3 Good traders listen to rumours and inside information to make their decisions.

a) True   b) False

4 Which type of analysis technique do you intend to use to trade? If you decide to use a hybrid of both technical and fundamental analysis, how do you intend to blend these two methods?

....

....

....

....

....

....

Answers

1 Fundamental analysis may help to provide an indication regarding which shares are likely to increase in value, but will not provide a timing tool. Technical analysis will help to pinpoint when to enter and exit a trade — it won't provide any information regarding whether the company is financially sound.

Fundamental analysis is based on the analysis of announcements, company balance sheets and profit/loss details. Technical analysis reviews actual price and volume action to reach conclusions about the likely direction of the future share price. Be aware that whichever method you choose, technical or fundamental, the analysis of the share must come first prior to working out which instrument or strategy is appropriate for you to use (for example, shares, options or futures).

2   False. Leverage often acts as a two-edged sword. If you have developed skill, it is a terrific way to multiply your success. If you do not have a track record in trading shares profitably, it is inappropriate to apply leverage.

3   False. Good traders rely on their own methods of analysing the market, and do not require rumour, newspapers, brokers or inside information to ensure their success. Developing skill in the area of technical analysis will assist you in analysing the market forces.

4   This is a personal decision. There is no particular correct answer. The right answer is the one that fits with your risk profile and personal beliefs about the markets.

The next chapter will take you a step closer to understanding that successful traders share the same characteristics as all profitable business owners.

2

Trust a broker? Are you crazy?

In this chapter, you will learn that:

- It is essential to set up your trading business professionally before you make your first trade. You don't need to trust a broker, financial planner or any other sharemarket professional. You can do this for yourself and achieve the lifestyle you deserve.

- Most people choose end of day data, but short-term traders may lean toward combining this with real-time data. Do not choose the cheapest option — data is as important to traders as oxygen!

- Your choice of charting software should be determined by your trading needs.

- It is essential to invest in your education. There is simply no better way to learn about the market than by reading books, attending seminars and listening to experienced traders.

HAVE YOU SEEN THE TELEVISION ad where an insect finds some leftover energy sports drink in a discarded can on the side of the road? After polishing off the drink, he flies down the highway on a direct collision course with a car. Instead of splattering on the windscreen, he breaks a hole in the glass with the sheer force of his body, and punches straight through the back window unharmed. In the background, you can see the car run off the road into a gutter. The insect smiles cheekily, and then zooms off into the distance with a maniacal laugh.

Many investors believe that they (the insect) can control the market (the car) in much the same manner. The TV ad is, of course, a work of fiction. In reality, a large number of these traders will suffer the financial equivalent of a real bug striking an actual car at high speed—splat! So, exactly what qualities set the best traders apart from the mediocre masses?

One of the key similarities between successful people in all professions is that they start with the end result in mind. If they want to make a million bucks out of their business, they set up a business that is capable of generating this amount of profit. This sounds like such a simple concept, doesn't it? Successful people tend to develop an income commensurate with their vision and level of effort. For some reason, however, when many people first begin trading, they seem to short-change their new venture and strangle their own potential results.

Successful traders make it a priority to develop their skills. They invest in their education and the tools of their trade. These tools include data, books, seminars, software and computer equipment. Unfortunately, it's not just a financial investment that will set you apart from other traders. (Otherwise any Gordon Gekko wannabe with cash to splash could buy his or her way into the upper echelons of trading excellence.) You'll, also need

The sharemarket is an equal opportunity employer.

to expend the necessary effort and put in some time to learn skills that will enable you to be profitable in the sharemarket. These will be lifetime skills that you will be able to apply in any market condition, at any time in the future. See the big picture from the beginning.

The sharemarket is an equal opportunity employer. You will be rewarded in direct proportion to the effort that you expend and the skills you develop and practise. Luckily, this doesn't mean that you need to spend every waking moment in front of your computer screen. It is completely up to you to decide what type of investment style you would like to cultivate. You'll need to put some effort into learning new skills, and I make no apology for this.

Many traders seem to think that they'll invest in the appropriate equipment or data after they begin to make money in the sharemarket. This will not work. You must sow before you reap.

To create a business-like profit, you cannot treat trading as though it is a hobby. If your goal to trade well is right down the bottom of your priority list, I can tell you with absolute certainty that you'll never derive a substantial income from the markets. The best investment that you can ever make is in yourself. If you look at successful people from all walks of life, you'll see that this philosophy acts as their common denominator. Trading follows this principle to the letter.

What do you *do*?

I'm so often asked 'What do you do?' It's a usual conversation starter when you meet someone, isn't it? For traders it's a difficult question to answer. When I'm with the other mums from school, I'm a 'full-time mum'. After my keynote presentations, to the audience I'm a 'professional speaker'. To the people who have read my books, I'm an 'author'. But, here is what I really do: I watch pretty little green and red candles do battle on a chart, assess which side is winning, and then back that winning side with my own money.

We're a funny bunch, us traders. We strive to perfect our entry, exit and position sizing, and we struggle with our own self-concepts as we realise we are creating money out of thin air.

My best friends are traders, and even though we have totally different backgrounds, we are magnetically drawn together by our pursuit. There is no higher calling as we are living by our wits, totally self-reliant and jubilant that our way of life has bought us back the years that others are frittering away by working too hard and for too little recognition.

I think a much more polite question to ask people, rather than 'What do you do?' is 'How do you spend your time?'. This will bring you a more interesting answer every time, and also prevent the possibility that someone will feel they're about to be pigeon-holed into a pre-conceived role. If I'm asked how I spend my time, I can tell people the truth: 'My passion is share trading and putting money into other trader's pockets and making it stick, even if they have only 30-minutes a day and limited knowledge about the markets. During the other 23 hours in the day, I'm a full-time mum, love to travel, and spend heaps of time drinking hot chocolate with the people I care about.' There, see? This is a much more complete answer.

What is your passion? How do you spend your time and is this the way you would choose if given the option? Trading is a skill set you can learn. I'm living proof! This isn't out of your reach. It's just a matter of learning the right skills so you can live life on your own terms as a trader.

Tell me, if you knew how to create money simply with the trading methods you implement, how much stress would instantly dissolve from your life? How confident would you feel? So, whatever your current role in life — wage-slave, business owner, career-junkie or 'between opportunities' — trading can dovetail right into your life and give you ultimate peace of mind. Before we discuss the specific areas that require a financial commitment from you in order to succeed, you will need to decide whether you fit the profile of an investor or a trader.

Are you an investor or a trader?

Investors typically have a long-term view and are prepared to sit out the inevitable downslide in share prices that the market periodically experiences. They usually consider that they own a part of the company in which they are investing and rarely implement strategies that make money from a downtrending market. Often investors view the fundamentals of the company (such as profit and loss statements or balance sheets) very carefully before buying a share. They are mostly passive, whereas traders are more active in their methods.

Traders are willing to adjust the term of their view depending on the market environment. Their trades may be shorter term or, depending on market conditions, medium to long term. They will adopt the most effective strategy to match the trend of the market, such as short selling or using derivatives. Some traders don't even know the full company name before they buy their shares. Traders are just looking for their entry criteria to be fulfilled before they purchase their bundle of shares. In many cases, they don't even care what the company does.

Traders typically buy and sell people's perceptions, whereas investors buy companies. Your own personality, aversion to risk, and time commitments will help to determine whether you lean towards trading or investing.

Throughout this book I will be referring predominantly to trading rather than investing, as I am assuming that you would like to know how to make money regardless of market conditions, and that you are willing to devote time to learn how to trade well. With these personal attributes, your journey, from being a beginner in the sharemarket to developing profitable trading methods, will be a lot simpler.

There are specific tax implications associated with whether you define your trading activities as those of an investor or a trader. You need to familiarise yourself with these taxation implications so you can make the best of your own situation. You should discuss this with your tax accountant or financial planner.

If you have already set yourself up to trade from home with a charting package and a data provider, feel free to skip to the next chapter. The following section is designed to assist the fledgling trader establish himself or herself professionally with the appropriate tools.

So what should you invest in to ultimately give you a fighting chance of extracting profits from the sharemarket?

Data

The data for fundamental software includes items such as dividend yields, assets, liabilities and profit and loss. Technical analysis software requires price and volume action in order to create charts. The standard technical information includes price data (such as the open, high, low and close for the day), as well as the volume of shares traded.

Short-term trades can last anything from a few minutes to six weeks. Medium-term trades could take from six weeks to one year to complete. Long-term traders might invest for anything over this period. The boundaries between these time frames are somewhat blurred, but hopefully this will provide you with a guide to investment horizons and the possible duration of trades. This has an impact on the type of data that you will require in order to trade effectively.

There are three main types of data available:

1   end of day

2   real-time

3   free.

End of day data

End of day data shows the share price action that occurred throughout the day as a snapshot that is available only after the market is closed. It is usually available via a download over the internet. Some data providers even send out the data to you via email. Download times also vary — some providers allow you to access the information at 5.30 pm, others at midnight.

Information may be provided on the Top 100 shares or on the entire market. I urge you to purchase all Australian Securities Exchange (ASX) share data, rather than buying only the Top 100. The price difference is usually not significant. Other information is also optional, such as for overseas indices. If you can afford it, buy it.

You will probably need to download the historical data to obtain past market information and to provide a base for the future daily downloads. This cost will be in addition to the monthly or annual price that you will pay for your daily information. Be aware that you get what you pay for. A good data provider should make an allowance for data corrections, such as when a share split occurs. Of course, a good provider will cost a little more than a shoddy backyard provider, but quality data is critical to your trading decisions. Fees vary dramatically, from about $10 per month to about $110 per month. This is one area in which you cannot afford to skimp. Your trading decisions will be based on the data that feeds into your charts, so your profitability depends on its accuracy. The best end of day data provider that I have found is <www.tradinggame.com.au>.

Real-time data

It is important that you know the approximate time horizon for your investment before making an entry or exit decision. If you are a short- to medium-term trader, you could consider using real-time data as well as end of day data. If you are a long-term investor, it is likely that you will only need end of day data. Be aware, however, that if you cannot trade profitably with an end of day system, it is unlikely that a real-time system will act as a fairy godmother and, with a wave of a magic wand, instantly convert you into a Cinderella (or a Prince Charming, as the case may be) of the trading world. This is a mistake made by many novice traders. A shorter term chart will not assist you any more than a long-term chart if your trading methodology does not stand up to scrutiny.

> It is important that you know the approximate time horizon for your investment before making an entry or exit decision.

Keep in mind that the intraday time increment you choose must be suited to the instrument that you are trading. If you are trading a highly volatile liquid instrument in the futures market, a five-minute time duration for your chart may be appropriate. However, if the instrument you've chosen to trade is less liquid, a one-hour chart may provide more meaningful results.

There are several real-time systems available for you to investigate. Many of these seem to be priced for the institutional trader rather than a private trader with budget constraints. Some systems require a dedicated online computer, while others allow you to access information via the internet for an hourly fee or a set monthly rate. Do your homework before purchasing the first real-time system that you see. Make sure you have located a system that is suited to your needs, or you may incur a substantial and unnecessary expense. Prices range from about $100 per month up to $18 000 per year.

With the increased competition between online brokers, many have begun offering real-time data as a part of their service. There will usually be a minor fee for this form of real-time data, but some brokers will provide you with this for free if you make a certain number of trades per month. Be aware, however, that even if you use this type of data and charting, you will still need end of day data in order to conduct your searches of the market. Any of the online brokers offering real-time data offer very limited searching facilities.

A real-time data system will provide figures on market depth. Market depth shows a bid and an ask screen of the price level and volume of trades as they occur. Some will even plot beautiful candlestick charts based on very small time increments. (You'll learn more about candlesticks in chapter 9.)

Free data

Now, before you get excited about the prospect of free data, let me remind you that we agreed that you were going to set yourself up professionally rather than always seeking the cheapest option. We had a deal, so don't back out of this agreement now. If people begin to drool when they think that they have found a way to avoid spending money, it provides me with a clear impression of their commitment to trading well. Let me make this perfectly clear: you will need to pay for decent information — there is no way you can avoid it.

... you will need to pay for decent information — there is no way you can avoid it.

The free charts that are available over the internet are usually not real-time charts, unless they are connected to an online broker's service. Widely available real-time charts are most likely to be 20-minute-delayed charts. In all probability, you will not be able to use any form of searching on them to assist in your share selection process. They will only be useful for checking your positions intraday, and not as a replacement for your end of day or real-time system.

Software

In the dark ages of trading, before the advent of computers, analysts of yesteryear used to draw their charts by hand. They performed long and complicated mathematical calculations to reach conclusions about a share. Sounds terrible, doesn't it? Luckily, software can now perform much of the grunt work for us — what a relief!

Some people find that hand charting can assist them in honing their skills when they are first learning about candlestick charting and bar charts. In this context, charting by hand can prove to be a useful lesson. However, relying on hand charting for the majority of your analysis work can end up being incredibly time consuming and labour intensive. You really need software to be able to do this for you.

The type of software I am talking about will read shares-related data and produce charts or other forms of analysis. If you are looking to analyse fundamental data, such as profit and loss figures, ratios and balance sheet information, you will often need a completely separate type of software, compared with the software required for charting. Some software is flexible enough to be able to analyse both technical and fundamental information, but the majority is not. You will need to decide in advance the type of trader that you want to be, the tools that you will require to do your job well, and then buy your software accordingly.

Software can be quite expensive. It is important to know what type of questions to ask the salesperson so that you don't get taken for a ride. Prices can range from approximately $400 to over $15 000. This is one area where additional price does not necessarily mean superior quality. Some remarkably inexpensive pieces of software can be incredibly effective. I have listed some considerations to assist you in evaluating the correct trading software for your requirements. You can use the following software considerations as your checklist:

- Are the graphics produced by the software visually appealing?

- Can you search the market easily for opportunities, or does writing a search routine require an advanced mathematics degree?

- What technical support is available if you run into difficulties?

- Are there training courses that you can attend to help you learn about the software? Is this via a classroom setting, a video, an online tutorial or a CD-ROM?

- How user-friendly are the manual and help files?

- Are there software user group meetings that you can attend?

- Can the software handle a variety of data formats from different data providers or will you be required to buy your data through only one source?

- Does the software have the ability to analyse fundamental data as well as technical data?

- Does the product have all of the indicators that you need to trade well according to your trading plan? If not, can they be added?

- What happens when the product requires an upgrade? How do you obtain the upgrade, and is there any charge?

- Where was the product originally created? Does this hinder future product-specific developments that may be required by local traders?

- What are the main reasons people stop using this product?

- How many locally based traders use this software? Can you talk to one of the users to gain his or her perspective on the software?

- Are there any ongoing maintenance fees?

- Does the product provide trading advice (that is, buy and sell signals) or is this up to the user to work out? (Software that provides buy and sell signals is not necessarily preferable to a product without this function. Refer to chapter 9 where black box systems are discussed in more detail to gain an understanding regarding this type of software.)

- Does the software contain all of the required tools in a single package or does it require additional components to enhance its functions?

If in doubt, find out the de facto standard software used by the industry and choose to use this. Often, this choice will mean that you have an abundance of help available to assist writing searches and understanding how to use the software effectively.

Computers

Buy the most up-to-date model of computer that you can afford, including a large monitor. A large screen will make things so much easier for you. Plus, consider getting two or three screens. Recent studies have shown that your productivity will increase by about 15 per cent by adding an extra screen. Speed counts.

Don't hold back on the purchase of necessary computers or computer peripherals. No matter what the salesperson tells you, buying a computer that is 'upgradeable' is largely a false economy. By the time you are ready to upgrade any components, it is usually cheaper to purchase a new system. Forget trying to find an equivalent model second hand — bite the bullet and invest in your future. Ideally, you will also need a broadband internet connection.

... bite the bullet and invest in your future.

Books

This is the cheapest form of education that you could possibly discover. When I started trading, books were just about the only avenue available to assist me. Back then there were barely any locally based books. Any interesting titles had to be ordered from overseas at great expense. I am completely envious of your situation if you are beginning to trade now — you have access to so much excellent information! Take advantage of the wisdom of others and benefit from their combined knowledge. Find some authors you can relate to and devour their information. Do everything you can to immerse yourself in this alien territory. Over time you'll catch on and the jargon won't seem quite so strange.

There is also value in re-reading books that you haven't touched in quite a while. When your foundation on some topics is a little shaky, many of the more advanced concepts can seem confusing. The benefit of re-reading is that you will be able to consolidate your knowledge and drive your trading to the next level.

Some people find that reading is a chore and they tend to avoid it wherever possible. This is absolutely no reflection on an individual's intellect. It is just the way that person approaches the world. If this describes your situation, I applaud you for reading this book. I promise you it will be worth your effort in the end. It may also pay you to investigate some of the other multimedia tools available in addition to reading books. (We don't want your foray into sharemarket education to be too traumatic!) For my list of recommended reading and further education tools, turn to page 299. You will see that many of the information sources I have released are available on CD or DVD. Remember as well that I've got a free trading pack set aside for you when you register at <www.tradingsecrets.com.au>. The five-part e-course will provide an audio version of the top areas you need to focus on in order to excel as a trader.

Seminars

The quality of seminars and workshops varies widely so choose carefully. If you are going to learn from someone, ensure that your faith in him or her is justified. Make sure you relate to their methods and preferably follow the referral of someone you trust. Read all that you can prior to attending a course. It goes without saying that you should fulfil any prerequisites of the course prior to attending. Discipline yourself before going to the course and you will derive far greater benefits from the information presented.

Traders often ask me, 'What is your number one secret to wealth?' and I tell them that it's essential to find someone you can respect and admire that has already achieved what you are hoping to achieve yourself. I believe it's best to never have another original idea when it comes to markets. You don't need to reinvent the wheel. You can copy someone else's system with their guidance. However, you'll need to customise essential elements to your own needs. The best traders on this planet follow systems that they have developed themselves, using the guidance of professionals. I'm here to help you do exactly that.

Before booking into any trading course, ask yourself these questions:

- Do the trainers have a combined experience of decades rather than nanoseconds?

- Will you get continuous ongoing support?

- Will you be taught how to make money regardless of the direction of the market?

- Will the methods you learn be tailored to your own personal circumstances?

How to choose a mentor

With the right mentor, hitting your goals can be achieved in half the time. Being trained by an experienced mentor who really cares about your achievements can be one of the most liberating experiences you'll ever have. The trouble is, finding the right mentor can make you feel extremely vulnerable. It can also be emotionally draining, scary and time consuming. So before committing to a mentor, check them out. See how long they've been around. Find out about the results their people have been achieving.

Why is this important? Well, there are so many people out there giving advice, it's hard to know who to trust and who is producing the top traders of tomorrow. To be blunt, there are a lot of flash-in-the-pan trainers out there who have only limited experience and couldn't produce a profit if you gave them Warren Buffett's best inside tip of the day.

Newsletters

The newsletters that are probably the least effective are the ones that present columns of buy and sell advice without any understanding of your personal circumstances or investment goals. Some newsletters can be effective teaching aids, especially if the writers are experienced professionals and value education. I would prefer to see you educate yourself so that you can make effective decisions and develop your trading ability rather than rely on external advice. You are welcome to register and subscribe to my free monthly educational email newsletter *The Trading Game Newsletter* by visiting my site <www.tradingsecrets.com.au>.

Stockbrokers

To buy and sell shares you will require the services of a broker. I will address the importance of using the correct broker for your needs in chapter 11. In general, there are three types of brokers available to accommodate your trading needs—full-service, limited-service and discount (including online) brokers.

Stingy behaviour

One thing that has been irritating me is stinginess. There's a heck of a lot of it floating around. If your fist is squeezed tight so money can't escape, it also means that money will have a hard time flowing into your trading accounts.

I'm not talking about frivolous wasting of money. I'm talking about investing in yourself and your own education, and having an abundant mindset with things that are really important to you. There will always be more money and more opportunities in your future for you. There isn't a shortage. However, if you are too self-protective, and you guard your own spending too vigorously, your money will find a different home (and it will probably be with that cow from work who keeps on talking about how great things are going for her).

Cheap behaviour breeds a scarcity mindset and poor thinking. Go out and do something small but special for yourself and savour it if money is tight. Buy a Lindor ball, or have a cuppa at a swish hotel and really own the experience. Remind yourself about why you wanted to be a trader in the first place.

Most people have spent their next pay rise before it even runs through their bank account. They have spent everything and more! They'll never be rich and they'll never live with an abundance mentality. Because you're reading this book, I know you'll never be that type of person.

The beauty of living below your means is clear, but few people actually do it. They stress and strive, trying to buy more and more things to impress people they don't even like—but they don't spend on the things that really count.

So what does count? Make your own list, but here is mine for your reference: education, meaningful experiences and appreciating assets. These are the things that will make a difference to me both now and in the future, and it's these values that I strive to pass on to my children, and my nieces and nephews.

'Things' don't impress me but experiences do. I'm not into expensive toys. Sure I can afford them, but it's just that I don't really want them. I live well within my means. Yes, I could buy more, bigger and better houses, couches and cars, but it's just not all that important to me.

Surrounding myself with great people who push me beyond my comfort zone, having top conversations and creating memories for my friends and family is what pumps me up. I'm not into competing with others about how much stuff I own. But forget about me. Focus on you. You are besieged by distracting, seductive, addictive smut every day, everywhere you look. Beware!

Just because others are sinking their money into the useless bottomless pit of the latest phone, TV or piece of technology that will be outdated almost instantly, it doesn't mean that you have to. The fact that so many are seduced tells me that you can't afford to be. Who wants to be just like the masses? Surely you want to stand apart from the masses and hold your head up high?

The only person you're competing with is you. Stop envying what others have got. Run your own race, focus on getting educated, and get your priorities in order. You create success by knuckling down and seriously applying yourself to something in a persistent, dedicated and focused way. Bruce Lee once stated, 'I fear not the man who has practiced 10 000 kicks once, but I fear the man who has practiced one kick 10 000 times'. Be clear on your goals, pursue education (with your feet flying and your arms flailing), and don't let distraction evaporate your dreams.

Being able to harness energy to perform at your peak is an essential component of effective trading. Keep reading to learn about how you can approach trading with enthusiasm, energy and focus, in a way that you may not currently think is possible.

3
Get ready for action

In this chapter, you will learn that:

- Getting the most out of our personal energy levels is an essential skill.

- When we are stressed we naturally take faster, shallower breaths to prepare us for action. This can lead to snap trading decisions that are ineffective and not based on cool logic.

- Breathing deeply and fully, and utilising your diaphragm is a way to dissipate stress and help you stay on top of the game.

- Separating your breath into three distinct sections can act as a pressure circuit breaker during times of stress — so practise breathing into your stomach, your lower chest and then your upper chest.

LIFE IS HECTIC. Every day it can seem as if there are more and more demands on our resources. Often, we have to deny our body the rest it craves and survive on energy drinks, coffee and chocolate bars. As you've probably experienced, it is impossible to stay completely pumped up, every moment of every day. Personal energy doesn't work that way — we get tired and we need time to rest and recover. Without a bit of down time we'll end up burnt out and totally ineffective. This also extends to our activities related to trading. Many traders succumb to pressure and this leads to ineffective decision-making.

When you first start trading, the importance of being able to handle your own stress levels may not seem to be a priority. Particularly if you haven't placed any money in the market, you may wonder why traders feel any pressure at all! Let me tell you, I felt the same way about golf until my first serious game of pitch and putt. I thought to myself, 'What's all the fuss about? You're only chasing a little white ball around a field. How hard can that be?' After my first ball dropped into the pond and my second ball failed to connect with my golf club … seven times (but who's counting?), I realised there must be more to this game. A minor hissy fit later, I now understand why golfers get the yips and have trouble performing.

…all it takes is a few stocks to misbehave, combined with a little time pressure, and you'll probably understand how easy it is for traders to blow their stacks.

Trading is a little like that. Before you begin, you imagine you'll be cool and calm, no matter what the circumstances. However, all it takes is a few stocks to misbehave, combined with a little time pressure, and you'll probably understand how easy it is for traders to blow their stacks. That's why it's important to learn some stress-reduction techniques, even before you put on your first trade.

Athletes

Athletes put huge amounts of effort into managing their personal energy levels. There is a lot we can learn from the field of sports psychology that we can apply to our own lives. Jim Loehr has been studying athletes' behaviour for over 30 years. In a particularly revealing study about tennis players, he noticed that it wasn't necessarily the most skilful athlete who won the match. In the 16 to 20 seconds between points, winning tennis professionals did something completely different with their time. They visualised success. They relaxed and refocused. They controlled their breathing and posture.

As a result, their heart rates dropped by up to 20 beats per minute. They recovered their energy, and this edge consistently led to winning behaviour on the court. Loehr concluded that a player's up time was only as good as his or her down time.

This chapter will give you some ideas to help you make the most of your down times between activities throughout the day. One essential skill is to learn how to harness the power of effective breathing techniques. This skill will also assist you in trading with calmness and clarity, and enable you to combat the mood swings that make following your trading plan the last thing on your mind. To describe this technique, I have taken an extract from my *Trading Psychology Home Study Course*. This course is the culmination of nearly two years of research and takes at least nine weeks to complete. Extensive background theory is presented and there is a series of mental exercises to complete, sometimes on a daily basis. It is available via my website <www.tradingsecrets.com.au>.

Breathing

Learning how to breathe properly is a central skill, core to the disciplines of yoga and meditation. Breathing properly is also a key skill harnessed by singers as they attempt to hit challenging notes.

When we are stressed, we naturally take faster, shallower breaths to prepare us for action. Traders under pressure can often gasp for breath when a position goes against them. Objectivity flies out the window and spur of the moment trading decisions can be the result. Most of us spend our days taking these shallow breaths, inadvertently creating tension — even when we are aiming to relax. Just because you are currently breathing, does not mean that you are breathing in the optimal way for health and relaxation.

By becoming more aware of your physical processes, you can develop a sense of calmness that can ultimately be summoned at will. Breathing correctly can help to lower your blood pressure, increase your concentration, and help you focus — particularly during times of trading pressure.

How to breathe

Place the palm of one hand on your stomach and the palm of the other on your upper chest. Inhale as you would when you take a normal breath. Which hand rises first? If the hand on your upper chest rises first, this means that you are taking upper chest breaths. If the hand on your stomach rises first, you are taking diaphragmatic breaths. If they both rise and fall in tandem, you are taking a mixture of the two.

Drawing in breath from the diaphragm is a core skill. By learning to breathe using our lower abdomen, diaphragm and lower chest, a message is sent to the brain that short circuits the stress cycle. When utilised with the correct posture, it will assist by conserving energy, as well as calming the mind to help you get into the zone of effective trading methods. Although initially this type of breathing may seem awkward, with practice it can become a part of your unconscious trading routine. Let's have a look at the distinct steps required to take a diaphragmatic breath.

Step one

In a seated position, sit up straight with both feet firmly on the ground. Place your two hands on your stomach. Your left and right hand should only be connected via the longest finger.

Step two

Take a deep breath in. Your aim is to fill your lower stomach with air. Breathe into the lower abdomen and, as you do, you will find that your fingertips will be drawn apart. If it helps, you may need to consciously puff out your stomach to achieve the desired effect. Repeat three times.

Step three

Move your hands upward so that they are now in line with your diaphragm, resting comfortably on your lower chest. You should be able to feel your lower ribs and your fingertips on each hand should be lightly touching. When you breathe in, aim to fill your lower chest with air, instead of your stomach. You should feel your fingertips move apart as you breathe in and, as you breathe out, your fingertips should naturally come back together.

Aim to breathe into your lower chest only. Try to inflate that as much as possible to get your fingertips to separate. Repeat three times.

Step four

Move your hands so that they are now positioned on your upper chest. With your fingertips touching, breathe in and aim to breathe only into your upper chest cavity. Now your fingertips should move away from each other when you breathe in, and come toward each other when you breathe out. Repeat three times.

Step five — the combination breath

Steps one to four give you the basics about how to take a complete breath — you just need to combine them. To complete a breath cycle, in the one breath, breathe firstly into your stomach, then into your lower chest and then into your upper chest. This is how to breathe in correctly. The one breath in should be capable of inflating each of the three specified areas in sequence.

Exhale naturally. Experiment with the exhalation by firstly deflating your upper chest, then your lower chest and finally your stomach. You have now completed one full breath cycle. I suggest that you complete at least three full breath cycles.

Breathing correctly will help you to focus and attend to the task at hand. I challenge you to practise this technique at least three times today. If you only have time for one full cycle, that's fine, but you will obtain the best results if you repeat it at least three times.

As a suggestion, try it before you get out of bed, then again at lunch, and finally before you go to sleep at night.

Here is what one trader, Caroline Semisi from <www.tradinggame. com.au>, had to say about the technique that we have just covered, 'This [method] has helped me in many areas of my life. If I ever feel like I am getting stressed I concentrate on my breathing and it helps calm and put things into perspective. It is quite amazing.'

Any time you feel stressed throughout the day, try a full breath cycle and observe how this makes you feel.

Any time you feel stressed throughout the day, try a full breath cycle and observe how this makes you feel. If you are asked to make a snap decision, try at least one full breath cycle before you give your answer. Before you speak to someone who you do not relate with, complete a full breath. This only takes you an extra second or two, but the results of your effort can sometimes last a lifetime.

It may take you a few days to fully develop this skill. As far as I am concerned, this skill should be taught in schools, and even children as young as five years old can master and apply it. As an asthmatic, I used to teach this technique to children for the Asthma Foundation. This method helped to calm the little ones down when they were in the throes of an asthma attack. It is incredibly effective at a deep level, and is one of the simplest methods available for calming your mind and body.

Throughout the day, practising this technique can make the most of your quiet time and sustain your energy during more taxing periods. When it comes time to trade, you will be more relaxed and focused, and much more likely to make effective decisions.

For some people, the effect of correct breathing will be immediate. Others may have to practise for a whole week before it begins to feel more natural. Wherever you lie on this spectrum is fine. Give yourself time to adjust to a new skill. Try this technique while you are trading and note the effects on your mindset.

Just because this is a supposedly simple skill, don't downplay the effect it could have on you and your entire life. Traders determined to excel realise that developing their mindset is just as important as learning the specifics of trading effectively.

Have you ever been attracted to the idea of quitting your job and living happily ever after? Who hasn't? Keep reading to learn about the best way to approach this issue and to work out whether you are ready to start trading full-time.

4
Got a job? Hang on in there ... for a while

In this chapter, you will learn that:

- The ability to trade successfully takes a long time to cultivate, no matter what you have been told. (There ... I've said it. Now don't run a mile because you're looking for a quick buck. Do this right and you'll set yourself up for life.)

- Many people quit their job prematurely and have not developed the skills, or capital base, required to weather all the sharemarket storms that lie on the horizon.

- Some effective traders have managed to combine their sharemarket activities with their regular work to derive the best from both worlds.

- It's important to work out in advance how you will handle combining trading and taking holidays.

WHEN I GRADUATED FROM UNI, I had it. When I had a job, I had it. After I lost my job, I still had it. Somehow I couldn't shake it. I could not shake the perception of myself as a share trader.

Goodness knows why I clung to this perception but I did. It has kept me chained to my desk peering at charts for more years than I care to number, and it's made it seriously impossible for me to entertain the idea of doing anything else for a living for very long.

I have a feeling that the tendency to perceive yourself as a trader is more than just a case of simple will. I think too that this self-definition plays a big part in who ultimately does and doesn't make it as a trader. I'm absolutely certain that this had a lot to do with the development of my career.

So, how do you describe yourself to others when they ask the question, 'What do you do?' Is trading somewhere near the top of your priority list or has it dropped way down to number 538? I can tell you now that the traders with determination and singleness of purpose will be the ones who come out on top in this game.

You know, so many people would love to be a trader but so many lack the discipline required to do so.

This is a good thing, my friend. Being a good trader is reserved only for the most committed, diligent people, determined to seriously impact their financial futures.

This is why I'm glad I'm with you on your journey towards becoming one of the elite — an exceptional trader with the skills, focus and freedom to live life on your own terms.

The statistic often quoted is that, at any one time, 70 per cent of workers dislike their job. (And the other 30 per cent lie?) It's only natural that whenever people are dissatisfied they start looking around for other opportunities. The market does not care what you've done in your life up to this point. It will provide instant feedback to indicate whether you are adhering to the laws of sound strategy and discipline. If you are tempted to give your job the flick and trade for a living, perhaps it would be sensible to first look at the pros and cons of being employed versus full-time share trading.

The dark side of employment

In my past 'working' life I was the sales manager of a national team — or so it said on paper. In actual fact, I spent the majority of my working hours contemplating whether I should raid the office supply cabinet and staple myself to death to avoid another pointless meeting. Ironically, in corporate life it seems that the harder you prepare for a meeting, the more likely it is to be cancelled.

Many of my colleagues took pride in their ability to assume the characteristics of a rubber plant and maintain perfect camouflage at the first sign of the managing director taking a tour of their department. Such a skill! Senior management dished out threats and treats as if prescribed by Dr Harry, the TV vet.

The positive side of working

When thinking about the benefits of working, if the words 'pay packet' do not immediately spring to mind then you've probably been receiving a salary as regular as clockwork for many years.

With most jobs it is possible to slack off for between one and eight weeks without any adverse effects. Loyalty money is a terrific invention — you get paid just for turning up. A perfect holiday in an air-conditioned, well-lit cubicle giving you time to relax while having money deposited directly into your bank account. Sounds like an advertisement for Club Med, doesn't it?

Free pens, free liquid paper and free coffee also score high on the list of perks. If you're in a role that provides a company car and travel, benefits also include free petrol and frequent flyer points. However, the grind of being constantly answerable to a higher authority can be frustrating.

If you own a business, the realities of overheads, employees, debtors and creditors are daily headaches that you may want to eliminate.

Carefully examine your motives for wanting to leave your job or business. If you think that trading for a living will be easy, glamorous and leave you with your days completely free, think again. Don't jump out of a relatively comfortable financial position if you don't need to. Consider working part-time or decreasing your hours at work to a more manageable level. This may be a more effective solution than dumping your job altogether.

Loyalty money is a terrific invention — you get paid just for turning up.

Trading is a discipline that can be developed while you are working a job or running another business. Remember the importance of cashflow and don't jump from the frying pan into the fire.

Every so often I really enjoyed the ambitious rush of climbing the corporate ladder. There is nothing like the acclaim of your peers and the feeling of accomplishment after beating hopelessly unrealistic targets. These are the main areas that bring a nostalgic tear to my eye when I look back over my career (so I quickly lie down until the feeling passes). However, trading for a living has its own drawbacks, as you will see here.

Share trading can be lonely

Before you quit your job or business, you should consider how you will handle the isolation. There may be times when you will want to dial your local emergency number purely to hear the sound of another human's voice. If you are quite social in nature, you may find that this aspect of trading represents a significant downside.

Some people also have trouble adjusting to organising their own time, especially if they are used to being kept on a fairly tight leash by their previous employer. As a rule of thumb, to have incredible trading results, you must really commit to an incredible amount of work.

Ask yourself a few pertinent questions before deciding to quit your job, such as:

- Have you honed the necessary skills to make money regardless of market conditions? If you do not know how to short sell and trade options and CFDs in addition to shares, then you are destined only to make money while in a bull market. This is not sustainable over the long haul. It would be horrible to have to go back to a job after you've managed to escape from it.

- Do you have sufficient capital to continue trading even though you may suffer a string of losses? Can you build your capital and increase your position size based on your trading results? If you can't add to your equity, inflation will ultimately bite you. Many traders begin their full-time trading careers undercapitalised and spend their first few months eating baked beans, remembering the days when money flowed freely and losses didn't matter.

- Can you exit a trade when it has turned against you? If not, you will eventually self-destruct. It's only a matter of time.

- Have you been able to bank your primary source of income for at least a year and live solely on the income that you have derived through trading? If not, the pressure of trading for a living when you do quit your job may affect your trading decisions.

- Do you have the support of your family? It's up to you to make sure that they understand your intentions and can accept your plans regarding how the future will unfold. It will mean a dramatic change of circumstances for all of you if you start trading full time.

- Do you have the support of a group of traders who have your best interests at heart and can act as your 'unreasonable friends'? You need people in the trenches with you facing the same battles you are facing. You need to have someone to celebrate your successes, but not let your ego run away from you. You're after some fellow traders to really provide a reality check so that you don't run amok. Years ago,

I didn't see that this was an essential component of full-time trading. However, the longer I've been a trader, and the more I have helped create new generations of full-time traders, the more I realise just how important a peer group is.

The good times

On about the third day of full-time trading, I realised that daytime clothes were completely unnecessary. Pyjamas are a much more comfortable trading attire and because the market doesn't open until 10.00 am, you can sleep in without fear of being late for work.

I am often asked, 'How much time do you spend each day trading?' There is a hidden implication behind this question. People really want to know, 'What is the minimum amount of work that I need to do to get the maximum returns from the sharemarket?' You're an adult so I'm not going to sugar-coat my response for you. Casual effort equals casual results. It's not like your average job—there is no set hourly rate. You will not earn the salary of a barrister with only a couple of weeks (or even a couple of years) experience in the market.

People are often used to starting their day in neutral and waiting for their boss to give them a push. With trading, *you* need to start your day in gear. You need to be the hardest boss that you've ever worked for in order to succeed.

Going on holidays

When you take a holiday from your job it's likely that you'll be able to find someone to look after your clients or tend to your accumulated workload while you're away. Trading shares is completely different. There is usually no backup. It's unlikely that there will be anyone to shoulder the burden of your open positions if you're not available to fuss over them with tender loving care.

Consider your choices. If you go on holidays without considering how to monitor your positions, I can bet that you won't have a decent break, especially if you're not in the same time zone. You'll be up at 3.00 am in a UK hotel room, trying desperately to catch a glimpse of a CNN cable broadcast that contains some snippet of information about the Aussie sharemarket. Not only will you disturb your holiday, but your family may also resent the intrusion.

If you are intending to go on a holiday with anybody other than another obsessed trader, make sure that your travelling companions can understand your trading requirements in advance. Unless you are very careful, you may find yourself sleeping on the spare couch in the hall instead of inside the five-star hotel room — hardly the exotic image that you had in mind before you left home.

It is possible to trade by using a laptop and a mobile phone, especially if you are in the same time zone. Depending on the type of holiday that you're planning, this could be feasible. Ensure that you check the mobile phone coverage at your destination before you leave home. Carefully assess whether this is an appropriate solution. Will you be able to relax if you have open positions?

Personally, if I am going to go on holiday for anything longer than one or two weeks, I close out all of my open positions. Now, before you gasp and exclaim, 'Really, how can you do that?' just think about how long you plan to be involved in the market. If you're planning to be involved for any longer than one year, you will need to factor in some relaxation time. Write down your thoughts about how to handle any holidays you want to take in your trading plan.

Write down your thoughts about how to handle holidays in your trading plan.

Your results in the sharemarket will be a direct reflection of your experience, efforts and persistence. I have heard rumours of a mythical creature that trades for only 10 minutes a week, with very little experience in the market, and made 50 per cent in one month. But I have never verified that this is a true story — it sounds like a fairytale to me!

People aiming to become full-time traders often quit their job prematurely. Even though trading for a living offers an uncommon freedom, make sure you have developed the necessary skills before telling your employers that they are no longer required.

What does 'being a trader' mean to you?

It continues to astonish me what a fantasy the general public has about 'being a trader'. It's a rare day that I don't encounter someone who wants to trade places with me. Otherwise sane people tell me how much they envy me: 'I wish I could trade for a living' or 'I envy your discipline', which they usually utter on the very same day that I've had to bribe myself with chocolate to fill in that bloody form my accountant has been nagging me endlessly for.

Interestingly, they never say: 'I wish I had your tenacity' or 'I wish I could stick with incredibly boring tasks for 20 years the way you have'. I find that rather fascinating. With trading, it's these qualities more than almost any other that create a bank account stuffed full of cash. The ability to stick with a task, even when you don't feel like it, is what counts.

Some trading days or weeks it seems that the market is literally throwing money your way and you can't put a foot wrong. These are not the times where you need tenacity. Other times it seems that no matter how closely you follow your trading plan, you have somehow fallen out of sync with the ebbs and flows of the sharemarket. Oooh, yes. These are the periods you need to dig deep.

Every once in a while somebody does become an effective trader by accident. However, rarely do these people stay as traders for very long. To excel over the long term, you generally have to desire it and be single-mindedly passionate about it. You just won't last the long haul in the markets without that spark of enthusiasm and that ever so rare and indescribable glow of energy that is strong and undeniable.

When I first walked out of my last actual job in the mid 1990s, I have to tell you I was more than a bit scared. After I shook off the shackles I realised that there would be no more nice fat deposits into my bank account from my employer. It gave me a jittery, butterflies in the stomach type of feeling. The type of feeling you get when you're a bit excited, but also the same feeling you get just before you're about to throw up — a bewildering mix of the two.

All of a sudden, I knew within every cell in my body that I was fully responsible for myself and my family, and I realised there was no-one else I could fall back on. At the time, I knew I had made the *right* decision, but there was still a little nagging voice of doubt in my head that seemed to amplify just before I fell asleep at night — it was the same little nagging voice that helps to protect us and keep us safe so that we don't make stupid decisions.

Even though I'd been earning profits as regular as clockwork from the sharemarket, I was still a little concerned that my transition to being a full-time trader might just stuff things up. I wish I had known other traders at that stage who had also gone through a similar set of emotions, and I yearned for a support network that really understood me.

You'll never need to go through a similar set of scary emotions, because you have my full support every step of the way — whether you're starting out as a trader, or you're already taking on the world as a trading dynamo.

As traders, we refuse to let other people call the shots and we know it's up to us to look after ourselves, and to develop more than one source of income. We know in our hearts that people who rely on their boss to plot their financial futures will be sadly disappointed. Our future is a direct reflection of our past decisions.

By reading this book, you've taken a step in the right direction. You've set yourself apart from the lazy or ignorant masses that are happy to stay in their misguided comfort zones. By your actions, you've shown that you don't want to be one of the people who get to the end of their lives and wonder 'what if?'

Now you may be wondering why we haven't looked at a chart yet, even though I have hinted that chart analysis is a cornerstone skill to effective trading. I'll let you in on a little secret. There are a lot of people who can analyse a chart but only a few who understand the benefits of trading psychology. Without the right mindset, you'll be destined to trade dismally, regardless of how well you understand the mathematical implications of the Stochastic Indicator. The sharemarket rewards people who put in the proper groundwork and display patience. We will move onto investigating charts soon enough. By the end of the third section of this book, you'll know all that you need to know about analysing trend direction.

The next part of this book will help you to identify the types of people who will become successful traders. Maybe you'll spot yourself among them? I certainly hope so! Keep reading to discover some of the key differences between how men and women trade.

Part II
It takes all sorts

5

It's all about sex

In this chapter, you will learn that:

- There are key chemical and physiological differences between men and women. These differences tend to influence the trading abilities of individuals.

- Men face several specific trading challenges, including overconfidence, overtrading and aggression.

- Women tend to encounter a lack of confidence, which results in a need to talk about their results and a concern that trading is a male domain.

- Being aware of these challenges and establishing action plans to overcome them is a great way to trade more effectively, regardless of your gender.

UP UNTIL THE 1980S, it was believed that the brains of men and women operated in much the same way. It was thought that any differences between the genders could be accounted for through social conditioning. Technological advances produced scanning techniques that revealed significant physiological differences between the male and female brain, differences that are present from the time we are born. It is important to be aware of how this can enhance or detract from your performance as a trader. (If you are planning in advance to take offence at something in this chapter, don't blame me—blame the improvements in technology! Just because men are different from women doesn't mean that one is superior to the other.)

A brief history lesson

In ancient times men and women lived in relative harmony. They knew their roles and respected each other for their unique differences. Each appreciated the other's efforts. According to Allan and Barbara Pease, authors of *Why Men Don't Listen and Women Can't Read Maps,* males were the 'lunch-chasers' and females were the 'nest-defenders'.

Lunch-chasers developed superior goal focus, excellent navigational skills and amazing physical strength. These men liked to win and see someone else lose. It reinforced their superiority over other males and enhanced their chances of breeding success. Social conditioning and the brain functions of the Neanderthal male prevented them from showing outward signs of fear or uncertainty. Their language skills were not heavily valued as they just had to kill the wildebeest, not sing it a lullaby. Males spoke only to relay facts, whereas females used words to build relationships. Men would compete and women would cooperate.

Women's thicker corpus callosum (the nerve cord connecting the left brain with the right brain) meant that they could juggle several tasks simultaneously.

The nest-defender's chief role was to look after her brood and form relationships with other nest-defenders. This ensured that the community would pull together in an emergency situation. Women's thicker corpus callosum (the nerve cord connecting the left brain with the right brain) meant that they could juggle several tasks simultaneously. They could watch the kids, have a meaningful conversation, trim the neighbour's hair and plan how to create the wheel, all at the same time. The presence of oestrogen enhanced women's language skills and equipped them to use creativity or insight to solve problems. Nest-defenders gathered fruit and nuts. They were not expected to hunt or fight.

Somewhere along the line, we became civilised. Mutual respect for each other's roles was thrown out the window. Men who are not sensitive to others' feelings are now often scorned by women. Women who decide that they prefer to nurture their children instead of hunting down a career may be considered brainless. Even though generations have passed, neither gender has changed much emotionally since prehistoric times. Our basic needs have stayed the same.

Many of these ancient skills have translated into the propensity for good trading habits. For example, men have the ability to focus when trading, and women always manage to fit trading around their already busy schedules. However, the vast majority of these hardwired behaviours propel us toward ineffective trading habits.

Rather than stand in judgement, let's have a look at the ways that both genders can use their unique skills to become better traders.

Chemistry

Hormone levels, as well as the physiological differences between the genders, make it seem as if men and women are from different planets.

When a man's brain is in a resting state, 70 per cent of its activity is shut down. Continual brain stimulation is an uncomfortable state for a man. This implies that men can mentally index their problems and put them on hold. To obtain peak effectiveness, guys need time to be master of the TV remote and become one with the couch. Men, take a break from trading from time to time to give your brain a chance to shut down. You'll trade much more effectively using this method instead of subjecting yourself to the constant stimulation of the sharemarket.

In a relaxed state, a woman's brain still functions at 90 per cent of its usual activity level. This shows that women are more likely to be processing information continuously. Females have difficulty putting their problems on hold and often need to talk through a situation in order to find a solution. Female traders may have a greater requirement to discuss their wins and losses with a friend. This can lead to several drawbacks, as revealed in chapter 22.

Men often consider that the sharemarket is a battlefield where there can be only one winner.

Men often consider that the sharemarket is a battlefield where there can be only one winner. If they have lost money by trading a share, they often actively seek revenge. Women may develop higher degrees of loyalty toward a share that has previously been profitable. Neither approach is effective. Become aware of your own psychology and you will increase your profitability.

Interestingly, women are (statistically speaking) 3 per cent more intelligent than men. Although this has nothing to do with how effectively each gender will trade, I felt compelled to draw your attention to this fact.

Confidence in decisions

Using a large US discount brokerage firm's account data for over 35 000 households, Brad Barber and Terrance Odean analysed the common stock investments of men and women from February 1991 through January 1997. Men traded 45 per cent more but earned 1.4 per cent per annum less compared with females. These differences are more pronounced between single men and single women. Single men traded 67 per cent more than single women and earned 2.3 per cent per annum less. The researchers attribute these results primarily to the negative effects of overconfidence and overtrading (as discussed in chapter 11).

Barber and Odean's study shows that the more a portfolio is turned over each year, the worse the ultimate performance. For example, when a portfolio is turned over more than 200 per cent a year, the average annual net return trails the market index by 10.3 per cent. In a study of 78 000 households, women turned over their portfolios about 53 per cent annually and men turned over their portfolios 77 per cent annually.

The research suggests that when feedback is unequivocal and immediately available, women are just as confident in their own abilities as men. It was found, however, that: 'when such feedback is absent or ambiguous, women seem to have lower opinions of their abilities and often underestimate [their sharemarket performance] relative to men'.

Feedback in the sharemarket is ambiguous. For this reason, women may be more inclined to await the perfect set up before investing. This could account for their more moderate trading levels compared with males, yet their higher levels of success.

Is trading a male domain?

According to Allan and Barbara Pease, about 90 per cent of women in the general population have limited spatial functioning. Navigation, maths and three-dimensional visualisation are not skills that come naturally to many women. Trading, especially from a fundamental perspective, is built largely on mathematics. Perhaps for this reason, as well as the huge impact of social conditioning, some women may feel that the sharemarket is largely a male domain.

Technical analysis relies on pattern-recognition skills and the ability to think laterally. An understanding of your own psychology is required, in addition to the psychology of the group behaviour that forms the tides of bullish or bearish emotion. If you are a woman, use your strengths to interpret these patterns. Make a decision to silence any nagging voice in your head that says that only men can excel in this field. It is simply not true. Your unique skills have set you up to achieve success in the trading arena.

Reaction to stress

Under pressure, some women eat chocolate and go shopping. Many women react emotionally, using theatrical body language and dramatic speech patterns. This has the effect of allowing the physiological signs of stress to dissipate—possibly explaining (in part) why, statistically, women outlive men.

A lot of upset women will talk about their problems. Sharing is a sign of trust. When dealing with a distressed woman, it is important to listen in order to validate her feelings. This shows that you are reciprocating the trust she is placing in you. Offering solutions at this stage is not necessary or productive. If you are the spouse of a female trader, please remember this.

When feeling stressed, men generally drink alcohol and invade other countries. They react aggressively and are more likely to lash out. There is often no socially acceptable way to disperse their anxiety levels, so negative emotions are sublimated to reappear at a later date—possibly disguised as a heart attack. If you are the spouse of a male trader, remember that many men do not like unsolicited advice. They need to feel that their spouse has confidence in their ability to sort out their own problems.

Testosterone

Professor James Dabbs of Georgia State University measured the testosterone levels of a variety of males in different fields. He reported that the superior achievers in any endeavour had higher testosterone levels than lower achievers. In addition, he found that the thrill of achievement actually caused more testosterone to be produced. A correlation between heightened testosterone levels and signs of aggression was also found.

Based on these findings, high-achieving males in the trading field presumably have heightened testosterone levels. However, to maintain terrific results, high achievers probably need to find a way to dissipate their testosterone. It's very difficult to punch the living heck out of the sharemarket, so you'll need to find another method of alleviating your aggression levels. Physical exercise is a great alternative. Taking revenge on your computer screen is not.

The need to be right

Many men like to be right. They often consider themselves a failure when they are wrong; they consider it to be a sign that they have not been able to do their job properly. In extreme situations, you may even hear a male trader declare that 'the market is wrong'.

The market is never wrong. Your interpretation of the market dynamics is the only logical explanation for why you have lost money. Get over it.

The top three gender-specific areas that could improve your trading, and of which you should be aware, are outlined in table 5.1.

Table 5.1: top three gender-specific ways to improve trading

Men	
Problem	**Solution**
Overtrading	Trading more often does not necessarily mean that you are trading more effectively. Quality, not quantity, is essential. Define your entry and exit rules explicitly and refuse to trade unless these rules are met.
Overconfidence	Overconfidence is correlated with underperformance in the sharemarket. Experienced traders have a healthy fear of the market. You are pitching yourself at a superior opponent. The market has infinite resources, more strength and more power than you. Remind yourself of this. Measure your results meticulously to add reality to your trading.
Aggression	Don't seek revenge if you have made a loss. Fight your battles with an opponent with whom you can make eye contact. Physical activity may assist. Following a written trading plan will help you avoid taking unnecessary risks when you feel like you could strut into a boxing ring like Rocky.
Women	
Problem	**Solution**
Lack of confidence	Start small then increase your position size as your confidence grows. Research the topic to gain knowledge about all aspects of a trading plan, predominantly entry and exit points, and position sizing.
The need to talk about results	Find an appropriate person with whom to discuss your trading. Choose carefully.
Concerns that investing/trading is a male domain	Look at the statistical track record of other female traders and realise that you have the essence of a good trader within you.

The next chapter will give you some pointers about how you can encourage your children to begin their trading careers.

6

The best gift you can give your child

In this chapter, you will learn that:

- Children of all ages can be encouraged to learn about the sharemarket. Set up your children with the right wealth mindset from the beginning. This can be your legacy and establish future generations with financial security for life.

- Young children can learn to colour in candlestick charts and may be capable of drawing trendlines.

- Adolescents can take a more active role and be assisted either to trade with real funds, or paper trade.

- Encouraging an interest in your chosen field may have the benefit of allowing you to share a common interest with your child. Many people find that by explaining trading simply, their own trading methods can improve also.

I AM OFTEN SENT EMAILS BY parents or interested adults asking how can they pass on the legacy of effective trading habits to benefit the next generation. I feel this is such a valuable quest. Learning about trading can provide a source of bonding with our children and significant littlies, as well as allowing them to develop a skill that could very well be among the most significant we could ever share. Developing the next generation and encouraging them to trade and become skilled with handling money is a magnificent goal.

One of parents' main roles is to inspire our children to find their own solutions to life's questions. If your child is showing an interest in what you are doing, this is absolutely ideal. In this chapter I'd like to share some ideas with you regarding how you can encourage your child's interest in your chosen craft. There are remarkable spin-off benefits to this. Not only will your own trading probably improve, but if it doesn't, there's always hope that the next generation will work out how this whole game works and keep you in the lifestyle to which you'd happily become accustomed in your old age.

Young children

According to Piaget, a renowned psychologist in the area of intellectual development, children between the ages of two and four are capable of interacting on a basic, abstract level. (Another way of putting this is that kids can manipulate adults on purpose and use them to attain their own goals.) They are egocentric, which means that they value their own needs above yours—as any parent can testify. Imitation is a primary means of exploring the world. Up until the age of four, children will only be able to grasp the most rudimentary knowledge of trading.

...children between the ages of two and four are capable of interacting on a basic, abstract level.

At this very young age, encourage your children to colour in charts and to set up an 'office' that resembles your own workspace. Your children can pretend to trade by drawing red and green candlestick charts, for example.

While you are trading, encourage your little ones to draw in trendlines. Help them spell the words 'up' and 'down', and get them to write these words on the charts. As your children get a little older, show them how to calculate profit and loss figures if the share price goes up or down by one dollar, for example. Attaching a dollar sign to maths problems can encourage basic skills development with meaning. Allow them to track the share prices and compare these prices with the share chart. Children as young as six years old can even draw candlestick charts, if they are shown how the charts are constructed. By doing this you are reinforcing your children's importance, as well as buying yourself a bit of time to concentrate on trading.

If you need some quiet time trading, some of these techniques can give you a few moments of peace, and help your children understand why it's important that 'mummy/daddy needs to concentrate at the moment'. A little comprehension goes a long way.

As expressed by Ross Campbell in *How to Really Love Your Child*, one of the main needs for children of all ages is sufficient eye contact. By concentrating on your computer, without focusing your attention on your child from time to time, it is possible that they will resent your involvement with the sharemarket. Sometimes it can seem that our children are out to sabotage our analysis time. However, try to see it from their point of view — trading is technically taking your attention away from them. Spending some time with your child and explaining what you are trying to achieve will result in many benefits.

If you don't have children of your own, borrow a neighbour's kid or consider hiring an eight-year-old child. About two dollars per hour and the bribe of a Tim Tam should suffice. After they have programmed your VCR and cleaned up the viruses on your computer, conduct a simple experiment: print out a chart and pin it up on your wall, take a few steps back and have a good long look. Explain to the eight year old that it is a picture of how the share has been performing. If your new mini-employee says that the share is plummeting then believe him or her! Children are much more objective than adults will ever be. Self-delusion is a wonderful thing. It can make the trauma of being a modern adult so much easier to bear and without the need for medication. However, convincing ourselves that the sharemarket is trending up when it is not can be a lethal mistake. Children can help sift through the clutter that we put up in an effort to help ourselves think more clearly.

Often people try to overcomplicate their trading method. By simplifying it to the point that you can explain it to a child, your trading results will improve.

Adolescents

Depending on the developmental level of your teenagers, you may want to consider setting up an account in their names or at least encouraging them to paper trade. Until individuals turn 18, they are not legally allowed to trade in their own name, so you will need to set up the account where an adult acts as the signatory.

One method to consider is to lend your teenagers a certain amount of trading money to utilise. If they follow their trading rules and make a profit, they get to keep 50 per cent of the proceeds. However, if they do not follow their trading rules, they don't keep any money at all. This will reinforce the principle of following a trading plan, regardless of the results.

Note that it pays to be aware of your teenager's limitations and to establish appropriate boundaries. Several studies have revealed substantial differences in the way those under 18 years of age approach problem-solving compared with the way adults function.

Cognitive scientist Abigail Baird suggests, 'Teenagers take more risks because they don't foresee the consequences adults do.' In one of Baird's experiments, teenagers and adults were shown different scenarios on a computer screen that ranged from images of people eating salad to divers swimming with sharks. When asked to judge whether each activity was safe or dangerous, teenagers took much longer than adults. Furthermore, brain scans showed that the teenagers had to put more effort into this decision as measured by the activity of the prefrontal cortex.

Adults tend to make decisions more quickly and with less effort than teenagers. They also judge the level of risk more appropriately because they either have more mature brain function or more life experience. Take this into account when aiming to pique your teenager's interest in the sharemarket. Make sure you don't just give them open slather with your trading account, as this will probably not bring about the desired objective, for either of you.

Ask your child's school whether they would consider entering the ASX School's Sharemarket Competition (visit <www.asx.com.au> for further details). It is quite feasible for some children to have accumulated almost a decade of trading experience by the time they hit their 21st birthday.

Some of the most enthusiastic and promising traders I have ever met happen to be under the age of 21. I just love it when I'm at a traders' expo or similar presentation and some high school or university students approach me for a chat. It's great to see that ambition can start at a relatively tender age. The market doesn't discriminate. It doesn't care whether you are 18 or 80 years old. If you are a young trader, or you are aiming to encourage a young trader, good for you!

Some of the most enthusiastic and promising traders I have ever met happen to be under the age of 21.

Children will follow the example that we set. Here is one trader's experience of the legacy left to him by his father: 'I wish I had spent more time observing my father and learning from my "master", while I had the chance. He was a terrific trader and he bought shares in a foreign company for me on the day I was born.'

These are just a few ideas about how you can get your kids involved in the sharemarket. Spend some time explaining why you are trading and what you are hoping to achieve. Encourage their participation from an early age and provide tasks appropriate for their level of development.

So, why is this important?

As technical analysts, we strive to gather facts and make hefty decisions in light of the evidence. We pride ourselves on being logical, focused and non-emotional. So you can imagine my surprise when I heard two traders talking about how money isn't really all that important.

'People make too much of a big deal about money. It really doesn't matter that much. I mean it's not like the rich people end up with kids who are more intelligent is it?' said one to the other.

Well, I have to say, that comment got me thinking. Do the children of people with money have more advantages in life than the kids of less well-off parents? Just what do the facts say?

To look at this very question, in 2010 there was a study conducted by Michael Marmot based on 17 200 babies born in the UK in one week in April 1970. It researched social factors against biology. Significant health inequalities existed between the poorest and the richest groups for a start. For example, even if you exclude the richest and poorest 5 per cent of people in England, the richest remainder can expect to live six years longer and enjoy an extra 13 years free of disability.

And that's not all.

It ends up that babies with low IQs at 22 months who were born to rich and well-educated parents had caught up by the age of six with kids who started out with high IQs born to those with parents less well-off and educated. Oh my gosh — read that sentence again! Far out!

By the age of 10, the kids from the well-off parents were still progressing well with IQ tests, whereas the less well-off group were falling further behind.

These findings have been duplicated in other studies, too (Robert Wood Johnson Foundation April 2009). So as a trader, what does this mean to you? Holy beegeebeez, when you're planning to significantly increase your wealth, *you're not just doing it for yourself!* You're also creating a ripple effect that spreads beyond your own generation, and could directly affect the IQ of your own children.

Next time someone tries to convince you that money isn't important you've now got some ammunition. You are different from the majority. You've taken action by working on your own education. Remember, it's not just for your benefit. It's also for the benefit of those you love.

It's no accident that you're reading this book. You can sense that you're in the right place and that this feels like home. You see a good idea and you jump on it. You know that you are destined for more in life than you're currently achieving and I'd feel privileged to be right beside you, every step of the way.

Trading insights

The Global Financial Crisis has rattled many people. People's beliefs about the basics in life have been shaken. The formula laid out by our parents where if you work hard and you're conscientious then you'll do well in life, just isn't accurate any more. However, it is my belief that turbulent economic conditions will produce more exceptional traders than any other time because these traders will use their life situations as mental ammunition.

When you trade, you trade your own money. If you wish to give it to someone else to manage, that's fine. However, if you want to be a trader, then it will take longer than three weeks to achieve any degree of success. To shortcut the process, focus on your education, surround yourself with like-minded people who can encourage you, and be prepared to stick at it for the long haul. The results will ultimately be worth it.

In the next chapter, I reveal some of my views regarding successful traders who have influenced me throughout the years.

7

Find a hero—the undervalued success secret

In this chapter, you will learn that:

- Trading can seem like a daunting new arena when you first begin. One of the easiest ways to learn about effective trading habits is to immerse yourself in the knowledge of people who have a method to which you relate.

- It is useful to take note of the teachings of others, but be prepared to develop your own plan for success. No particular writer or trader will have knowledge of the unique circumstances you deal with, so tailor their ideas to your own requirements.

- If any claims about the results you could make from trading sound too good to be true, you're probably about to have vast amounts of money surgically extracted from your hip-pocket and implanted into the bank account of the seminar organisers. Beware of the sharemarket guru.

To EFFECTIVELY LEARN A NEW skill, it is often important to find someone to emulate. Anthony Robbins says, 'If you want to be a success, find someone who has achieved what you want and copy them.' Trading can be confusing. Even when you think that you've mastered the necessary skills, often you will come up against a completely new experience that will take your breath away. Personally, I have found that reading books written by successful traders has been invaluable in my own trading development. It is not only their techniques that I am seeking, but also their attitudes and views on life. Find someone to whom you relate and saturate yourself with his or her knowledge.

Market gurus

Just a quick word regarding putting people on pedestals—if you revere someone too much, you may be disappointed when you find out he or she is only human. Everyone has their flaws. Even though you can admire people in the markets, don't expect them to never put a foot wrong. Take what you can from their teachings but make sure that you develop and follow your own personalised plan.

There are three things that we need to achieve happiness in life: someone to love, something to believe in, and someone to blame when things go wrong. Enter the sharemarket guru.

> *... if you revere someone too much, you may be disappointed when you find out he or she is only human.*

The guru cashes in on our major needs, combining popular psychology and extreme promises to hypnotically entice us to pay copious amounts of money for seminars that will supposedly help us achieve sharemarket happiness. I've heard some of these gurus proclaim that you can quit your job with less than a year of trading experience! Let's allow logic to prevail here and work out the validity of statements such as this. Yes, some people may have achieved this but I can almost guarantee that most won't—only a very small percentage of people manage to achieve instant success.

All of this may be okay in a raging bull market; however, from time to time the bull will sprout claws. Just like sharks confined to a fishpond, the seminar presenters gnash their teeth and show signs of aggression. To encourage seminar attendance, and stand out among the other presenters, they make outrageous advertising claims.

How to spot a guru

In place of the flowing swami robe, the sharemarket guru is resplendent in Armani and appears to have all the hallmarks of success. If your sharemarket trainer makes any of the following boasts, be wary. Such statements are usually indications that your sharemarket trainer may have his or her heart in the wrong place.

'You'll make returns of more than 70 per cent per year.'

Here is a quick reality check. Ed Seykota is one of the greatest traders in the world, with returns of 60 per cent per year (no, this is not a typing error). Unrealistic benchmarks will sell a seminar, but they will also set you up for catastrophic losses. What makes you think that you can outperform Ed?

'I've been trading for the last three years.'

Even the worst traders can make astounding profits if the market conditions are right. Find someone that has weathered a few sharemarket crises and knows how to make money out of a downtrend. Three years is a blink of an eye in the context of the sharemarket.

'I make profits 80 per cent of the time.'

This is a ridiculous yardstick. Most good traders will talk more about their losses and the lessons they have learned as opposed to their profits. This is not just a case of admirable humility—the sharemarket has a way of punishing those with inflated egos.

Any statements or testimonials jam-packed with impressive figures about profit should be regarded suspiciously. In Australia, the Australian Securities & Investments Commission (ASIC) is the industry watchdog that ultimately cracks down on these types of schemes. Most countries have some sort of equivalent body set up to protect traders; however, in many cases it is too late to save the innocent and gullible people who have already paid thousands of dollars to pursue a pipedream. If you are in the buying zone for a seminar on the sharemarket, check the credentials of the presenter and organisers very carefully, and don't get sucked in by over-the-top claims.

'Here is a no-risk strategy.'

The search for the no-risk trade has achieved Holy Grail status in the sharemarket. Novices believe that it exists. Professionals know that it doesn't. If there is no risk, then there is no reward, it's as simple as that.

'Entry is the key.'

There are three distinct parts to a good trading plan: entry/exit methodology, risk management and money management. Entry signals will only help you to engage trades that have a high probability of success. They will not tell you how to exit or how much money to place into a trade, which are the very things that will determine your long-term success. Risk and money management are not sexy topics and they will not sell a seminar, but they do separate the professionals from the mediocre masses.

Natural selection dictates that for a particular characteristic to evolve it must be attractive to those we seek to impress. The gurus have emerged because we have encouraged them to do so. We have no-one to blame but ourselves. In our desperate and pathetic hunt for a higher authority, we willed them into existence. Unfortunately, the guru of yesterday is the despised charlatan of today.

There are no shortcuts to trading success—you will need to stop relying on fairytales and begin trusting your own written trading plan. The best traders have read widely, sparingly attended high-quality seminars, and exercised discernment when it came to listening to other traders. Don't blame the guru for your trading results—they only had power over you because you gave it to them.

Wisely choose the seminars that you attend and aim not to be duped by the 'wealth creation' specialists who do not have your best interests at heart. Seminars can be a fabulous way to learn about trading, but just be aware that some presenters are more interested in the money you can donate to their own piggy banks than providing you with sound, conservative strategies based on solid financial-planning principles.

Ultimately, to achieve greatness you will need to do more than just copy someone else. Your trading must be individualised to suit your own circumstances.

With trading, you can't leave your choices to guess work. If you do, you will fail. You've got to challenge common assumptions about trading, your mindset and your progress.

Understand this: people generally don't question. They meekly accept their miserable fates. Rarely do they strive to achieve. Rarely do they stand up and shout, 'Over here, success. Pick me! Pick me!'

If you're the type of person who can search for answers, back your trading hunches with cold hard facts, test your ideas and develop the skill and tenacity to stick at trading, then a lack of money will never be an issue in your life. The markets will throw money at you.

Great traders

One of the best sources of information about great traders is interviews. The *Market Wizards* series of books by Jack Schwager will provide valuable additions to your library. There are some similarities between all of the traders interviewed in Schwager's books. These can be distilled into the following three components:

1   There is no one particular grand secret to trading the markets, even though this is difficult for people to accept. There are a million ways to make money in markets. The irony is that they are all very difficult to find and will require hard work and exertion. Tips, insider information or black box systems will not lead to trading success. If it sounds too good to be true, it probably is.

2   The secret to success lies within each individual, not in finding a new indicator
     or a unique set-up. Your background does not determine your success. Qualities
     such as tenacity, fluidity, lateral thinking and experience will propel you toward
     trading excellence.

3   Success in trading is a terrific goal, but it is worthless if the rest of your life is in
     a shambles. Most good traders have achieved a level of balance in their lives. They
     value their health, their personal lives and often their spiritual lives.

Why do traders write books?

The Dalai Lama once stated, 'Share your knowledge. It's a way to achieve immortality.'
This reflects my personal beliefs as to why some traders are quite willing to share
their knowledge.

The longer I have been trading, the more humble I have been forced to become. I do
not consider myself to be a great trader. If I were ever tempted to feel this way, then I
was probably on the brink of making a catastrophic trading mistake. Writing books is an
interesting sideline for me, but it is not my primary source of income. Popular novelists
get paid well, good technical writers do not.

Three heroes

Throughout my trading life there have been some significant turning points that have
been initiated by the books I have read. Although I have never met these authors, my key
trading influences have been Darvas, Weinstein and Tharp.

Darvas

Nicolas Darvas, who was a dancer in the 1950s, wrote the timeless classic *How I Made
$2,000,000 in the Stockmarket*, and his insights into the sharemarket are terrific. His breakout
method of trading is something that I use in my own trading, and prepared me well for
when I encountered the works of Stan Weinstein. Many of the psychological principles of
trading successfully are revealed in this charming story about Darvas' own life.

Here are a number of Darvas's main concepts that I have found invaluable:

* trade alone

* apply a trailing stop loss

* don't listen to well-meaning brokers

* find a method that suits you

- stick to your rules

- take responsibility

- keep a trading diary.

Weinstein

Stan Weinstein's process of analysing shares according to different stages is somewhat legendary. His book *Secrets for Profiting in Bull and Bear Markets* refined my own breakout and retracement trading strategies and builds on the tactics explored by Darvas. When I combined my own theories about candlesticks with Weinstein's stage analysis, I could hardly believe the results. I cover this in more detail in my book *The Secret of Candlestick Charting*.

Weinstein's premise is that, in a share chart, a pattern will form that resembles the chart shown in figure 7.1. By figuring out what stage a particular share is in, you will be able to develop appropriate strategies to make money.

Figure 7.1: MIM weekly chart—share stages

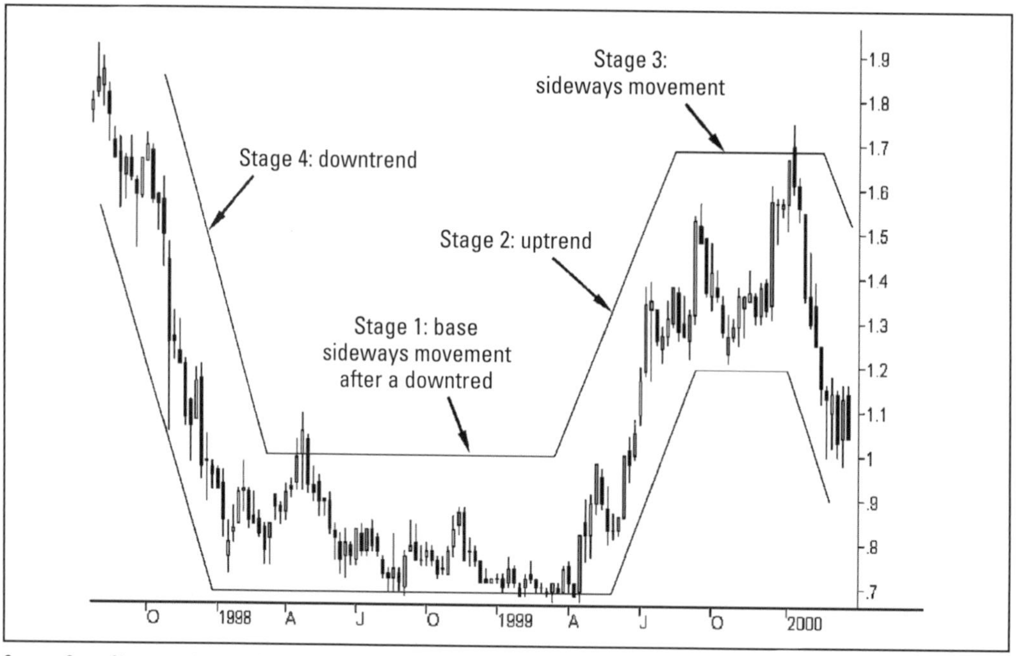

Source: SuperCharts version 4 by Omega Research © 1997.

Weinstein also emphasises the importance of the Relative Strength Comparison, in addition to short selling. These are essential components of my own trading. I recommend Weinstein's book for beginners in the sharemarket as well as more experienced traders who have not explored the share stages concept.

I realise this chart is really quite old now. I'll bet you that you could find some more recent examples. There are heaps of them. Just pop your charts onto weekly, zoom out and then look to see if you can spot any apparent share stages. This little exercise will give you a much deeper understanding of this concept.

Tharp

Dr Van K. Tharp's *Trade Your Way to Financial Freedom* is the quintessential book on trading psychology and money management. Tharp is a world authority on these subjects and if you are at the intermediate or advanced level, you will derive maximum benefit from this book. An awareness of his concepts of risk/reward, expectancy and win/loss ratios is essential to be able to trade professionally. Tharp emphasises that entry set-ups are only a minor component of a winning trading system, which fits very well with my own trading philosophy.

The more you can absorb from books, the more sophisticated your trading will become.

The most successful people in any endeavour tend to have a high level of self-awareness. This is true of profitable traders as well. Keep reading to learn how to develop some of these key skills.

8

Trader—know thyself

In this chapter, you will learn that:

- Controlling your own mindset will contribute just as much to your trading success as developing appropriate trading strategies.

- It is essential to develop detachment from your trading positions and be consistent with your approach to trading. The best traders continually educate themselves about trading psychology and seek to attain balance in their lives.

DURING THE HEIGHT OF THE technology boom in the late 1990s, I heard about a group of Silicon Valley psychologists who specialised in the treatment of Rapid Wealth Syndrome. This modern-day affliction was reaching epidemic proportions in the '20-something-geek' demographic at the time. I wonder if, after investors subsequently fell out of love with the word 'dotcom', these psychologists went on to treat clients suffering Rapid Wealth Depletion Syndrome? What will they be up to next?

There may be an easier way to gain personal insight than hiring a team of psychologists. By working on yourself as hard as you work on your trading plan, you're more likely to achieve financial success.

One of the main hindrances to superior trading performance seems to be that people are limited by their own mindset. Your level of self-awareness will determine your level of financial success. As the late Jim Rohn said, 'Success is not to be pursued; it is to be attracted by the person you become.'

The pursuit of self-awareness will be a lifelong journey. To condense this process into a chapter that you can read in your lunch break is a somewhat daunting task. The concepts I am about to discuss should be just the tip of the iceberg. I would like to encourage you to do whatever you can to improve your mindset. This will provide you with an emotional buffer that you'll need when things are not going well and you feel like quitting.

Trading has a way of forcing you to bare your soul. It will often make you come face-to-face with your inadequacies. The sharemarket tends to highlight all of your flaws while minimising all of your strengths. Sounds like a picnic, doesn't it? Only the persistent and emotionally strong will ultimately achieve trading prowess.

> *Trading has a way of forcing you to bare your soul. It will often make you come face-to-face with your inadequacies.*

It you are relatively happy with your trading strategies but have a sneaking suspicion that something is standing between you and incredible profits, then you owe it to yourself to read on.

Balance is important

Reading between the lines of *Market Wizards* by Jack Schwager, the majority of superior traders have attained a healthy balance in their life. Occasionally an obsessed, power-hungry person will become a good trader — but these people are the exception rather than the rule.

Initially, you may find that learning about trading is occupying your every waking moment. Over time this feeling should dissipate. Outstanding traders spend time taking their dog for a walk in the park; they volunteer for tuckshop duty at their kids' school; and they often help their community by giving money to charity. They look after their health, their spiritual development and their families, as well as their wealth.

Know when not to trade

Do you honestly understand the current emotions prevailing in the markets? Unless you can answer with an unqualified 'yes', then I suggest that you do not trade, or at least minimise your position size until you honestly feel you can trade with relative confidence. This is one of the rules that most traders tend to overlook. It's important to know when not to trade. Trading when your view of the market direction is unclear is no better than being an amateur blackjack player.

Changing personal circumstances will sometimes create pressure that can lead to underperformance in the markets. If you are sick, moving house, getting divorced or having a baby, then you are probably not trading from the ideal emotional foundation. (Especially if you are having the baby while you are trying to trade. Linda Bradford Raschke, a US-based trader, was apparently trading while in the last throes of labour, and again within just a few hours of giving birth! Yikes!)

During periods of stress you will probably overlook details and second-guess your analysis. When you subsequently experience a loss, you may persecute yourself mercilessly and perhaps propel yourself into a mini-depression.

Often in life we are either spiralling up or we are spiralling down in attitude. If you keep making poor trading decisions while you are in a vulnerable situation, you will only exacerbate your own negative mindset. Wait until the tide turns in your life, and it's likely that your trading will improve also. There will always be opportunities in the market. Whether you start trading later this week or later this year will be of little significance in the long run. Give yourself a chance to recover if you have experienced a recent emotional shock.

Self-sabotage

Often it can seem as if the market is alive and is out to get you. Believe it or not, the share won't drop from a great height because it knows that you bought it the day before. Even though the markets are dynamic and can seem to be self-aware from time to time, let me assure you that the market doesn't know that you exist. Your own hand has perpetrated any damage that you have experienced as a result of being a player in the sharemarket. The enemy lies within. Luckily, so do the seeds of your own greatness.

Often in life we are either spiralling up or we are spiralling down in attitude.

Many people have an inbuilt drive towards self-destruction. We all know the type of people who consistently choose the wrong job, crash their car or are burgled because they left the front door open. All of these symptoms could be an outward display of a deeper issue. As Ed Seykota, one of the world's most successful traders, says, 'Some people seem to like to lose, so they win by losing money.' Sort out your own mindset or the market will manifest your darkest thoughts.

Personalities

If you are a trader who has an impulsive personality, you may find that you constantly enter trades on rumour, opinion or hearsay. You may even fall in love with a stock so that you are blinded to the true behaviour of the share. If you are overly analytical, you may miss a trading signal because all the traffic lights on your drive interstate were not green before you left your home. Working on your weaknesses doesn't sound like much fun but I'm willing to guess that neither are elements of your day job. Your profitability will increase in direct proportion to your desire to learn about yourself, as well as the market. Trading utopia is unfortunately at the end of a road known as hard work.

> *Your profitability will increase in direct proportion to your desire to learn about yourself, as well as the market.*

Do you know the best way to encourage a rat to push a lever incessantly? (That's assuming that this is a desirable behaviour in rats — after I spent four years studying psychology at university, the professors had almost made me believe that this is how rats achieve self-actualisation!) All you need to do is provide a pellet for the poor hungry rat, on a random basis. With an intermittent reward like this, the wretched little rat will keep on pushing that lever until it develops carpal tunnel syndrome.

Partial reinforcement is the most powerful method of behaviour modification. This is exactly what the markets provide for you. Sometimes when you follow your rules you will make money. Occasionally when you break your rules, you will make money. By examining these events, you may think that there is no correlation between your own behaviour and the changing tide of your fortune. This is a recipe for addiction. It is how casinos encourage a never-ending stream of punters to walk through their doors.

Here are some of the symptoms that could mean you have a problem:

- You find it difficult to ever take a holiday and close your positions.

- Your trading time frame has become shorter and shorter until you are practically day trading.

- You become increasingly annoyed when your family distracts you from looking at the computer screen.

- After a loss, you feel compelled to increase your position size to win back the money that the market 'owes' you.

- The little noises and bleeps that your computer makes now cause you to salivate like one of Pavlov's dogs.

If you can relate to any of the symptoms in this list, you should close out your open positions and take a break. Get some perspective. Trading because of an addiction is a sure route to disaster.

Focus on more than the current trade

Traders tend to perceive that their current trades have the ability to make or break them. Selective perception kicks in and every glimpse of information about 'your special share' seems to take on an overwhelming importance.

There is no one particular trade that will determine your ultimate trading success. By extending your knowledge about stop losses, money management and position sizing, you will come to realise this.

Admit when you're wrong

The ability to review your mistakes and to quickly admit when you are wrong is essential. The market is always right and there is no point in arguing. It is futile to stubbornly hold your ground when all evidence suggests that your analysis is no longer correct.

Learn from every trading experience, whether you incur a win or a loss. The Dalai Lama says, 'When you lose, don't lose the lesson.'

Learn from your past results

Dr Alexander Elder, a great trader and author of *Trading for a Living*, explained to me that there is a popular Russian saying that translates as: 'Don't step on the same rake twice.' Learn from your past errors. Also, learn from your past successes.

Keep a trading diary and review it at least once a month. Analyse your results dispassionately as if you were looking at someone else's trades. It is within your grasp to learn everything that you'll ever need to know about trading. Recognise patterns in your own behaviour.

Stop envying other people

As a teenager with crooked teeth and a few too many kilos, I remember looking at the popular girls with abject envy. I would ask, 'Why were they born so pretty, skinny, clever or blonde?' As my grandmother always told me, 'Comparing yourself to others only leads to heartache.'

Although it seems as if everyone around you is making a killing on the markets, it is likely that they are only telling you about their good trades. Any trader who tells you they consistently get in at the bottom and out at the top of a trend is either a liar or suffering from an advanced case of self-delusion.

While I'm on this topic—stop telling people about your trades! Most people feel an overwhelming need to fill any silence with words. If you keep telling others about your open positions, you are encouraging them to respond. Dr Alexander Elder says, 'Don't talk your book.' While you have active trades in the market, it is far better to keep this private, and not discuss your successes or failures with another living soul. You do not need to hear another person's response regarding your effectiveness or ineffectiveness as a trader. The market will tell you soon enough. Your role is to introspectively work on yourself and your trading plan, and not rely on others to sympathise or to congratulate. What other people think about you is none of your business.

Develop detachment

When traders lose money, they usually blame bad luck or poor advice rather than their own personal qualities of arrogance, fear and greed. External attribution of blame is a sign of immaturity. This is called 'external locus of control'. Aim to develop an 'internal locus of control' and take responsibility for your own actions. Assume that all trading results are your responsibility and aim to find ways to improve your own behaviour. This is the quickest way to improve your trading ability.

Good traders have achieved a sense of detachment from the market and have divorced themselves from chasing elusive profits. The way that you handle trading can come down to the following formula:

$$A + B + C = D$$

$$(A = \text{the event}$$

$$B = \text{self talk}$$

$$C = \text{emotions}$$

$$D = \text{reaction})$$

The only thing that you don't have full control over in this formula is 'A', which represents a loss or a profit. How you compile every other part of this formula is up to you. Even if you take high probability trades, it is still only a probability and not a certainty. All traders must adjust to the concept that even high probability trades can sometimes create a loss. It is how you talk to yourself about this event (for example, a loss and the emotions that you feel) that will determine your reaction to the event (for example, revenge trading or quitting).

Professional traders treat profits and losses with calmness and emotional objectivity. Amateurs oscillate between joy and despair repeatedly (see figure 8.1).

Figure 8.1: emotional swings of a trader

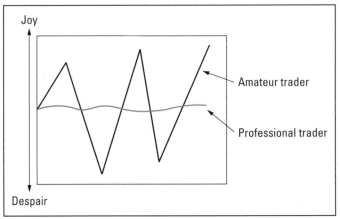

You choose how to react to every event in your life. No-one can force you to feel a particular way. Stop allowing external circumstances to prevent you from achieving your potential.

Fear

There are so many things to be fearful of in the markets. Fear of taking a loss, fear of learning a new skill, fear of failure, fear of being wrong—the list goes on and on. To achieve in the sharemarket you must overcome these fears and strive to achieve trading excellence. To quote Lao Tzu, 'Conquering others requires force, conquering oneself requires strength.'

There is one other predominant fear that people struggle with in the markets—the fear of success. Can you visualise how your life would be if your net worth doubled or tripled? This skill is essential in order for us to achieve our goals. To attain greatness, you have to have the courage to visualise it.

Traders brought up in a religious environment may also struggle with the question of ethics. Is it okay to be rich? Is there a higher level of nobility in suffering and being the revered 'battler' who is almost worshipped in our culture? You will need to come to grips with these issues in order to develop wealth. Money doesn't change

Money doesn't change people— it only amplifies their natural predisposition.

people—it only amplifies their natural predisposition. If it is in your nature to be kind and good to others, then money will assist you in this goal. For example, your contributions to charity can be more significant.

Be consistent

The irresistible lure of a big win, the propensity to compare ourselves to others, and the fickleness of markets all combine to teach us poor trading habits. The only way that you'll make a better return than the fund managers is to develop a robust trading system and follow it to the letter. Unless you follow a system consistently you will have no chance of making the necessary modifications to improve your trading.

Be willing to appear goofy

I received an email the other day that kind of shook me. Here's what it said:

'Louise, I'm a fan, but I have a piece of advice for you that I do hope you'll follow. You're telling people too much. As an example, I know that you openly tell people how it took you three years to break-even on the sharemarket. You need to be aware that people don't want to hear this if they're going to follow your strategies. They need to feel they can put their faith in the things that you do, so they'll be able to trade well.'

Ahhh ... isn't this an interesting topic?

Is it wise to be so open and share so much personal stuff? Wise? No. But honest? Yes. Are people more likely to follow someone without a few bullet holes and scars? Personally, I'm not so crazy about listening to those with the Midas touch. They're not all that interesting, relatable or knowledgeable about the strategies you get to create when your back is to the wall. Also, when the bullets do start flying about, I'll bet that they'll be running for cover, crying 'mummy, mummy ...!'

So yes, I do risk showing you my heart in this book and pointing out the things I've done wrong with trading, as well as right. However, it seems to me that the overwhelming majority of people go through life literally crippled by not wanting to be embarrassed in front of other people. They live their lives of quiet desperation and dissatisfaction—subservient when they should take charge, quiet when they should be speaking up, dependent when they should be independent and poor when they should be rich.

As I walk beside you on your trading journey, pointing out the hidden landmines (because I have stepped on them before), just realise that I'm willing to look a bit goofy on the occasion, because I care about your trading success. I'd rather tell you what I've done wrong so that you can learn from my experiences, and don't need to go ahead and repeat them.

And besides, those initial three years taught me valuable lessons, so I really don't look back on them as a failure. Without those first few traumatic ups and downs, I wouldn't be the person I am today.

Five ways to overcome trading barriers

Need some specifics? Here are the best things you can do to become the best trader you can be:

1   One of the main ways I have found to overcome these hurdles is to develop a written trading plan that you believe in. If you're convinced that your plan is effective, you will have much less difficulty following it.

2   Simply pull the trigger and get involved in the market. Start with a small amount of money while you have your training wheels on. The more trades that you do, the easier it will be to take a loss. Do not react egotistically to a profit. The markets will teach you all that you need to know.

3   For traders facing issues related to procrastination—break down your trading task into steps, rank them in terms of priority and set yourself a deadline to complete each step. Tell someone that you trust about this deadline and ask this person to question you regarding your progress. Find someone to be answerable to. Work out how to discipline yourself or the market will discipline you.

4   Write down the top three things that are stopping you from trading well. Examine these issues. The reason you hold on to certain aspects of your personality is because, on some level, you want to. A small part of you may relish the by-products that come about through not trading well. When you have become aware of your own behaviour, you can alter it immediately should you choose to. Write down the benefits that you derive by holding onto these trading afflictions. Be honest with yourself. Make everything about your own behaviour as explicit as possible, and you will dramatically improve your own performance.

5   You can try self-affirmations, meditation, yoga or whatever method that you find to be of benefit in creating clarity in your life. There is no one method that will work for every individual. Keep trading in perspective and maintain balance in your life. If you cannot sleep because you are worried about your trading performance,

lower your position size until you find that you can handle the pressure. Trading should be monotonous—if it isn't, then you need to improve some aspect of your attitude or system design.

A trading system typically includes three components:

- entry/exit methodology

- risk management

- money management.

Handling your own individual psychology is essential if you are to become a successful trader. If you would like more information on this topic, listen to my *Psychology Secrets* CD program. On this CD, with the help of fellow trader Chris Tate and Dr Harry Stanton, I explore the top 10 trading blunders and how to overcome them. *My Trading Psychology Home Study Course* is also available to help you become more self-aware. These products are available from <www.tradingsecrets.com.au>.

If you haven't picked up your free trading pack from my website, run to the computer and do this now. You can't afford to put it off for another minute. It's free. It's waiting for you. I guarantee I've put my heart and soul into it for you. You deserve it.

The next part of this book will take you through some specifics relating to effective technical analysis. I'm sure that, by now, you've been dying to get your teeth into analysing some charts and to learn about trend detection. Well done for being so patient. The best traders are willing to work as hard on their own psychology as they are their technical analysis skills. Let's get down to the nitty gritty. Keep reading to develop your skill with charting and to learn about the 'darling' of technical analysis—the candlestick.

Part III
Trading tools

9

History never repeats.
Are you sure?

In this chapter, you will learn that:

- Sure *History Never Repeats* is a catchy song title. However, when it comes to trading, this saying is wrong. Dead wrong. Past share price behaviour can be used to estimate future share price direction and I'll show you exactly how.

- The basic building blocks of a chart involve a graphic display of price and volume action. You may choose to use bar charts, line charts or candlestick charts.

- Candlestick charts are the best charts to use. Bar charts and line charts look boring and ugly.

- When looking at the patterns candlestick charts show, take into account the candle colour, the candle length and the tail location.

BY USING PRICE AND VOLUME action, you can form a view about the likely direction of the trend in the future. This is the essence of technical analysis. Money is made in the markets by calculating the probability of likely direction and responding to market conditions. The aim is to estimate whether a share is likely to continue in a specific direction or if a change in trend is probable. It is impossible to make a prediction with 100 per cent certainty, unless you have a crystal ball (if you've got one of those, then please email me to let me know the winning TattsLotto numbers). Technical analysis is far from a perfect discipline and your degree of success will depend on your skill and experience.

Black box systems

From time to time you may hear a slick sales pitch where a sharemarket guru predicts future share price movements and claims an amazing level of accuracy. I guess if such gurus make enough predictions, then they are sure to be right once in a while. Even a broken clock tells the time correctly twice a day.

This is the easiest way to get the general public to part with their money — tell them that there is a method that will always predict the direction of the market.

This one ploy helps to line the pockets of the promoters of the particular technique, but does little for the purchaser of this mysterious market system. If someone really knew the direction of the future market activity, why would they tell you? Why wouldn't they just trade in the direction of their prediction and become overnight millionaires? They wouldn't need to impress upon you the effectiveness of their system — they could just trade with it and not suffer the burden of an expensive advertising budget!

I don't know of any successful trader who uses a black box system. These mysterious packages are often called 'black box' systems. With such systems, you are not informed about how the buy and sell signals are generated and the software makes all of the decisions. Even if the system worked well at one stage in the past, the dynamic nature of market behaviour lessens the chances of this reliability continuing into the future. Good systems require subtle alterations over time. The chances that an off-the-shelf trading system will match your own trading objectives and personality are very slim indeed. I don't know of any successful trader who uses a black box system. If black boxes were effective, then surely great traders such as Ed Seykota and George Soros would stop working so hard and just use a black box to create their incredible returns.

Grey boxes can include elements of undisclosed buy and sell indicators and proprietary indicators unique to the company that developed them. Tool boxes provide you with a variety of indicators but they do not provide guidance about which shares to buy and sell. The closer a grey box is to a tool box, the better.

Share behaviour

In many ways, shares behave in a similar way to children. Each child has its own personality from birth. Some are obstreperous and incredibly difficult to look after. Others are placid and calm, never causing a moment of grief. If you can get to know the child, then looking after him or her suddenly becomes much simpler. Likewise, if you begin to understand the share's price action characteristics, you will learn how to treat it. The particular idiosyncrasies of that share will suddenly seem within the realms of normal behaviour. Technical analysis provides us with tools to assist us in realising this goal.

If this is the first time that you have come into contact with technical analysis, it may be beneficial to re-read this chapter and the following chapter a couple of times to consolidate the principles. Remember your first day on your job? It was terrifying, wasn't it? You didn't know where the lunch room was located, or what was expected of you. Yet, over time, you adjusted and your work became second nature. Trading is exactly the same. Initially, it will seem confusing and strange, but with a bit of effort you will finally work it out. Be patient with yourself. All it takes is a bit of elbow grease and persistence and you'll be well on your way to being profitable.

If you are already a skilled trader, then you will find that the following section will act as a form of revision. In any endeavour, the people who excel are those who conquer the basics. When playing cricket, there are actually very few skills that you need to have. For example, catching, batting, bowling and running. Yet it is the application of these basic skills that will separate the cricket professional from the backyard superstar.

Bars, lines and candles

As technical analysts, it is our goal to form a view regarding whether a particular share is going up, going down, or moving in a sideways band. Even though there are only three directions in which a share can move, it is sometimes a tricky task to see exactly what a share is doing. Simplicity is essential. When first looking at a chart, get to the grassroots level and have a good look at a share's price action. You can use a bar chart, a line chart or a candlestick chart. Indicators can ultimately assist us in our quest and these will be covered in the following chapter, but the first step is to look at the chart itself.

The markets are made up of people's emotions toward shares. If they predominantly feel fear that they will lose their capital or profits, then the share price will ultimately decrease. If the participants mainly feel greed or hope, the share price will go up. A chart will show this interplay of emotion in a graphic format.

The individual building block of a bar chart is a single bar. Drawing a single bar requires an opening price, a high, a low and a closing price (see figure 9.1, overleaf). The vertical line shows the high and low of that period. The two horizontal lines depict the open and the close. The open is the horizontal line on the left of the vertical line, and the close is the horizontal line on the right of the vertical line. On a daily chart, one bar will show the share price action for one day. If you look at a weekly chart, the open price will be the opening price at the start of the week and the closing price will be the final price recorded at the end of the week. The high and low will be the overall high for the week and the overall low for the week. Whichever time period you utilise, the bar can show the activity for that session.

Figure 9.1: a single Western bar

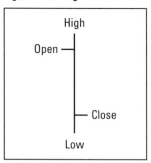

When many of these single period bars are plotted on a chart, with the horizontal axis representing time and the vertical axis showing the share price, a traditional bar chart is created (see figure 9.2). The interrelationships of the bars show whether the share is generally going up in value (bullish) or going down in value (bearish). Periods of sideways progression are also evident. Indicators may help assist you to understand whether the predominant direction is likely to continue.

Figure 9.2: CBA daily bar chart

Source: SuperCharts version 4 by Omega Research © 1997.

A line chart connects the closing prices for each period, and so provides even less information, but is perhaps a simpler chart to interpret compared with the bar chart (see figure 9.3). This type of chart is generally used in newspapers when a journalist depicts share price action.

Figure 9.3: CBA daily line chart

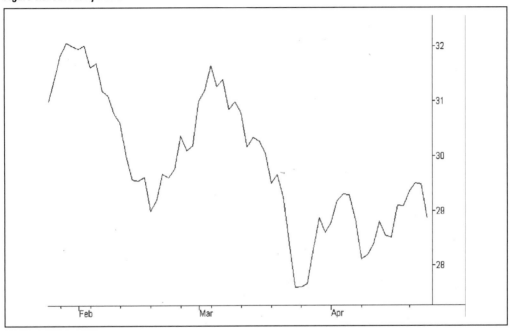

Source: SuperCharts version 4 by Omega Research © 1997.

A single candlestick represents the same data that you will find in a single bar; however, the two look completely different. The origin of the name is obvious when looking at the chart. A candlestick chart looks like a series of candles with tails at either end of the candle. Every part of the candle has specific implications (see figure 9.4, overleaf).

The three charts shown in figures 9.2, 9.3 and 9.4 all represent the same information, and the same time scale, yet their graphical format ensures that each chart looks very different from the others.

Figure 9.4: CBA daily candlestick chart

Source: SuperCharts version 4 by Omega Research © 1997.

Why use candles instead of bars?

There is a silent war going on between two distinct groups of technical analysts — bar chartists and candlestick chartists. Which is the best type of chart to use for your needs? Let's rate them according to the following dimensions.

Colour

Bar charts usually show up in boring black. This is hardly adventurous, is it? Such an unimaginative monochrome! Red and green (or black and white) are much more exciting to look at than a boring one-colour depiction of share price action. As you will discover in the next section of this chapter, the colours of the candles instantly epitomise bullish or bearish intent and will let you see at a glance whether the trend is moving up or down, even from the back of an auditorium. This clarity is essential during periods of trading pressure. Candles clearly win on the 'colour' dimension.

Number of patterns

An advantage of the candlestick chart is the variety of reversal and continuation patterns these charts reveal. The majority of these patterns are unique to candlestick charting and are not available by using any other method. While bar charts do provide some recognisable patterns, using candlesticks will provide a greater number of triggers into positions and, if you are using them to exit, they provide many more indications of trend completion. Again, in this category, candlesticks clearly outperform the bar chart.

Psychology

If you develop an understanding of the psychological principles that drive the creation of a candlestick, you will be more likely to understand its potential impact. This skill can be applied to any new candlestick pattern that you may come across in the future. The psychology of the candle is simpler to conceptualise and see because of the immediately apparent size of the real body and the colour of the candlesticks. Bars just aren't as easy to read.

Visual appearance

The visual display of a candlestick chart provides a valuable method of analysing price information. As you attune your eye to candlestick patterns, signals will practically jump off the chart and wrestle you to the ground. All of the information in a standard bar chart is already included in a candle chart — it is just represented in a different format.

Interesting names

Would you prefer to talk about an 'outside day' (a bar chart pattern) or 'a bullish engulfing pattern above an open window'? Candles have cool names that make them an interesting alternative to the mostly anonymous bar pattern. The specific names of a candlestick pattern will help you speak with clarity to other traders familiar with these charts. The names of the patterns are steeped in Japanese history and will quite likely increase your IQ a few percentage points, just by uttering them!

If you develop an understanding of the psychological principles that drive the creation of a candlestick, you will be more likely to understand its potential impact.

So, all in all (and as illustrated in table 9.1, overleaf), the candlestick is clearly the chart of choice for today's technical analyst! (You were not expecting a different conclusion from the girl who wrote *The Secret of Candlestick Charting*, were you?)

Table 9.1: a quick comparison of charts

Feature	Bars	Candles
Colour	☒	☑
No. of patterns	Less	More
Psychology	Not obvious	Obvious
Visual appearance	Boring	Pretty
Interesting names	☒	☑

In my view, using a candlestick chart is clearly superior to using a bar chart or a line chart. It may take a bit of effort to learn how to interpret these types of charts, but it will give you an edge over other traders in the market. Initially, these charts may look as if they were created by Salvador Dali while he was inebriated, but I promise you that over time the fog of confusion will lift. I will be using candlestick charts throughout the remainder of this book, so you'll have plenty of chances to apply your newfound knowledge. For a complete description of how to use candlesticks to formulate strategies and profit in the sharemarket, refer to my book *The Secret of Candlestick Charting* and complete my *Candlestick Charting Home Study Course* or watch *The Secret of Candlestick Charting* video program available on DVD through <www.tradingsecrets.com.au>. If you already possess a good understanding of candlestick principles, it may be appropriate to skip forward to the review section starting on page 91. Let's have a closer look at these little beauties and learn how to use them effectively.

Candlestick charts

The thick part of the candle is called the 'real body'. This shows the range between the opening and the closing price (see figure 9.5). When the real body is white (or empty), it means that the close was higher than the opening price. When the real body is black (or filled in), the close was lower than the opening price. As you can imagine, if a share price is driven up for the day, this is a bullish sign, and results in the creation of a white candle. A share price that decreases during the day is a sign that the bears have been in control, which results in the creation of a black candle.

The thin lines above and below the real body are called the 'wicks', 'tails' or the 'shadows' of the candle (regardless of which side of the real body they are located). The upper tail (the high for the day on a daily chart) is located above the candlestick's real body, and the lower tail (the low for the day on a daily chart) is located below the real body. The tails are usually seen to be of less importance than the real body, as they represent extraneous price fluctuations. The open and the close are considered to be the most emotionally charged points of the day and therefore contain the highest level of significance in candlestick analysis.

Figure 9.5: definition of a candlestick

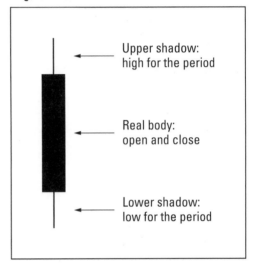

There is a saying that 'the amateurs open the market and the professionals close the market'. The amateurs have had all night to absorb the rumours and news items about certain shares, and their anxious flurry of activity on the opening of the market reflects this. In the first hour of trading, there is a scramble of punters trying to establish their positions. Once the early morning activity calms down, the market settles into a less volatile period during the middle of the day.

The final hour of the sharemarket also experiences a definite increase in volatility as buyers and sellers review the price action that occurred during the day. They must quickly assess whether they can live with their trading decisions overnight, so they must be decisive and brave to buy or sell at the final hour. Emotions again run high as traders buy and sell their shares in accordance with their view of the direction of the market for the following day.

The white candle

As I mentioned earlier, the colour of the candle depicts whether it is bearish or bullish. When the day closes higher than it opened, this is a positive bullish sign. There is demand for the share and buyers are willing to pay higher and higher prices. The price is driven up as demand outstrips supply (see figure 9.6).

The black candle

When the day closes lower than its opening price, it is a sign that sellers have fear in their hearts. This has the effect of driving the share price down. The market sentiment is pessimistic, creating a far greater supply of shares. Therefore, the close is lower than the opening price, and the colour of the candle is black. A black candle will clear show that the bears were in control for that period (see figure 9.7).

Figure 9.6: the white candle

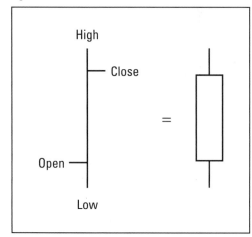

Figure 9.7: the black candle

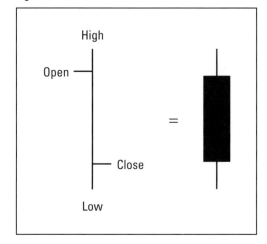

The bulls' and the bears' (buyers' and sellers') struggle for dominance forms the basis for each candlestick pattern formation. A single candlestick, or a group of candles, often has particular bullish or bearish significance.

When to use candlesticks

Candlestick patterns fall into the following two broad groups:

1 continuation patterns

2 reversal patterns.

Continuation patterns suggest that the share will continue in a particular direction over the short term.

Reversal patterns mean that a share is likely to change direction completely or simply flatten into a sideways trend (see figure 9.8). If they occur once the share is trending, reversal patterns suggest that the trend may change. They will be the focus of the following discussion.

Figure 9.8: reversal patterns

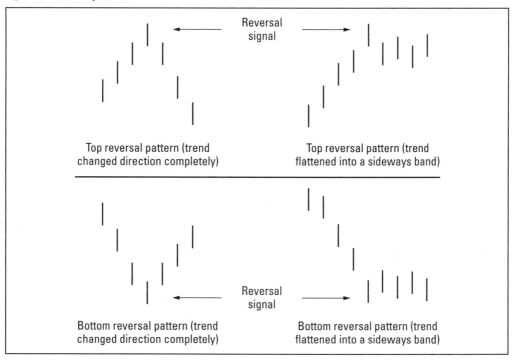

Some common candlestick patterns

Let's kick off our discussion about candles with some of the ones that you're most likely to spot on a chart.

The shooting star

This pattern displays an upper tail length that is two times the length of the real body (see figure 9.9). When a gap (or a hole in the share price action) is present between the previous candle and the shooting star, the formation becomes more significant. This principle applies to all candlestick patterns. A discussion of the types of gaps present in charts can be found starting on page 116. This pattern, as with all top reversal candlestick formations, has greater significance if it is black. Shooting stars appear at the top of a trend and signify that the bears are likely to move in with strength and that a downtrend could occur.

Figure 9.9: the shooting star

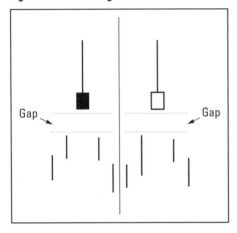

The small bars before and after the candlestick formation will show you the direction of the preceding and following prices on the chart. They have no other special significance in these examples.

Figure 9.10: the doji

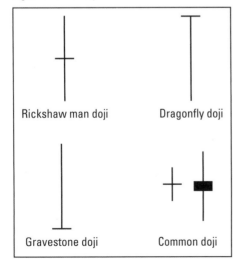

The doji

The doji displays an extremely small real body (see figure 9.10). The open and close are at the same price (or nearly at the same price) for that period. A doji is representative of the market temporarily coming to an agreement about the fair value of the share. The reason for the awesome strength of the doji is the psychological importance of its message. A doji suggests a balance of supply and demand, whereas trends require imbalance. Either the bulls or the bears must actively drive the market for a trend to endure. The doji signifies the end of one trend and the beginning of another. The share will typically reverse its direction the day after a doji appears in the chart of an uptrending or downtrending stock.

Spinning top

Spinning tops are similar to a doji pattern, as they both display a small real body (see figure 9.11). The real body in a spinning top formation depicts a greater range from the open to the close compared with a doji pattern. The tail length is largely unimportant and the candle can be either white or black. This pattern represents a tug of war between bulls and bears and is accentuated by the presence of a gap before and after its formation.

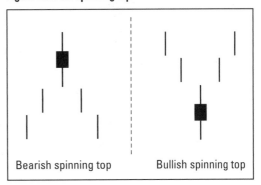

Figure 9.11: the spinning top

Bearish spinning top   Bullish spinning top

Hammers and the hanging man

These patterns display a long tail above or below their real bodies (see figure 9.12). There is likely to be no tail, or a very short tail, on the other side of the real body. The tail length is required to be two-times the length of the real body to fulfil the exact definition of this candle. Gaps increase the significance of the pattern. Look for these patterns at the top or bottom of trends to signify that a reversal is likely.

Figure 9.12: hammers and the hanging man

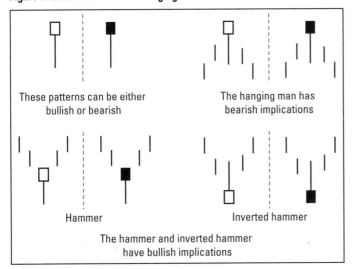

These patterns can be either bullish or bearish

The hanging man has bearish implications

Hammer

Inverted hammer

The hammer and inverted hammer have bullish implications

Figure 9.13: the bearish engulfing pattern

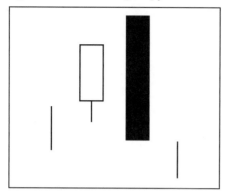

The bearish engulfing pattern

This two-candle combination is an extremely effective pattern that often signifies the dramatic end of an uptrend (see figure 9.13). After the appearance of this pattern, prices typically plunge downwards steeply. The second real body of this pattern totally engulfs the first real body and is a bearish sign, as the price has closed lower than it opened for that period. The first candle must be white, and the second candle must be black.

Figure 9.14: the bullish engulfing pattern

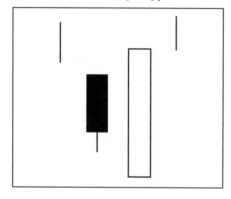

The bullish engulfing pattern

This candle pattern often signifies the end of a downtrend (see figure 9.14). After the pattern has been formed, prices often surge upwards. The colour of the first candle must be black, while the second candle must be white. If the second candle is accompanied by high relative volume, this is a particularly bullish sign. As with any bottom reversal pattern, the presence of heavy relative volume as the share trends upward will help confirm the effectiveness of the candlestick.

Figure 9.15: dark cloud cover

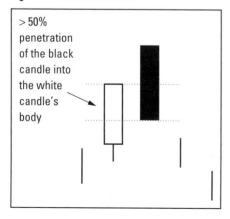

> 50% penetration of the black candle into the white candle's body

Dark cloud cover

This two-candle formation is a top reversal pattern (see figure 9.15). The second black candle must penetrate 50 per cent or more into the white candle's body. In candlestick philosophy, the more significant patterns display greater penetration of one candle into the body of another. Therefore, this pattern is not as significant as the bearish engulfing pattern. Confidence is essential to ensure the continuation of an uptrend. The dark cloud cover suggests a loss of confidence by the bulls, and this may lead to a future downturn in trend.

Piercing pattern

This two-candle bottom reversal pattern is the inverse of a dark cloud cover (see figure 9.16). The 50 per cent penetration level of the second candle into the body of the first is essential to fulfil the definition of this pattern.

Evening star

This bearish three-candle top reversal pattern (see figure 9.17) shows a long white real body (1), a small star of either colour (2), then a black real body (3). The evening star pattern is especially significant if there are gaps between each candle.

Morning star

This bullish three-candle bottom reversal pattern (see figure 9.18) shows a long black real body (1), a small star of either colour (2), then a white real body (3). If a bottom reversal pattern occurs within an existing medium-term uptrend, often the effect will be very bullish. However, a bottom reversal during a medium-term downtrend will not show such a vigorous bullish response.

Figure 9.16: the piercing pattern

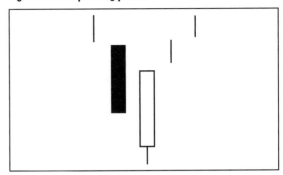

Figure 9.17: the evening star

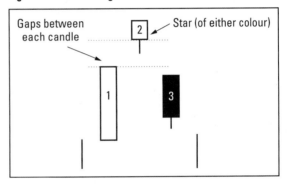

Figure 9.18: the morning star

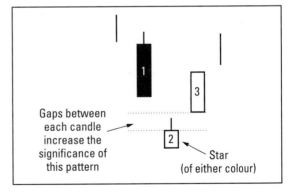

How to use candlesticks

There are many other candlestick patterns that appear in charts. Rather than memorising every definition, it is more important to internalise the meaning behind each pattern. The specifics of the formation of candlestick patterns may initially seem a little confusing.

To help simplify the use of candlesticks, try focusing on the following aspects:

- *Candle colour*. Look at the chart, and see whether there are more white candles or more black candles. If there are more white candles, it is probable that the predominant emotion in the market is bullish. If there are more black candles, the bears are more likely to be in control of the bulls.

- *Candle length*. Observe the length of the candles. Look at the real body length as well as the length of the tails. If there are longer white candles compared with black, then the bulls are in control. If the black candles are longer than the white, the bears are winning the battle. Roughly equal numbers of black and white candles means that the share is likely to be travelling in a sideways band, and neither the bulls nor the bears are dominating.

- *Tail location*. If there are lots of tails sticking upward, this indicates selling pressure and that the share is likely to fall in value. If there are many tails pointing downward, then the buyers are moving into the market and the share is likely to increase in value.

Available on my website <www.tradingsecrets.com.au> are two candlestick-based special reports that may interest you. The *Special Report — Candlestick Pattern Summary* is a handy, quick reference guide that can help you remember the patterns and confirm the validity of any pattern that you come across. The *Special Report — New Candlestick Patterns* will introduce you to some brand new, unique candlestick patterns that I have observed from my years trading the markets.

Trading insights

Effective learning is error-driven. Failures grab our attention. In fact, researchers have found that the more wildly wrong our predictions are about the markets, the more quickly we learn. Our brain needs failure to create success. So next time you make a mistake, embrace it and then move on.

Review

1   Have a look at figure 9.19. Do you feel that the predominant direction is upward, sideways or downward? Why have you reached that conclusion?

....

....

....

....

Figure 9.19: Wesfarmers weekly

Source: SuperCharts version 4 by Omega Research © 1997.

2   Identify any candlestick patterns that you can see in figure 9.20.

....

....

....

....

....

....

Figure 9.20: Toll Holdings daily

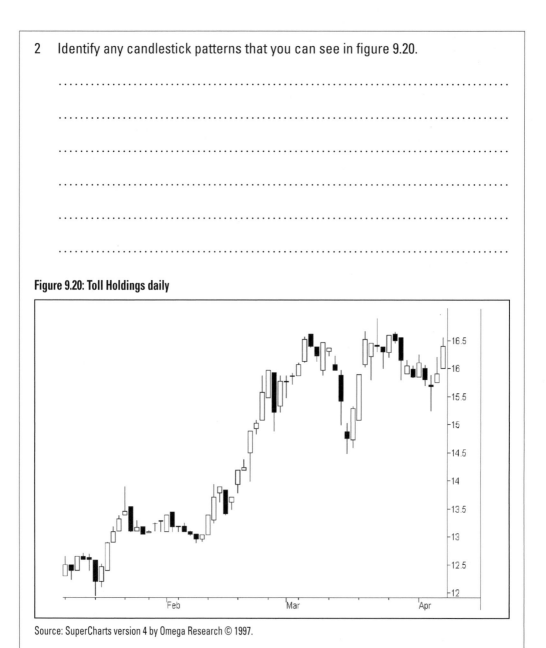

Source: SuperCharts version 4 by Omega Research © 1997.

Answers

1   Figure 9.21 shows how I have interpreted the chart.

Figure 9.21: Wesfarmers weekly interpretation

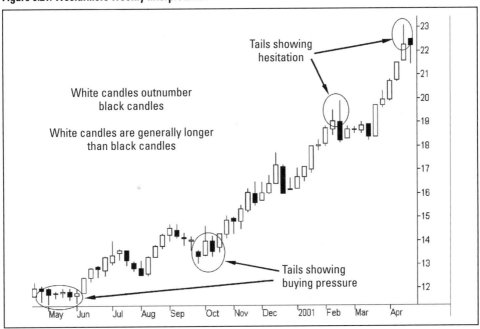

Source: SuperCharts version 4 by Omega Research © 1997.

- *Candle colour.* There are more white candles than black candles, suggesting an uptrend.

- *Candle length.* The white candles are generally longer than the black candles, which suggest that the uptrend is quite strong.

- *Tail location.* Any tails pointing upward have been easily transcended by bullish activity and did not result in a significant barrier.

All these indications suggest that the share is in an uptrend and that the uptrend is likely to be enduring.

2 Figure 9.22 shows some of the candlestick patterns you have learned about. You may have found other patterns on the chart in addition to those I have indicated. This is perfectly acceptable. Even though I have sought to quantify each pattern with a scientific approach, the art of recognising the implications of candlesticks is somewhat subjective.

Figure 9.22: Toll Holdings daily interpretation

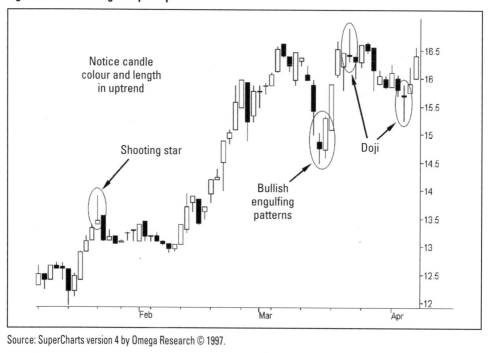

Source: SuperCharts version 4 by Omega Research © 1997.

The next chapter will help you refine your skills in detecting trends.

10

Stop playing blind archery

In this chapter, you will learn that:

- There are a few techniques I utilise in order to make a decision about the likely future direction of the share price action. I use trendlines, support/resistance lines, moving averages, a momentum indicator, volume and pattern recognition to analyse any share chart. If you don't have a consistent way of analysing the market, you're throwing money away.

- By using at least one indicator from each of the major indicator 'families', I am seeking to apply a weight of evidence theory to my trading, and maximise my probability of making a profitable trade.

- There are literally hundreds of other indicators available to traders. By adding more indicators, you will not necessarily be increasing your effectiveness. The majority of successful trading systems are only right up to 50 per cent of the time. Because shares trend only about 30 per cent of the time, 50 per cent is slightly better than random probability. Entry systems are only part of the collage of components that make up a professional trading system.

INDICATORS TAKE THE RAW DATA shown on a share chart and present it in a different format to help you to make trading decisions. Often, some form of calculation is involved. In the majority of cases, your charting package will be able to do this at the flick of a button. Let your computer crunch the numbers and display the information so that you can focus on the analysis component of trading.

Gut feel

There is no room for gut feeling in the markets when you are starting out. Over time, you may develop an inkling that a trade will work out well, but this will take many years of successful trading. When experienced traders talk about a gut feeling, it often means that they have internalised many of the indicators that imply an enduring trend, after years of honing their skills. Trading is about making money — it is not about feeling 'right'. Stop trusting your gut feelings; traders can only afford to trust their trading plans.

Develop a scientific process for analysing signals, and do not let your emotions dictate your trading habits. You need to define your signal in words so that another trader unfamiliar with your technique can duplicate your strategy. If it cannot be duplicated, it's not a system.

Trading is about making money — it is not about feeling 'right'. Stop trusting your gut feelings; traders can only afford to trust their trading plans.

Many analysts add unnecessary confusion to the art of trading by analysing too many indicators. These rocket scientists are often theoretical practitioners who are the equivalent of the know-it-all brother-in-law that you try to avoid at the family Christmas party. The addition of more indicators is more likely to hinder effective trading habits. Don't look for 15 indicators to be pointing skyward as well as for Jupiter's moon to break out of orbit — or you may be waiting for a very long time to make your next trade.

Develop a simple entry system. This will serve you better than a convoluted set of signals that even a nuclear physicist will have trouble understanding. Find a maximum of four to six methods or indicators that you are happy with, and then look for each of these signals to confirm your entry procedure. Apply a weight of evidence principle to your trading. For more information about how to apply technical analysis skills that involve using formulas and indicators, as well as macro pattern analysis, refer to my book *Charting Secrets*.

Weight of evidence

When several chart patterns and indicators point in the same direction, their signals are reinforced. If the weight of evidence of several indicators suggests that the share is uptrending, then the bulls have probably taken control of the market. Without using a strong weight of evidence on your charts, you're playing blind archery and you're likely to bomb in the near future.

If you receive conflicting signals between any of your favourite indicators, wait for heightened levels of confirmation prior to acting. By seeking consistency between all of your entry signals, you stack the odds of experiencing profitable results in your favour. Another method of risk control is to attribute less money to shares that do not have the ideal set-up. It is acceptable to act on a set-up that is not considered perfect, as long as you acknowledge the risk inherent in this strategy.

Before you decide to enter any trade, ask yourself, 'Is this the highest probability trade that I can make right now?' This may help you act only on trades that comply with your rules, and ignore those trades that are less scientific in nature.

Indicators tend to fall into several distinct families. Use at least one of the indicators from each family in order to form an opinion about the share price's likely direction. This is an ideal application of the weight of evidence theory. These families are:

- the line family

- the moving average family

- the momentum family

- the volume family

- the pattern family.

The line family

Let's explore each of these families in turn. We'll start with the line family.

The trendline

To ascertain the direction in which a share is trending, you can use a trendline. When drawing a trendline, use a bar chart or a candlestick chart rather than a line chart. A line chart only shows one piece of the information (the close), compared with four pieces of information (the open, close, high and low). You may as well act on the most information that a chart can display at any particular time to make your decisions.

'Is this the highest probability trade that I can make right now?'

Uptrends

An uptrend may be defined as a situation where prices consistently make higher lows. Each trough in share price action is followed by a trough that occurs at a higher price level. A trendline can be drawn on the chart to connect these low points and, when there is sustained movement below this line, the uptrend is likely to be broken. When drawing a trendline, try to connect at least two low points for a tentative trendline and three or more to confirm a trendline (see figure 10.1).

Figure 10.1: Cochlear monthly chart showing an uptrend

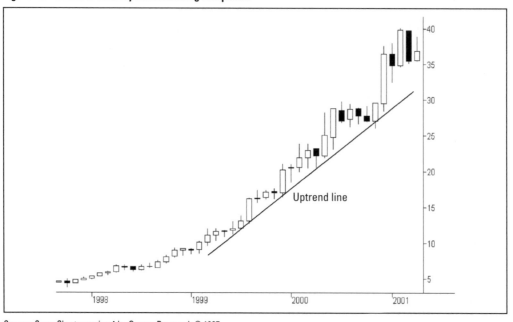

Source: SuperCharts version 4 by Omega Research © 1997.

If the share is forming consistently higher highs and higher lows, a trend channel is formed. This is a very bullish sign. It shows a consistency of uptrending behaviour that is wonderful territory for share trading (see figure 10.2).

Have a look at the share in figure 10.3. Try drawing an uptrend line connecting the lowest share prices. To do this, the line will need to be drawn underneath the majority of the share prices. There is no one perfect answer, but to see whether you are on the right track, you can turn to the answers section at the end of this chapter and look at figure 10.25. I purposely put it at the end of the chapter to remove the temptation to immediately flick forward. I want to give you a chance to fill out this section first. You will learn the principles with a much greater degree of precision if you do not immediately turn to the answers. Pick up your pencil and have a go. Don't worry about marking the book; with the money you will make as a result of your new skill in drawing trendlines, you'll be able to buy many more copies!

Figure 10.2: ANZ weekly chart with a trend channel

Source: SuperCharts version 4 by Omega Research © 1997.

Figure 10.3: Lang Corp weekly chart

Source: SuperCharts version 4 by Omega Research © 1997.

Downtrends

A downtrend may be described as a share that makes consistently lower highs. A trendline can be drawn on the chart that connects the highest prices of a downtrend (at least two for a tentative downtrend or preferably three or more for a confirmed downtrend). This will result in a downward sloping line drawn above the majority of the price action. The downtrend is considered to be broken when prices move above this line in a sustained upward direction, ideally accompanied by good relative volume levels. It is important that volume accompanies any upward movement after a prolonged downtrend, otherwise it is likely that the sustained downtrend will continue. The bulls have to move in with force to conquer the bears. When a share increases in price on heavy relative volume, this is a sign that the bulls are exerting their dominance (see figure 10.4).

Figure 10.4: Sausage Software daily chart showing a downtrend line

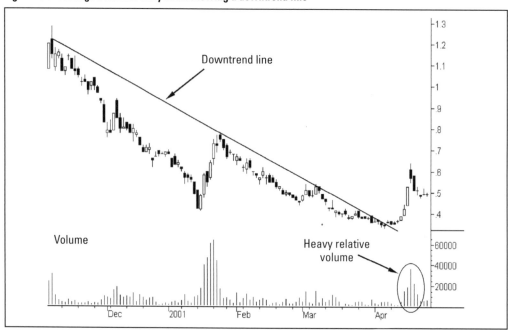

Source: SuperCharts version 4 by Omega Research © 1997.

If the share forms lower highs and lower lows, a bearish downtrending channel is created. This characteristic represents quite a sustainable downtrend (see figure 10.5).

Figure 10.5: Coates weekly chart with a downtrend channel

Source: SuperCharts version 4 by Omega Research © 1997.

Sideways trends

Other than these two conditions of uptrending and downtrending, the share may trade in a sideways lateral band for extended periods. Some analysts have suggested that this sideways movement can occur up to 70 per cent of the time.

The unfortunate implication with a sideways-moving share is that your capital is tied up, preventing participation in other, more lucrative, opportunities. This opportunity cost is a frustrating consequence of being involved in non-trending shares. Opportunity cost means that your money could be working harder for you elsewhere. When using shares as a vehicle, a clear trend is necessary to benefit and make substantial profits.

The unfortunate implication with a sideways-moving share is that your capital is tied up, preventing participation in other, more lucrative, opportunities.

Support and resistance

Diagonal support and resistance can be seen along a trendline. To avoid any confusion, however, I will refer to support and resistance lines as running horizontally. For trading purposes, a closer examination of the daily chart after viewing the weekly chart is suggested. I usually start with a weekly chart and then review charts of increasingly smaller time increments for the share that I am interested in trading.

The support line can be seen along the base of a share's price action, and resistance can be seen along the top of a range of consolidation. It's almost as if a share is jumping up and down on the floor to hammer out a support line, and hitting its head on the ceiling to create a resistance line.

The change of polarity principle suggests that once prices break through a significant resistance line, then this line should act as support for future trading activity. This will only occur if the uptrend is strong. Also, once a line of support has been broken, it is likely that this line will act as resistance in the future. This is a sign of a downtrend that is likely to continue.

If the share shows an overall uptrending behaviour, a period of consolidation is very healthy. This pause allows the share to recover from its vigorous trading activity. Often, the longer a share is within a consolidation band, the more violent the eventual breakout.

Figure 10.6 shows an example of support and resistance lines, as well as the change of polarity principle. There are probably quite a few extra lines that you could draw in, but the concept of less is more is appropriate here.

Figure 10.6: Wesfarmers daily chart with support and resistance lines showing a change of polarity

Source: SuperCharts version 4 by Omega Research © 1997.

Now it's your turn. Have a look at figure 10.7 and try drawing in uptrend lines, downtrend lines and support/resistance lines. When drawing any lines on charts, try to connect at least two low points for a tentative line and three or more to confirm the line. Once you've finished, you're welcome to turn to the end of the chapter and see my interpretation of this chart in figure 10.26.

Clearly, entry and exit signal back-testing is a complicated area of trading but thankfully there are people that can help. If you do not wish to undertake the research yourself, there are credible businesses that do this type of research specifically for private investors.

One such business is Share Wealth Systems, led by founder and head research analyst Gary Stone. You can learn more about Share Wealth Systems by downloading their free guide to successful systems trading at <www.spa3.com.au/freeguide>. The team at Share Wealth Systems have been personally very supportive to me for over a decade and I know you'd get a lot out of exploring the way they approach the markets. Tell them I recommended you so they'll know how keen you are about pursuing your own education.

Figure 10.7: Lion Nathan daily chart

Source: SuperCharts version 4 by Omega Research © 1997.

The moving average family

A moving average takes the sum of the closing prices and averages them across a particular period. This indicator plots points that form a line that smoothes out the fluctuations present when looking at the share price action. They can also be applied to smooth out the gyrations of any indicator, such as a momentum indicator.

There are some basic principles to consider when using a moving average:

- Moving average lines that intersect have very important implications.

- A golden cross is where an indicator, moving average or share price crosses up through a moving average. This is a bullish sign.

- A dead cross is where an indicator, moving average or share price crosses down through a moving average. This is a bearish sign. See figure 10.8 for an example of a golden cross and a dead cross.

- When the share prices are located above the moving average, this is a bullish sign.

- When the share prices are located below the moving average, this is a bearish sign.

- Moving averages are not as effective if the share is trending sideways.

The most common question that I am asked at the trading seminars I conduct is, 'What moving average do you use?' Let me assure you that there is no magic setting for using a moving average that will give you the best results at all times. The search for the Holy Grail with this particular indicator seems incredibly ingrained in the trading psyche of the majority of people. Novice traders tend to develop an obsession with finding one indicator length that will be the answer to every trading situation in the universe. This search is futile. Even if a particular indicator has worked perfectly in the past, the changing nature of markets will ensure that this level of predictability is unlikely to repeat in the future. Even though the majority of trading can be defined with meticulous detail, there still needs to be a certain amount of fluidity in your decision-making process in order to trade well. One of the areas in which you may need to be flexible is your choice of moving average.

Let me assure you that there is no magic setting for using a moving average that will give you the best results at all times.

As a rule of thumb, I suggest that you use a 30-period moving average. Use this until you attune your eye to the impact of using different time periods—do not regard this as the ideal setting! Interestingly, your results will not deviate significantly if you use a 28-period, a 30-period or a 32-period moving average.

If you are looking to try a shorter term moving average, use a 15-period moving average. When using a daily chart, the 15-period moving average will average the closing prices of the last 15 days. When using a weekly chart, the 15-period moving average will average the closing prices of the last 15 weeks. If you decide to use both the 15-period and 30-period moving average on the same chart, then you can experiment with looking for golden and dead crosses between these two moving averages.

Figure 10.8 shows a 30-week Exponential Moving Average (EMA) and a 15-week EMA on a weekly chart of the National Australia Bank. Notice where the golden cross and the dead cross occur. The golden cross is formed when the 15-week moving average crosses up through the 30-week moving average, which is a bullish sign. The dead cross is formed when the 15-week moving average crosses down through the 30-week moving average. This is a bearish sign. Also notice the location of the prices in comparison with the moving average lines. When the prices are located predominantly above the moving average, this is bullish. When the prices are located mainly below the moving average, this is bearish.

Figure 10.8: National Australia Bank weekly chart showing a 15-week EMA and a 30-week EMA

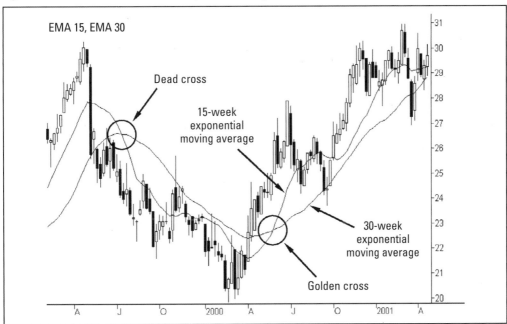

Source: SuperCharts version 4 by Omega Research © 1997.

There are several types of moving average with a variety of complicated names such as weighted, displaced, or exponential. For the time being, stick with an EMA. It won't make a lot of difference in the long run which one you use, but for the sake of consistency, I'll be using EMAs throughout this book.

Make it a rule never to buy a share that is trading below its 30-week EMA. It is likely to be in downtrend. Even if you are a short-term trader, it is prudent to check that the overall weekly trend is upward. You will conduct higher probability trades by trading in the direction of the overall trend.

The momentum family

Momentum refers to the rate of change of a price trend. Indicators under this banner help traders to establish whether prices are increasing or declining at a faster or slower pace. The Relative Strength Indicator (RSI), Rate of Change (ROC) and the Stochastic (STO) are all momentum indicators, and there are many more. When people's maximum level of pain or fear has been hit, a trend will change. Momentum indicators track this sentiment and provide a quantifiable method of evaluating it.

This is one area that brings the rocket scientists out of their closets. They will do their best to add complexity. Complexity doesn't mean that you will trade more proficiently. Let's see if I can explain the concept behind momentum simply.

Momentum indicators look at the speed of the progression and estimate a turning point.

Imagine you threw a ball up into the air. If you used a video camera, you could track its movement in slow motion. To begin with it would go very fast indeed, then it would gradually slow down. Ultimately it would stop in mid-air before gravity ensured that it came back down to earth. If you were going to apply a momentum indicator to the movement of the ball, the indicator would track the speed of the movement of the ball. The indicator's purpose would be to pinpoint the time when the speed of the upward movement was waning. Ideally, the indicator would provide you with a signal at the highest point of the ball's progression, when gravity reverses the ball's direction and pulls it back to earth. Momentum indicators look at the speed of the progression and estimate a turning point.

At the highest point of the ball's progression through the air, the indicator would describe it as overbought and a downtrend in the ball's action from that point would be likely to occur. An oversold area could be observed at the bottom of a downtrend and show a time when it is likely that the share would begin an uptrend. You don't have to understand the exact calculation of the indicators, but a basic understanding of what these indicators are measuring will help you to interpret their meaning. Trading can be skilfully conducted even by the mathematically averse, so don't drop the book and run screaming out the door. Persist and it will all become clear.

Some momentum indicators have predetermined overbought and oversold lines, such as the Relative Strength Indicator (RSI) and the Stochastic Indicator (STO). These are called indexed momentum indicators. For example, on a scale of zero to 100, when looking at the RSI indicator, 30 signifies an oversold condition and 70 represents an overbought condition. Other momentum indicators may not display these lines, but require the analyst to make a decision based on whether the indicator has reached a historical high or a historical low (see figure 10.9).

Figure 10.9: momentum indicators

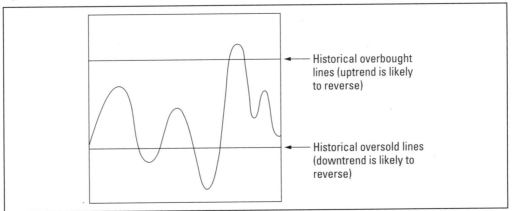

Interpreting momentum indicators

Initially, many people find that these indicators are confusing to interpret. If you have found that my quaint little discussion of balls flying through the air has left you cold, then that's fine. Even if you simply trade with trendlines, support/resistance lines and moving averages, you can still be a perfectly adequate trader. The majority of people in the market haven't even used these effective tools to help them isolate shares that are likely candidates to buy. To refine your skills, though, momentum indicators measure the strength of potential moves and may keep you out of a new trend because it may be weak in nature, and be likely to reverse in the near term.

Here are a few simple rules that may assist you when using momentum indicators:

- When the indicator crosses down through an overbought line, this suggests that the uptrend is likely to reverse.

- When the indicator crosses up through an oversold line, this suggests that the downtrend is likely to reverse.

- If the indicator has been trending down and turns up, this is a buy signal.

- If the indicator has been trending up and then turns down, this is a sell signal.

- The strength of the above two points is intensified at historical high points for sell signals, or historical low points for buy signals.

- It is wise to watch for confirmation of these signals from actual changes in share price action, rather than trusting the momentum indicator in isolation.

- It is generally a bullish sign if the momentum line on the weekly chart is rising, and the momentum line on the daily chart is rising. This is even more significant at historically low levels.

- It is generally a bearish sign if the momentum lines on the weekly and daily charts are declining. This is even more significant at historically high levels.

Consolidation and momentum indicators

If a share has formed a base, or a range of consolidation, you will notice that momentum indicators will react in a peculiar manner. If the share breaks upward from the consolidation range, the momentum indicator will, in all likelihood, show signs of becoming overbought. This is because most momentum indicators are designed to register a change in the range of prices represented over the past several periods. As a result, the indicator will often be propelled upward and this will often signify the beginning of a new uptrend, or the continuation of the existing uptrend. Usually, this propulsion into overbought territory after a range of consolidation is a positive, bullish signal. This is a widely misunderstood fact regarding momentum indicators. Normally, an overbought area is a region that may show that an uptrend is running out of puff. After a period of consolidation, though, an overbought momentum indicator is likely to show that the uptrend is probably going to continue.

When I first learned about the momentum indicator, I thought it was the best indicator that I had come across in ages (yes, there is a bit of the rocket scientist in all of us). I went so far as to use an RSI, an STO as well as an ROC, all on the same chart. What a silly girl!

My weight of evidence theory was unbalanced. These three indicators roughly measure the same thing, so they were very likely to tell the same story. It was as if I was using one indicator and allowing it to assume 90 per cent of the decision-making. Learn from my mistake and choose one of the three momentum indicators listed here and don't use all of them to confirm each other. It is akin to using three related car mechanics to tell you that you need to replace your entire engine — of course they will tell you the same thing. At least try to find a mechanic from a different family!

Normally, an overbought area is a region that may show that an uptrend is running out of puff.

Figure 10.10 shows overbought and oversold zones, and the related share price behaviour at these levels. I have used a 10-period RSI on this chart. Notice that the share price at the overbought zones began to downtrend. The share price at the oversold zones began to uptrend. When you combine this information with your existing knowledge about trendlines and moving averages, you can see the weight of evidence principle in action.

Figure 10.10: National Australia Bank weekly chart showing overbought and oversold zones

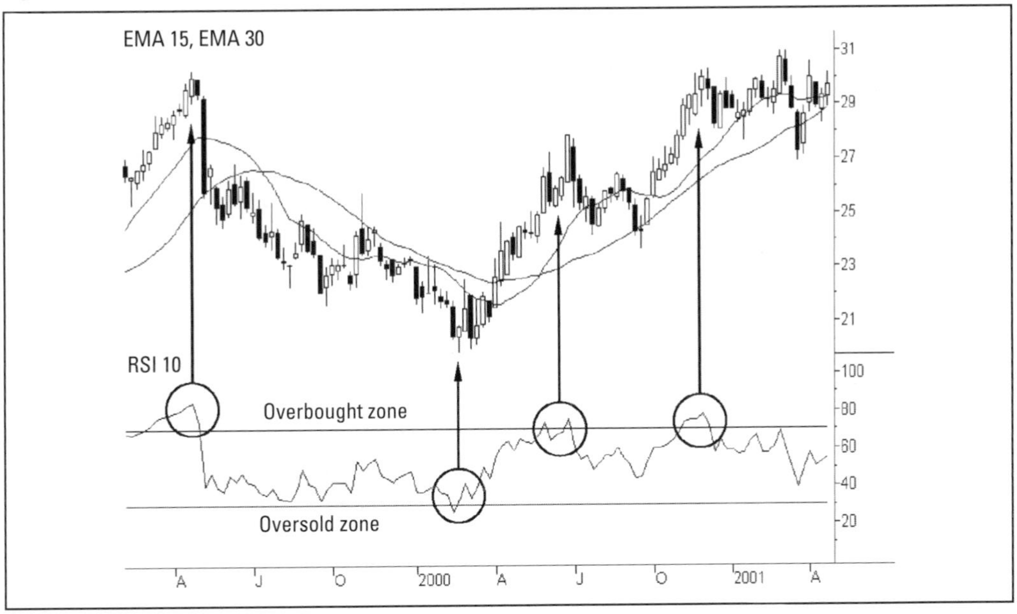

Source: SuperCharts version 4 by Omega Research © 1997.

Divergence

Some momentum indicators are displayed as histograms at the bottom of your share chart, rather than as a squiggly line (for want of a better description). This type of display lends itself to the study of divergence. You can look at divergence when using the RSI, the STO or the ROC, but there is a histogram momentum indicator that I find to be particularly useful called the Moving Average Convergence Divergence or MACD.

There are several types of divergence, but the basic concept behind them all is the same. Divergence means that the share chart is forming higher and higher prices, but the momentum indicator is failing to make higher peaks. This is most easily visible when using a histogram. The same argument applies to a share that is making consistently lower lows, but the histogram is showing a higher low. Divergence suggests that the defined trend of the share price is likely to be weak and therefore unsustainable. Remember that this is only a likely event, so check your suspicions with the actual share price action, rather than reacting on the basis of the momentum indicator alone.

You can use a histogram type of momentum indicator in conjunction with a line momentum indicator. Stop at two types of momentum indicators though. Resist the urge to think that the more momentum indicators you use, the better your analysis will be (see figure 10.11).

Figure 10.11: Colorado Group weekly chart showing MACD histogram

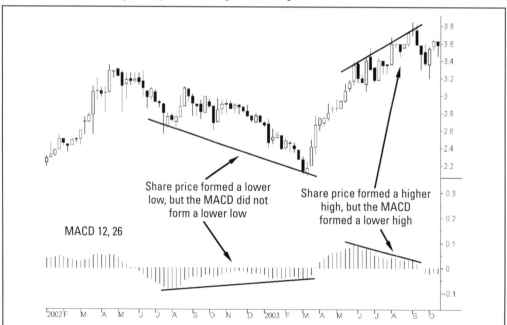

Source: SuperCharts version 4 by Omega Research © 1997.

The chart of Colorado Group shows clear divergence when comparing the share price with the MACD. I have used the default MACD settings of 12 and 26 periods. When the share formed a lower low, the MACD formed a shallower low, which suggests that the downtrend was running out of puff. At a later date, the price formed a higher high, but the MACD formed a lower high, showing that the uptrend was unlikely to be sustained.

The volume family

If you are to evolve into a profitable trend follower, then it goes without saying that you will not get in at the lowest price and out at the highest price. Many people have great difficulty with this concept. The goal of the trend follower is to take profits from the middle chunk of the trend, and not resort to the egotistical desire to buy at the lowest price and sell at the highest price. If you are aiming to enter at the cheapest price, how do you know that the price won't go lower, taking your capital with it? Find a share that is trending upward or your capital will erode.

At a recent seminar, I stated, 'The aim is to buy when the share price is going up, and to sell when it is going down.' To my amusement, I was tackled on this issue. The attendee seemed to believe that the key was buying a share that was going down in value. People with this view are affectionately known as bottom-pickers. In a raging bull market, their strategy may work, but in any other type of market, the idea of trying to buy at the lowest possible price is a quick route to the poor house.

Wait for volume to confirm the direction of a trend, especially if you believe that you have identified a turning point in a downtrend. Here are some rules that work with astounding effectiveness:

- If volume is increasing and the price is increasing, then you are likely to be monitoring a share that is trending up or beginning to trend upward strongly.

- If volume is increasing and the share price is decreasing, then ripples of fear are flooding through the shareholders and more people are likely to sell their shares in the near future.

- Look for upward moves in share price on heavy volume and temporary moves down in share price on light volume to show a strong uptrend.

- Make sure that the overall volume of an instrument is sufficient. If the share only trades every second day, you may not be able to exit from your position easily when you need to. As a general rule, if in doubt, calculate the average daily volume over the past three months and never buy more than one-fifth of this amount.

There are several indicators that calculate the impact of volume, but I find it just as useful to observe the raw data by looking at the volume spikes on a share chart to make my observations.

Figure 10.12 shows a daily chart of BRL. As you can see, it is in an uptrending state.

Figure 10.12: BRL Hardy daily chart showing volume spikes

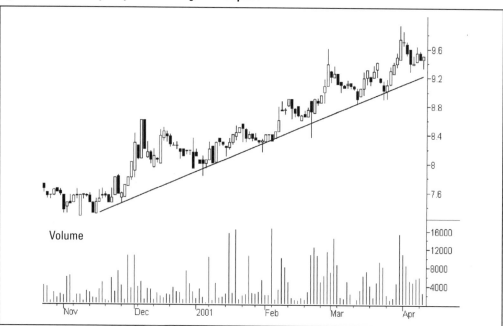

Source: SuperCharts version 4 by Omega Research © 1997.

Let's expand the last few candles of this chart and take a close look at how volume reacts during an uptrend (see figure 10.13). The volume expands when the share bullishly breaks above the resistance line. Then, when the share price pulls back to the resistance line, which now acts as support, volume contracts. This is a very bullish sign.

Figure 10.13: BRL Hardy daily chart showing volume reacting to an uptrend

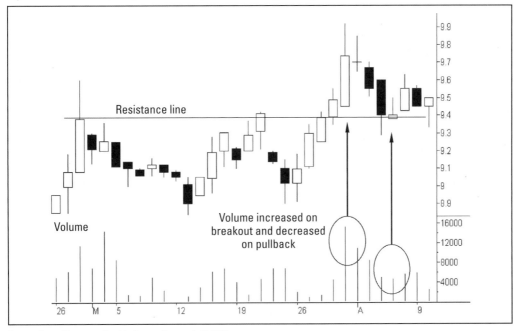

Source: SuperCharts version 4 by Omega Research © 1997.

The pattern family

There are hundreds of patterns formed by the share price action. People sometimes attach particular significance to these patterns, especially if they have made money using them in the past. Don't become overwhelmed by the large array of patterns available. You can spend a trading lifetime looking for patterns and be left with no time to trade effectively! Find a few methods of analysis that you relate to and use them.

You've already become familiar with some of the more popular candlestick patterns described earlier. With time, you will become experienced in how to interpret these patterns and profit from them. The types of patterns discussed in this section consist of several days or weeks of activity rather than only a few sessions of price action.

When you understand the concepts of support and resistance, volume and trendlines, the majority of patterns can be deduced. Stay true to the concepts that you understand and you will end up trading well.

It is important that the overall trend is established in order for these patterns to work with any level of consistency. Isaac Newton said,

It is important that the overall trend is established in order for these patterns to work with any level of consistency.

'Once a body is set in motion, it is likely to continue in that direction.' This principle applies to shares also. If the overall trend is upward, then it is likely to continue. Patterns will assist in timing your entry point, but the indicators already discussed will aid you in determining the overall trend direction. Patterns are generally a micro tool, not a macro tool to determine the predominant trend.

As an example of pattern recognition, here are two effective patterns to get you started: the breakout trade and the retracement trade. The vast majority of shares that I buy display one of these patterns to trigger my entry, in addition to a favourable combination of the other indicators already described. There are several other patterns that I use, but they are just the icing on the cake.

The breakout trade

On a weekly chart, check to see if the share is in uptrend and at least trading above its 30-week EMA. If it fulfils this qualification, then seek an entry trigger to buy the share. The breakout pattern can provide this entry trigger on either a weekly or a daily chart, depending on your preferred time horizon for trading. Short-term traders, in particular, could even use an intraday chart displaying this pattern. You have already seen an example of a breakout trade in figure 10.13 with BRL Hardy.

Here is a description of an ideal set-up for a breakout trade. After a period of consolidation between two significant support/resistance lines, the share is primed for action. Don't be impatient and jump in before the share price suggests the direction of the ensuing trend. The entry trigger consists of a break through the established resistance line (preferably initiated with a white candlestick) with heavy relative volume. A gap in an upward direction would also be a favourable signal. This pattern is one of my favourite buy triggers, especially when the support/resistance lines occur along psychologically significant price points; for example, $2.00 and $3.00. A discussion regarding why this is important is included in chapter 12.

The length of the consolidation range can provide a clue regarding the size of the ensuing breakout. The longer the consolidation period, the more dramatic and enduring the ultimate breakout is likely to be. I am more likely to enter a position if there is little overhead resistance close to my entry price. If the trend is to remain intact, it is unlikely that the share price will collapse back to within its previous trading range. Should the prices bearishly penetrate the previous level of breakout, my stop loss will generally be triggered and I will exit the trade immediately (see figure 10.14).

Figure 10.14: Fosters Brewing daily chart breakout

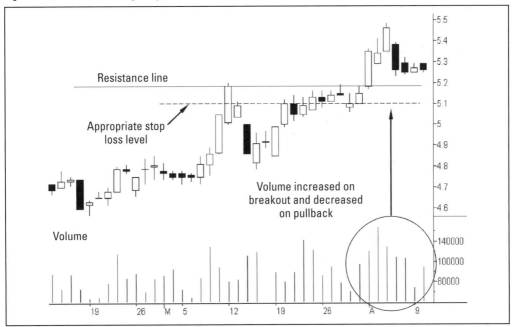

Source: SuperCharts version 4 by Omega Research © 1997.

The retracement trade

If a share is in an existing uptrend and trading above its 30-week moving average, then you can wait for a pullback to a lower price level prior to entering. This situation can be fulfilled using a daily, weekly or intraday chart. The art of this strategy is to ensure that the share has not begun a fully fledged downtrend and that the pullback is a temporary pause prior to the share uptrending again. The pullback can retrace to either an existing trendline, or perhaps a moving average line.

Entry can be made with a high degree of probability if there is a confirmed bottom candlestick reversal pattern. This is one strategy that requires definite confirmation to ensure the effectiveness of the bottom reversal candlestick pattern before purchasing the share. If the closing price of the share has punctured a level of support or an uptrend line, prior to producing a bottom reversal, this has a different implication compared with when the reversal was apparent above a support line. I do not enter a trade based on a bottom reversal pattern if support, the moving average or the trendline has been broken.

The weight of evidence in this situation would suggest that the share has commenced a downtrend (see figure 10.15).

Figure 10.15: Lang Corporation weekly chart retracement trade

Source: SuperCharts version 4 by Omega Research © 1997.

The spinning top candlestick pattern occurred in alignment with the uptrend line in figure 10.15. It is ideal to await confirmation prior to entering, to increase the probability that the uptrend remains intact.

Gaps

Any dramatic overnight drop in share price will form a gap down in the price action of the chart. The dramatic decrease in share price due to an ex-dividend situation often forms such a gap, or a hole that can be seen on the chart. There are several types of gaps that may be evident when viewing a chart:

- Sucker's gaps occur when a share goes ex-dividend and the corresponding share drop is visible in the chart. You will need to know the ex-dividend date in advance in order to observe the subsequent gap in the share price.

- False gaps occur without an accompanying volume increase.

- Real gaps in a share chart have an associated increase in volume. In general, there are three types of real gaps:

  - A *breakaway gap* is a big gap on heavy volume at the start of a trend.

  - A *continuation* or *runaway gap* mostly leads to prices continuing in the direction of the trend.

  - An *exhaustion gap* may indicate that a trend is running out of puff and that a change in the direction of the trend may occur.

Many traders will trade in the direction of the real gap. For example, if a share is in an existing uptrend, and gaps upward on opening, then it is preferable to buy the share as soon as the gap has become evident. The breakout is more likely to be sustained if the gap hurdles a previously well-established level of resistance, accompanied by heavy volume.

Feel the pulse of the market

One of the concepts that most beginner traders have never heard of is a macro filter. The more that I've traded and the more that I've back-tested my own personal trading systems, the more I've realised how important this concept is.

A good macro filter will examine the state of the overall market and tell you whether to trade long (so you can make money out of a down trend), trade short (make money out of a downtrend), or whether you shouldn't be trading the current market at all.

If you think of the Global Financial Crisis that swept through the world, billions of dollars would have been saved in people's superannuation portfolios if only they had learned when *not* to trade. Instead of believing that the market was falling like a warm knife through butter, they buried their heads in the sand and didn't want to face reality. There are times when you should trade like a bandit, and times when you shouldn't be trading at all — and I urge you to develop rules to help you decide under what conditions you will trade.

There are lots of ways to approach this, but as a simple idea, if the overall market index that you want to trade is showing activity below the 30-week Exponential Moving Average, it's likely to be going down, and you should consider entering short positions. If the Index is above its 30-week Exponential Moving Average, enter long positions. If the market is going sideways, according to your rules, consider not opening any new positions at all.

This is trading gold. I know it's a simple idea, but don't just breeze over this thinking it's too simple to work. I can tell you now that the Mentor Program participants that I'm working with are using this concept, and their results have been exceptional. Develop your own, or investigate my Mentor Program further by going to <www.tradingsecrets.com.au> and I'll give you the specifics of what I use to make these types of trading decisions.

The impact of dividends

'But it pays a good dividend' is the justification that many traders use for hanging on to a losing share trade. This is equivalent to saying that you are a compulsive gambler because they provide free coffee at the casino. Even rats will put up with being zapped by an electric current if they are regularly fed tasty pellets!

A dividend is part of a company's net profit paid to shareholders as a cash reward for investing in the company's shares. This periodic profit payment to the shareholders is often made on a quarterly basis. It is usually paid out as a number of cents per share. Companies that are performing well typically pay larger dividends than their non-performing counterparts.

Contrary to popular opinion, companies that pay dividends may not have their shareholders' interests at heart. Companies that retain their dividends, and invest in developing strategic superiorities over competitors, automatically increase their earnings per share. Investing in a share buyback scheme, rather than paying a dividend, would naturally drive the share price upward. Whenever demand outstrips supply, a significant return on investment for shareholders is the result. This is inherently more beneficial to investors than a dividend (or a tasty pellet) to keep them interested.

Regardless of your views regarding dividends, it is important to know how to treat them and trade with them if you are planning to use them as a part of your strategy.

When the market is preparing for a dividend payment, the share price will often increase in value. Demand increases due to the promise of a dividend payment. Once a stock goes ex-dividend, the price of the share will often fall significantly.

Share price fall

How much is the share price likely to drop when it goes ex-dividend? This is an important question to consider. In order to assess this situation, another question needs to be asked regarding whether the dividend is fully franked or unfranked. A fully franked or partially franked dividend means that the company has paid tax on the dividend before you receive it. This makes it possible for you to pay less tax on income from shares due to dividend imputation tax credits.

Unfranked dividends are considered to be of less value to shareholders. With unfranked dividends, the shareholder must shoulder the full tax burden. The level of franking has important implications in regard to the ultimate price drop that the share will display after it goes ex-dividend.

As a rough guide, for unfranked dividends, the share will fall by approximately the price of the declared dividend. Fully franked dividends will mostly show a share price decrease of more than the declared dividend. Although the corresponding share drop will be dependent on market conditions, I will provide some general guidelines that may provide a basis for your calculations. It is a good idea to be conservative in your estimates and consider the worst-case scenario if your calculations do not come to fruition.

The level of franking has important implications in regard to the ultimate price drop that the share will display after it goes ex-dividend.

From my observation, the corresponding drop in share price for a fully franked dividend will usually be between 20 per cent and 60 per cent in excess of the declared dividend price. To make calculations simple, perhaps use 50 per cent in excess of the declared dividend as a guide. For example, a fully franked dividend of 50¢ per share may result in a share price drop of 75¢.

This rule does not always hold true, but serves us by providing a sound estimate of share price activity in an ex-dividend situation. In times of heightened volatility, the effect of this phenomenon will vary. In times of rapid sharemarket rallies, the ex-dividend share price drop will be less than this amount. The converse is also true. In bear market conditions, the ex-dividend drop may be accentuated.

For partially franked dividends, you will need to calculate the share price drop by taking the percentage of franking into account. For example, a 75 per cent franking on a 50¢ dividend may result in a share price drop of approximately 69¢. This is calculated by the following:

$$50¢ \times 50 \text{ per cent} = 25¢$$

$$75 \text{ per cent (franking) of } 25¢ = 18.75¢$$

$$50¢ + 18.75¢ = 68.57¢ = 69¢ \text{ (rounded)}$$

Therefore, the approximate drop in share price will be 69¢.

Despite this observation of share price decreases, it is important that you satisfy yourself on this issue by monitoring the ex-dividend share gaps over time. As another observation, for uptrending shares, the ex-dividend share price gap will often recover within five to seven trading days. The gap shown in the chart will close as the subsequent price activity continues its upward trend. In the case of downtrending shares, in some situations the share price does not recover. Determine the trend of the share to estimate the likely change in share price after an ex-dividend situation.

Once you have located a share that is in an existing uptrend, it may pay to buy the share before it goes ex-dividend, and to be aware of the expected approximate share price drop. Following this strategy, it is important that you make sure to factor in this share price drop when setting your initial stop loss, and calculating your position size. For example, if the fully franked dividend is 20¢, set your stop at 30¢ lower than your initial stop would suggest (that is, 20¢ plus 10¢ to cover the effect of the franking implication). The likely event is for you to receive the benefit of the dividend, and to have the share that you have purchased trend up to your initial entry price within five to seven days. By setting your stop further away than usual, you are still staying loyal to the concept of exiting a position if it behaves beyond the limits of its usual trading range.

The benefit of the franking credit, from a taxation perspective, can vary depending on the time you have held the share. I asked Jason Cunningham, director of the Melbourne accounting firm The Practice <www.thepractice.com.au> for his views on this topic:

> **There is a regulation known as the '45-day rule'. Under this general rule, franking credits received from shares held for less than 45 clear days cannot be used to reduce your income tax liability. This only applies where you have received more than $5000 in franking credits during the financial year. The 45-day rule aims to prevent individuals trading in franking credits and applies to ordinary shares. For more information on franking credit trading regulations, you should consult your taxation adviser.**

Each share does not always go ex-dividend on the same day each year. You can keep track of the ex-dividend dates by monitoring your newspaper or asking your broker. Most online brokers provide a list of ex-dividend dates.

An example

ASX went ex-dividend on 7 March 2001. The dividend was 100 per cent franked and 26.8¢ in value. How much would you expect the subsequent share price drop to be when the share went ex-dividend? The expected drop would be calculated as follows:

$$26.8¢ \times 50 \text{ per cent} = 13.4¢$$

$$26.8¢ + 13.4¢ = 40.2¢$$

ASX was in a medium-term downtrend when it went ex-dividend. The suggested drop in price would be approximately 40.2¢. In fact, the actual price decrease was 33¢ (see figure 10.16). As expected, the gap added momentum to the existing downtrend.

Figure 10.16: ASX daily chart showing ex-dividend gap

Source: SuperCharts version 4 by Omega Research © 1997.

This has been quite a complex chapter, especially if you haven't been introduced to these concepts previously. Let's see if I can summarise the main points for you and then you can review your progress so far. There are a few techniques that I utilise in order to make a decision about the likely future direction of the share price action. I use trendlines, support/resistance lines, moving averages, a momentum indicator, and volume and pattern recognition to analyse any share chart. Candlestick charts are my preference due to the variety of patterns that they display. By using at least one indicator from each of the major indicator families, I am seeking to apply a weight of evidence theory to my trading, and maximise my probability of making a profitable trade.

Review

Often it will take a while to understand the implications of a particular charting method until you practise your newly developed skills. By the time you've analysed about 100 charts or so, you'll gain some level of proficiency. Take the time to answer the following questions and you will be more likely to consolidate the principles discussed in this chapter.

1   Take a look at the following chart in figure 10.17. Describe all of the bullish signals that you can observe. Practise drawing trendlines and support/resistance levels.

Figure 10.17: Pac Group daily chart

Source: SuperCharts version 4 by Omega Research © 1997.

....

....

....

....

....

2 Look at figure 10.18 and describe all of the bearish signals that are evident. Practise drawing trendlines and support/resistance levels.

Figure 10.18: PMP weekly chart

Source: SuperCharts version 4 by Omega Research © 1997.

....

....

....

....

....

....

....

....

3   Is this share trending upward, downward, or sideways (see figures 10.19 and 10.20)? What is the likely future direction of this share? What makes you say that?

Figure 10.19: Paperlinx weekly chart

Source: SuperCharts version 4 by Omega Research © 1997.

....

....

....

....

....

....

....

....

Figure 10.20: Paperlinx daily chart

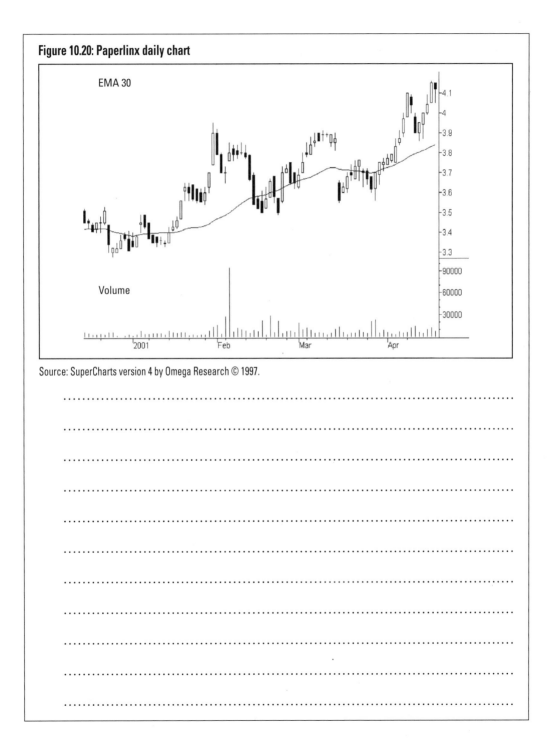

Source: SuperCharts version 4 by Omega Research © 1997.

....

....

....

....

....

....

....

....

....

....

....

Answers

Because technical analysis requires a degree of subjective interpretation, it is quite likely that you drew your trendlines and support/resistance lines in slightly different locations to where I drew mine. The main point of this exercise is to determine the direction of the trend, so if you have achieved this goal, don't be too concerned about the differences. When you are learning this technique, it is incredibly tempting to cover the chart with lines and be voted the new Spirograph User of the Year! This is counterproductive. Try to resist this impulse and only draw lines where the majority of price points touch. This will restrict any tendency to obliterate the view of the chart with lines that do not assist in your ultimate analysis.

Answer 1

Let's see how you went with these exercises.

Figure 10.21: Pac Group daily chart interpretation

Source: SuperCharts version 4 by Omega Research © 1997.

Bullish signals include:

1   more white candles than black

2   generally longer white candles than black candles

3   breakouts through several different layers of resistance (ideally volume should increase when this occurs; this was not evident)

4   share price above the moving average

5   share price above the trendline

6   a series of higher lows.

There may be other bullish signals, but as long as you named some of the signals listed here then you're on the right track.

Answer 2

Keep in mind that most people find they need to analyse about 100 charts before they get their training wheels off. Here's my interpretation for this one.

Figure 10.22: PMP weekly chart interpretation

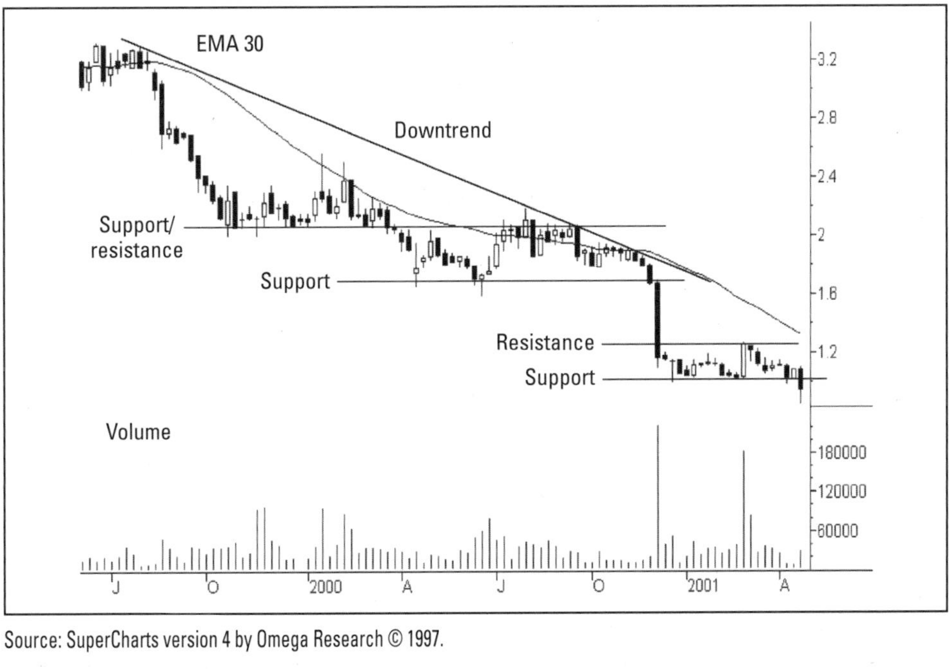

Source: SuperCharts version 4 by Omega Research © 1997.

Bearish signals include:

1   more black candles than white

2   generally longer black candles than white candles

3   breaks in a downward direction through several different layers of support

4   increased volume with share price movements downward

5   share price below the moving average

6   share price below the trendline

7   a series of lower highs.

As you become more adept at technical analysis, you will be able to interpret the trend direction with more precision.

Answer 3

Here's how I interpreted these charts.

Figure 10.23: Paperlinx weekly chart interpretation

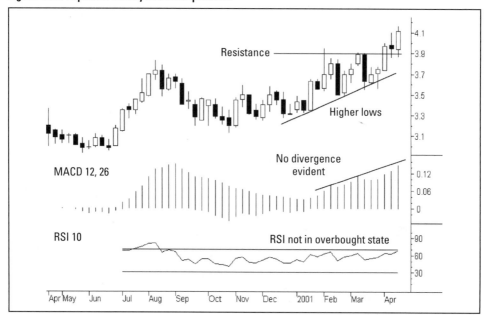

Source: SuperCharts version 4 by Omega Research © 1997.

Figure 10.23 shows several bullish signs, including:

1   Breakout occurred through a significant level of resistance.

2   There is no divergence evident on the MACD. The share is forming higher highs and so is the MACD histogram.

3   The RSI is not in an overbought state, even though it is approaching the line. If the RSI was above the 70 line and turned downward, it would be a bearish sign.

4   A series of higher lows is evident.

Figure 10.24: Paperlinx daily chart interpretation

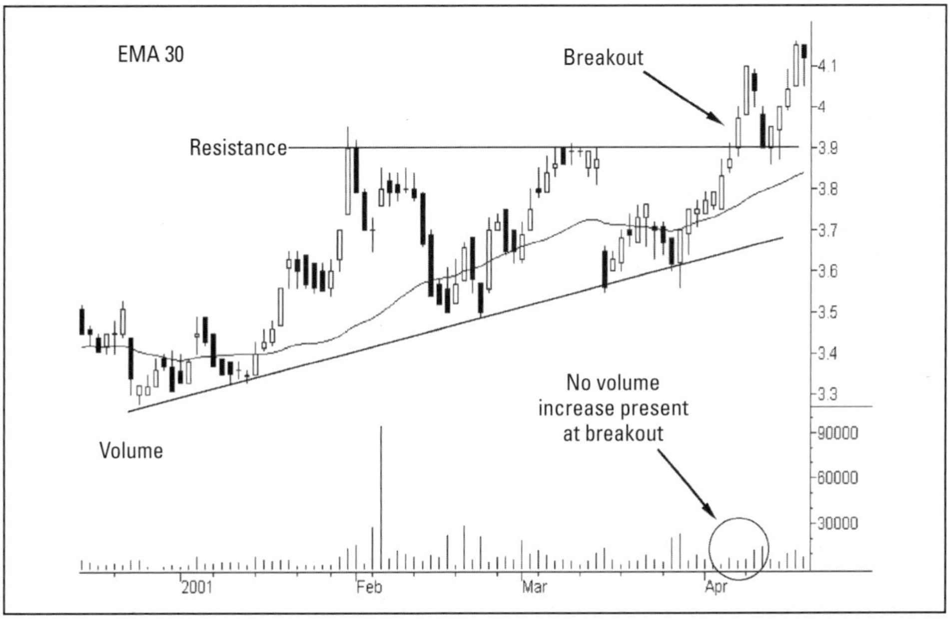

Source: SuperCharts version 4 by Omega Research © 1997.

The predominant direction of this share is upward. Bullish signals include:

1   more white candles than black

2   generally longer white candles than black candles

3   breakout past a significant level of resistance, but this is unfortunately not supported by an increased volume level

4   prices are above the moving average line.

> Based on the weight of the available evidence, the share is in an uptrend after a fairly long period of consolidation both on a weekly chart and a daily chart. Given there is a lack of volume supporting the upward move, a temporary short-term pullback is to be expected. The momentum indicator on the weekly chart shows no sign of divergence, so the pullback is not likely to affect the share price action in the medium term. The overall movement is upward, so it is probable that this movement will continue. There are no guarantees. The best traders act on incomplete information, as by the time the market set-up is perfect, often the timing for entry is no longer ideal.

As I've mentioned, there are hundreds of other indicators available to traders, but adding more indicators does not necessarily increase your effectiveness. The majority of successful trading systems are only right up to 50 per cent of the time (no, this is not a typing error). Because shares trend only about 30 per cent of the time, 50 per cent is slightly better than random probability. Entry systems are only part of the collage of components that make up a professional trading system.

Entry isn't everything

Professional traders realise that indicators and entry signals are the most minor part of any trading system. A system that is correct even 80 per cent of the time can still send you broke if you do not know how to size your positions correctly. A system that is correct only 35 per cent of the time can make you vast amounts of money if you know how to pyramid (that is, add to a winning position) appropriately and how to ride a trend until it ends.

The Turtles are one of the most successful groups of traders the world has ever seen. The group was formed due to a bet between two very profitable traders, Bill Eckhardt

...adding more indicators does not necessarily increase your effectiveness.

and Richard Dennis. Dennis was convinced that trading was a skill and could be taught, so he set out to prove his assertions. He chose a variety of different people from all walks of life who responded to a newspaper advertisement. Only about 50 per cent of this original group continued trading. The others who quit could not follow the simple trading system set out for them due to some form of psychological resistance. The remaining group is called The Turtles because less than 50 per cent of wild turtles actually make it to the ocean to have a chance at survival to adulthood — 50 per cent die on their way to the ocean from predators or other dangers.

The Turtles consistently derive annual returns in excess of 70 per cent, yet their trading system only produces correct entry signals 35 per cent of the time. The probability of a win is insignificant when you consider the importance of the size of your wins compared with the size of your losses. Subsequent chapters will deal with these concepts in greater detail.

Most professional traders would be able to teach you how to trade their system in about two hours. Why, then, do so few traders go on to achieve profitable results, even after being taught by some of the best minds in the trading world? It is because the majority of people are not instinctively set up to trade. About 95 per cent of traders never seek to improve their overall mindset and, as a result, inadvertently deprive themselves of extraordinary profits. These profits are achievable only by the 5 per cent of traders who are prepared to get out of their comfort zone and work on their innate deficiencies and acknowledge their personal strengths.

Further answers

Figure 10.25: Lang Corp weekly (suggested answer to figure 10.3)

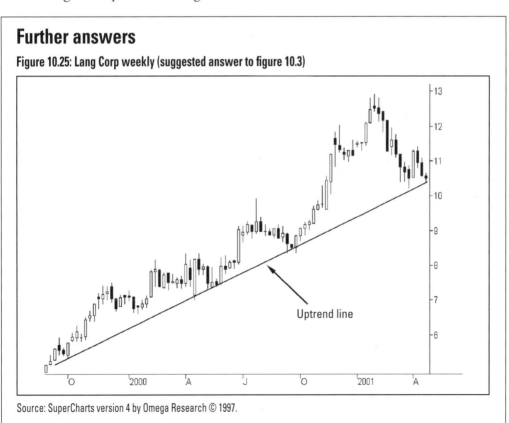

Source: SuperCharts version 4 by Omega Research © 1997.

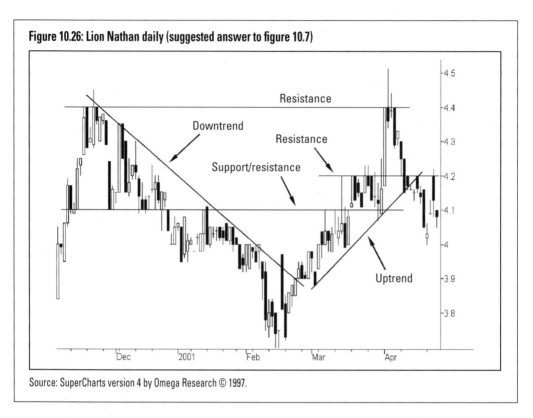

Figure 10.26: Lion Nathan daily (suggested answer to figure 10.7)

Source: SuperCharts version 4 by Omega Research © 1997.

Keep reading to learn about some of the more colourful characters of the sharemarket world — stockbrokers — as well as the fascinating world of online trading.

11

Speed counts. Should you get online?

In this chapter, you will learn that:

- To execute your trading orders, you will need to use the services of a broker of some description. In general terms, brokers fall into three categories—full-service brokers, limited-service brokers and discount brokers (which includes online brokers).

- Before jumping into the online environment, be aware of the drawbacks. Online traders often overtrade, are overconfident and earn less money than traders using a human broker.

THERE IS AN OLD WALL STREET adage that advises, 'Don't confuse brains with a bull market.' During a bull run, people tend to think that they have found the combination to the bank vault. Many traders reach the conclusion that it is easy to trade and that markets always go up. This is not the case.

Up until the GFC, there were a lot of swollen egos and swollen bank accounts. The advent of online trading has meant that almost anyone with half a brain and a bank balance can now call themselves a trader.

When the world started to realise that leverage had a downside, lots of traders found their bank accounts teetering close to the brink of extinction. It's a difficult thing to accept for many. Those who flourished took the lessons and learned how to make money out of a down trend, and how to determine what up and down looked like. Those who held onto their old way of trading went the same way as the dinosaurs.

Just because trades can be executed with the click of a mouse, inexpensively, from the comfort of your own home, doesn't mean it's a simple thing to derive profits. Trading online can produce terrific benefits, but, in the wrong hands, it can be a perplexing, capital-reducing activity.

Types of brokers

There are three levels of brokers in the trading community:

1   full-service

2   limited-service

3   discount.

Full-service brokers tend to provide all of the bells and whistles that you would expect, especially given the amount of brokerage that they will extract from every transaction! They will provide you with research, invite you into a plush city office with imported Italian designer furniture, and usually provide personalised attention whenever you call. For these perks, you may pay between 0.5 per cent and 2 per cent in brokerage fees per transaction. Everything is negotiable though, so the more you trade and the larger your account size, the more likely you will be charged less brokerage per transaction. Full-service brokers usually offer a range of advanced services, such as providing you with access to floats and enabling you to trade options, as well as executing any short-sale positions that you require. These types of trades will be defined in subsequent chapters.

Full-service brokers tend to provide all of the bells and whistles that you would expect, especially given the amount of brokerage that they will extract from every transaction!

Limited-service brokers will provide you with fewer perks; they probably buy their furniture from Ikea instead of importing it from Italy, and offer cheaper brokerage rates. These rates may range from 0.3 per cent to 1.5 per cent per transaction. The growth of online trading has severely diminished the client bases of many full-service and limited-service brokers. Today, if you venture into the vicinity of any of the major stockbrokerage firms, you will hear the sound of the last remaining brokers sobbing quietly into their cafe lattes, lamenting the time when clients were plentiful, and brokerage was easy money. Poor darlings!

Discount brokers fall into two categories—the human variety, or online brokers. Human discount brokers will talk to you over the phone and offer very cheap rates. (To continue my practice of measurement by furniture, I imagine they might be sitting on a milk crate.)

They won't provide advice or send you any flashy newsletters and often you won't be able to deal with the same person every time you make a transaction. They may charge you $50 to $75 per trade, but these figures vary widely.

The other type of discount brokerage firm is an online broker. Online brokers often charge a flat fee per transaction up to a certain value of shares traded (for example, $50 000). Fees may be $19.95 through to $30 per transaction but, again, these fees vary from broker to broker. Fees for online brokerage seem to be decreasing all the time, due to the level of competition in this area. The power of the internet has given traders access to information previously available only to the broking industry. You can now get access to the news, company information, prospectus information, option prices and all the fundamental or technical data that you could possibly wish for. Even though the online environment has been responsible for adding sex appeal to the activity of trading, as well as allowing more people to conduct this activity easily, there are some drawbacks.

The pitfalls of online trading

There is statistical evidence that traders who switch from a broker to an online service receive a lower return on investment per annum. Brad Barber and Terrance Odean, well-known US-based researchers, studied 1607 traders during the 1990s. Prior to going online, these traders experienced strong performance, beating the market by more than 2 per cent annually. After going online, they traded more actively, and less profitably than before—lagging the market by more than 3 per cent annually.

These days, most traders don't use a human broker at all. They trade online from the very beginning. However, trading mistakes are expensive, so it makes good sense to learn how to avoid them. So let's have a closer look at why people lose money when they begin trading online.

Overconfidence

Traders typically enter the market with an inflated opinion of their abilities, while simultaneously underestimating the amount of work required. They tend to attribute too much of their success to themselves. Unfortunately, traders have a tendency to sell winning investments and hold on to losing investments, and to recall their successes more easily than their failures.

Trading is a precise and somewhat boring activity, where decisions are made long in advance of any contact with the market. The world's best traders realise this and they plan with meticulous care. Every contingency is considered, then reconsidered. This approach may not appeal to those who believe that trading should be about frantically yelling 'Buy!' or 'Sell!' to your broker on a mobile phone while admiring the upholstery on your new Porsche. However, it is a truth that must be faced in order to join the ranks of professional traders.

When there is no human broker available to perform a reality check for the trader, the online environment can exacerbate these negative effects. Most traders who switch from a human broker to online trading do so after a period of unusually strong performance. This may have inflated their confidence levels.

If you are intent on trading using an online facility, you will need a high reserve of emotional maturity. Take responsibility for your own actions. Learn from your mistakes, as well as your triumphs. Every trade can be considered a success if you derive a lesson from it.

Overtrading

Online investors have access to vast quantities of information. This serves to create an illusion of control and encourages overtrading. These aspects of online trading tend to boost the ego of traders to gigantic proportions. In this situation, traders are inclined to trade too often and inflict damage on their bank balance.

Evidence suggests that those who overtrade make a lower percentage return than those who trade less. The more actively investors trade, the less they earn. Barber and Odean divided 66 465 households into five groups on the basis of the level of turnover in their common stock portfolios. The 20 per cent of investors who traded most actively earned an average net annual return 5.5 per cent lower than that of the least active investors.

Personally, I don't know any successful day traders. Day traders take a very short-term view of the market, and close out their positions by the close of trading each day. I used to know of some supposedly successful day traders before the tech wreck at the start of the new millennium, but this market correction tended to wipe them out of the trading pool. Basically, if you cannot make a profit when trading with a medium-term or long-term view, shortening your time horizon will not assist.

Computer skills required

There are some traders that may lack the necessary computer skills required to trade online effectively. An eye for detail is an essential skill for trading online. Placing orders incorrectly can quickly erode a hard-earned profit. It can be a tricky situation if you are new to the computer environment, as well as trying to really focus on punching in your trades correctly.

I often feel empathy for traders who come into trading without having ever touched a computer before. It can be quite an intimidating prospect. Sooner or later though, you'll need to stop making excuses and begin learning about the new technology available to help you make money. You can make excuses or you can make money. Go to a TAFE course or befriend a computer boffin. They're always happy to talk about their greatest love — computers.

Experienced traders who avoid the traps of overconfidence and overtrading will find that the online environment offers an ideal opportunity. However, if you are inexperienced in the market, or subject to dramatic flutters of ego, trading online may represent a potential catastrophe.

…if you cannot make a profit when trading with a medium-term or long-term view, shortening your time horizon will not assist.

Trading online will not miraculously transform you from a losing trader into a winner. If you have decided to steer clear of online trading until further notice, it is important to understand some of the pitfalls of dealing with a broker. To have a full understanding of the strengths and weaknesses of the style of trade execution that you choose is essential.

My suggestion

These days, most people find that trading online is necessary, because many brokerage firms have gone out of business, or consolidated their activities with other firms. That means there are fewer and fewer brokers to choose from. Plus, there is enormous pressure on traders to jump straight into the online arena.

If you've decided you'd like to trade online, without going through the learning curve of using a human broker, I do suggest that you establish an account to learn on. Some online brokers allow you to do the equivalent of a sophisticated paper trade. They 'give' you an account of a particular size, then you trade it as if there were real money in that account. This is more sophisticated than the usual paper trade where you alone are keeping records. It adds an additional component of accountability. I definitely recommend that this is a great way to get started, or to test out a new trading system in a semi-realistic environment, before you pop real money into your account.

Using human brokers

Now, before I get a barrage of emails criticising me for having a go at brokers, I want the chance to defend myself. Some of my best friends are brokers and I have met many fine members of the species in my time. I have had dinner with brokers and spent long hours on the phone with them discussing the sharemarket. Let's put these warm and fuzzy feelings aside for just a moment. As traders, we need to recognise the limitations of this profession. Here is a guide to assist you when dealing with these verbose, yet charming, creatures. Be wary if your broker tells you any of the following.

'Trust me, I'm a professional'

A sophisticated 45-year-old gentleman will almost certainly utter this statement. He is likely to have just the right amount of respectable, credibility-inspiring grey hair. He may have been working as a truck driver last week, but it's amazing what a plush office, a Hugo Boss suit and a big boardroom table will do for a guy, isn't it? 'Trust me, I'm a professional' is a classic statement of roughly the same calibre as 'Trust me, this won't hurt a bit . . .'

(Before anyone seeks to correct me, I realise that there are female brokers also. The majority of brokers are still men, however, so I am generalising by referring to brokers as men.)

Admittedly, brokers are required to fulfil stringent requirements in order to gain their qualifications. Your broker may have scored 99 per cent on his exams, but this doesn't mean that you have to take everything he says at face value. In fact, I'll bet that by taking the pressure off the poor guy, and taking responsibility for your own decisions, your trading results will improve. Your broker will breathe an audible sigh of relief if you behave as though you're an adult. If you're lucky, he may even invite you over for a latte, if you happen to notice him at his favourite restaurant.

'It's a good stock'

This implies that good stocks only ever go up in value. It's those bad stocks that you've got to look out for. Did you know that by the light of a full moon, the bad stocks all gather in the graveyard to plot your ultimate demise? It's true, you know!

'Leave some on the table for others'

This statement sounds so wholesome and good-natured — it's got Doris Day written all over it. It is actually designed to make you feel better about selling a share just prior to a magnificent mind-blowing rally that would make even George Soros — one of the world's richest traders — quiver in his boots. That's if Uncle George wears boots. With the amount of money that George has, he can wear whatever he darned-well likes!

Trade to the best of your ability and create as much capital as you possibly can. At least you can then choose a charity that means something to you, rather than altruistically donating money to the sharemarket under the guise of foregone profits.

'You liked this share when it was $9.00. It's only $4.50 today, so it must be twice as good now'

I don't think I'll even comment on this one. It has just been awarded a place in the Stupid Statements Hall of Fame, and wants to enjoy its moment of glory in private. Please don't ever be tempted to average down (that is, buy more of a downtrending share). The implications of this counterproductive strategy will be discussed further in chapter 16.

'It can't go down forever'

Oh yes it can! Shares can drop from the sky with astounding speed. The bulls slowly climb the stairs while the bears abseil down the elevator shaft. The sharemarket robs the ignorant and undisciplined, and throws overwhelmingly large armfuls of money toward astute traders.

Only buy shares that are uptrending and remember to set a stop loss, for goodness' sake. Later chapters of this book will cover how to set stops.

'This one's a sure thing!'

'In a couple of weeks, with the money you're going to make, you'll be able to buy New Zealand!' says your broker confidently. If you believe this, and engage in the trade without doing your research, you are the chump, not your broker. Your broker will still profit from the commission that you have to pay, while you are licking your wounds and mournfully expecting sympathy.

Finding the right broker

When you begin looking for a broker, interview him or her as if you were looking for a new employee. After all, your broker is there to assist you in making decisions about your future. Here are the top 10 qualities to look for in a broker when you're starting in the sharemarket.

Top 10 broker qualities (for beginners in the sharemarket)

1   experience

2   patience

3   commitment to helping you

4   accessibility

5   commitment to education

6   excellent execution of orders

7   easy-to-understand paperwork

8   great range of services offered; for example, short selling and options

9   good people skills

10 reasonable brokerage rates.

After you've gathered some experience in the sharemarket, you will probably look for different qualities when interviewing brokers. Here are my top five brokerage requirements for experienced players.

Top five broker qualities (for experienced traders)

1   excellent execution skills

2   great range of services offered, for example, short selling, options, automatic stop loss facilities

3   ability to process an order without any comment

4   easy to understand paperwork

5   reasonable brokerage rates.

As you can see, fees should be among your lowest priorities when evaluating a new broker. A friend of mine who sells new cars is always concerned when a potential

BMW purchaser asks about fuel economy. Likewise, if you're really worried about the brokerage rates, then you probably can't afford to trade.

Your broker's role is to execute your orders. Any additional benefits that he or she provides is like receiving a free apple pie with your Big Mac—nice, but not strictly necessary, and it may even burn your tongue. You are in control of your own destiny. Take responsibility for your finances, and don't you dare blame your broker if he gives you advice that results in a loss. It was your decision to listen to him in the first place.

You could choose to use a combination of online execution and a broker's services. I predominantly buy and sell shares online, but short sell and trade options using a human broker. Make your own decision about the method that best suits your individual style. For a list of brokers, refer to the 'Support' section at <www.tradinggame.com.au>.

The next chapter focuses on refining your entry and exit triggers and provides you with an opportunity to test your knowledge.

12
Show me the money!

In this chapter, you will learn that:

- It is essential to articulate your exact entry and exit signals in specific terms in order to trade effectively. This will shave hours off your analysis, and get you to the money much more quickly. If you want me to show you the money, you'd better pay close attention to this chapter.

- If you can define a trend in words, it is more likely you'll be able to recognise one in real time.

- Once you have detailed your thoughts about trend definition, it is important to back-test these concepts. See if they are effective over a large variety of shares and market conditions.

THERE ARE SOME FASCINATING PSYCHOLOGICAL principles that recur in the markets. Before examining your entry and exit triggers, let's have a look at a principle that occurs with surprising regularity.

Rounditis
Rounditis is an interesting affliction that takes a ferocious hold on even experienced traders in the market. Traders will generally be drawn to buy and sell at round dollar values. For example, it feels comfortable to buy a share at $5.00 and sell it at $6.00. The comfort of round figures, or regular price increments, seems ingrained.

Levels of support and resistance are often visible at psychologically significant values. It is uncanny to see how many times a reversal in share price will occur at $2.00, $2.20 or $2.50, for example.

It is perception that drives the market. When you buy a product for $24.00, why does this sound more expensive than if you bought the same product at $23.99? This minor difference in price is incredibly important to our subconscious. Just as marketing managers make use of this information, you can utilise the same approach in your share trading.

Rather than selling your shares at $12.00, try placing your sell order at $11.99. I can bet you that there will be fewer sellers at this level, and buyers will be attracted, as they are likely to subconsciously perceive that the price is closer to $11.00 than $12.00.

A real-time data system that provides figures on market depth will allow you to observe this effect for yourself. Market depth shows a bid and an ask screen of the price level and volume of trades as they occur. I am constantly amazed at the number of sellers at round figures in comparison with odd numbers. By making your offer perceptually more attractive to other buyers, you have a higher probability of exiting the trade at that price. You may have to sacrifice a small amount of profit, but if you require your sell order to be filled within a set time frame, this psychological trick can give you an edge.

When a share pushes upward through a round figure with little or no hesitation, it can be a bullish sign. If it hesitates and seems reluctant to close past a certain round figure, it's a sign that the bears are whispering in the ears of the bulls and driving fear into their hearts.

When a share drops easily through a round value, it shows that the bears are firmly in power. If the share finds support at a round figure, it may be a bullish sign, at least in the short term. Often, shares will bounce along this rounded price and then use that figure as a springboard to propel themselves into higher territory.

In order to trade effectively, it's important to be as mechanical as possible. Pretend you are a computer and can only respond to written commands. By writing down all aspects of your entry and exit methods you'll be able to follow these commands to the letter.

Entry signals

Two chapters of this book so far have been devoted to entry signals that you can use to engage the market. Often you can observe an uptrend, but unless you specifically define the situation that will lead you to enter a trade, then all you have is a scintillating piece of academic knowledge. Sooner or later, you will have to pull the trigger and put your money into the market. Paper trading and imagining that you are trading will only get you so far. Rehearsing the scene of a 200-metre swim in your mind is a poor substitute for competing in the actual event—eventually you will actually have to dive in. You must act on your knowledge and actually buy a share.

I challenge you to stop reading this book until you have filled in this next section. I know the temptation is to refer directly to the answers, but you'll only be cheating yourself out of a learning opportunity. By progressing without internalising what you have learned, you will not derive the maximum benefit from the following chapters. Have a shot at summarising some of the key signals that you would look for that indicate that a share is in an uptrend, and the conditions that would trigger your entry. List as many as you can.

Entry signals

....

....

....

....

....

....

....

....

....

If you mentioned any of the bullish signals listed here, then you are on the right track:

- ☑ share prices are predominantly above a 30-week EMA
- ☑ a golden cross with two moving averages of different time durations; for example, a 30-week EMA and a 15-week EMA
- ☑ a rising momentum indicator at a historically low level
- ☑ an upward-sloping trendline
- ☑ a breakout through a significant resistance line on heavy relative volume, preferably initiated by a white bullish candle or a gap

- ☑ a recovery from a period of retracement
- ☑ a resistance line that becomes a line of support
- ☑ heavy relative volume when a share moves upward in price
- ☑ low relative volume when a share moves down in price, compared with when it moves upward
- ☑ a predominance of white candles compared with black candles
- ☑ longer white candles compared with black candles
- ☑ a series of candle tails pointing downward, indicating buyers moving into the market
- ☑ ease in the share's ability to break through round-dollar-value figures; for example, $5.00, $5.50, $6.00
- ☑ a series of higher lows and higher highs
- ☑ a momentum histogram showing higher highs while the share price is also displaying higher highs
- ☑ a gap that hurdles a previously established level of resistance, particularly on heavy relative volume levels.

You may have added in a few more, which is terrific. The key is to put into writing the signals that you find will trigger your entry into a particular share. Make the wording unambiguous, and define each signal as carefully as possible. In times of trading pressure, you will need to have some simple methods to ensure that you are thinking clearly. Try not to make your entry signals complex, as you need to be able to recognise an uptrending share at a glance. Being able to thoroughly express your ideas in writing is a great reality check to see that you've thoroughly grasped the concepts that we have discussed.

Exit signals

How do you define a downtrend? Would you be able to instantly spot whether a share is in decline? This may assist in avoiding buying a share that is currently trending downward. It can also help when trying to identify shorting opportunities, which is a specific strategy that enables you to make money out of a downtrending share. Details about this strategy will be explained in chapter 19. Try writing down the indications that you would use to suggest that the sellers are more aggressive, and that the share has turned bearish.

Exit signals

....

....

....

....

....

....

....

....

You are doing well if you wrote down any of the following signals:

☑   share prices are below the 30-week EMA

☑   a dead cross between two moving averages of different time durations; for example, a 30-week EMA and a 15-week EMA

☑   a falling momentum indicator, especially at a historically high level

☑   a downward sloping trendline

☑   a break downward through a significant support level — especially on heavy relative volume — preferably initiated with a black bearish candle or a gap

☑   share prices closing underneath an upward-sloping trendline

☑   heavy relative volume when a share moves downward in price

☑   low relative volume when a share moves upward in price

☑   a predominance of black candles compared with white

☑   longer black candles than white candles

☑   lots of candlestick tails pointing upward

☑   failure to push upward through round-dollar values; for example, $2.00, $2.50, $3.00

☑   a series of lower lows and lower highs.

Without thoroughly defining a trend in your own mind, you are destined to lose money in the sharemarket. Unless you know what you're looking for, in all probability you will not buy an uptrending share. These are by no means definitive lists of uptrend and downtrend signals, but they will perhaps provide you with some inspiration to more closely stipulate your own entry conditions.

Back-testing

Back-testing seeks to test an indicator's or a system's performance by applying it to historical data. Numerous methods result in an incredible success rate when dealing with the left-hand side of the chart. Unfortunately, you are not permitted to trade any trends that have occurred in the past. It's so easy to be a hero in retrospect.

A system that is over-optimised—that is, designed with heavy reliance on past data—will show incredible clarity when back-tested. It will be completely capable of detecting turning points in the past, but how will it perform in the future? This is called postdictive error. It is an unfortunate consequence encountered by many rigid, inflexible systems. Remain flexible, and allow your trading system to evolve based on new market information, but do not use this premise as an excuse for not following a system at all. The best traders utilise systems in order to minimise the effects of emotion while experiencing periods of pressure.

Discover entry signals that you relate to and use them consistently. Stick with those methods and give your system a chance to prove its worth before altering all of its inherent principles.

Once you have been able to express in writing your exact entry and exit conditions, then you may be able to program these parameters into your trading software package. This will help you search for buy and sell signals that fit your unique trading style, but be sure to remember the old systems analyst's creed: GIGO (garbage in, garbage out). Your computer will not miraculously learn how to read your mind. You need to spell out your search requirements precisely or the results derived will be useless.

Depending on the system you plan to implement, your entry signals (based on the uptrend observations you have just listed), may prompt you to open a position. However, your downtrend observations may not be a suitable trigger for you to sell your shares. Once a share is in a fully fledged downtrend, you may have given back too much profit or suffered a large depletion of your trading equity. Other exit methods may avoid these consequences. There is a variety of other methods that may trigger your exit decision prior to a downtrend being in place. Often actual exit signals have more to do with capital preservation than trend reversal. We discuss this further in part IV of this book.

Trading insights

The majority of people suffer from scarcity thinking. This type of affliction sees only limitations, and expects poverty and lack of opportunity. On the other hand, prosperity thinking allows you to believe that the more money you have, the better off society will be as you will be able to provide for charities, your own family and anyone that you know in need.

Scarcity consciousness questions whether it is ethical to have more than just your basic needs provided for. People stuck in a scarcity rut denigrate the efforts of others to rise above the masses. They can even believe that successful people are unethical, greedy or immoral. Shake free of your scarcity thinking and you will stack the odds in your favour of excelling in the markets.

The next chapter will take you through one of the macro influences on share behaviour — how particular sectors are performing.

13

Sector analysis— your shortcut

In this chapter, you will learn that:

- There are two broad approaches to searching the market for opportunities—top-down analysis and bottom-up analysis.

- Top-down analysis compares each sector index with the All Ordinaries to see which sectors are outperforming the overall market average. Sectors that are outperforming the All Ordinaries are more likely to contain shares that have a higher probability of increasing in value in the future.

- Bottom-up analysis involves searching for shares that have a series of bullish indications, regardless of which sector they are associated with. This can be an effective way to identify trading opportunities.

- An advance/decline line (A/D line) measures the absolute number of shares increasing in value, in comparison with those decreasing in value. A positively sloping A/D line is a bullish sign, as it indicates that the majority of shares in that particular sector are increasing in value. If you mainly buy shares while the A/D line is in bullish territory, you are maximising your chances of making a profitable trade.

- You do not need to trade floats in order to be profitable. Before you fill in the paperwork to buy an initial public offering (IPO), you may want to establish that the sector is trading positively in comparison with the All Ordinaries.

So MANY SHARES, SO LITTLE TIME...just how do you go about searching to find the best opportunities in the market? It can be quite an overwhelming proposition! There are two broad approaches that consistently locate shares with a high probability of trending upward. (The identification of shorting opportunities, which require a downtrend to become profitable, is also assisted by these methods. Simply reverse all of the signals discussed to identify shares with a high likelihood of trending downward. Chapter 19 discusses this concept in more detail.) Before reviewing these two search methods, let's have a look at a critical concept to assist us in our quest to discover a high probability trade—the Relative Strength Comparison (RSC).

The RSC is a concept that is often confused with the Relative Strength Indicator (RSI). The RSI is a momentum indicator. The RSC is the technique of comparing shares, sectors and indices. It is shown as an indicator in many charting packages.

A share may be trending upward but, in comparison to the All Ordinaries index, it may not have been performing as well as the other shares represented. This would suggest that a different share might represent a more appropriate instrument to purchase. However, if the share in question displayed a positive relative strength in comparison to the All Ordinaries index, this would be a bullish sign. This share would have, in effect, been outperforming the index.

I aim to identify shares that have been outperforming their sector, in sectors that have been outperforming the All Ordinaries index. Once I isolate these types of shares, I will enter a long position based on a favourable combination of bullish indicators.

> *I aim to identify shares that have been outperforming their sector, in sectors that have been outperforming the All Ordinaries index.*

Searches for 'hot' and 'cold' sectors can often be programmed into the search routines of your charting software, so your computer can crunch the numbers for you. I tend to search for the sectors showing positive and negative relative strength once a week to assist my decision-making for long and short positions in the market. If you would like a free list of all of the hot and cold sectors that I have identified, on a weekly basis, refer to my website <www.tradingsecrets.com.au>.

Top-down analysis

Top-down analysis involves using the RSC to relatively compare each sector index with the overall market average (for example, the All Ordinaries index). This will lead the investor to the sectors that have the most positive market sentiment (see figure 13.1).

When the RSC line on the chart is located above its moving average, it is an indication that the sector is outperforming the All Ordinaries index. Once these sectors have been identified, the next step is to find the stocks in those sectors that are outperforming their respective sector index.

Figure 13.1: the healthcare sector

Source: created using Beyond Charts <www.beyondcharts.com>.

A mechanical method of using the RSC is to ensure that it has been trading above a medium-term moving average for a set number of weeks. This will lessen the chances of a sector performing well for only a limited period of time, prior to collapsing back into underperforming the All Ordinaries. For example, if the sector has been trading positively in comparison to the All Ordinaries index for the past five weeks, this is a bullish sign.

Another important filter when using the RSC is to look at the advance/decline lines for these sectors. An A/D line measures the absolute number of shares increasing in value, in comparison to those decreasing in value. A positively sloping A/D line is a bullish sign as it depicts that the majority of shares in that particular sector are increasing in value. Alternatively, an A/D line (as shown in figure 13.2, overleaf) shows that since 2007 more shares have been decreasing in value in comparison with increasing in price, in the S&P/ASX100.

Figure 13.2: S&P/ASX100 advance/decline line

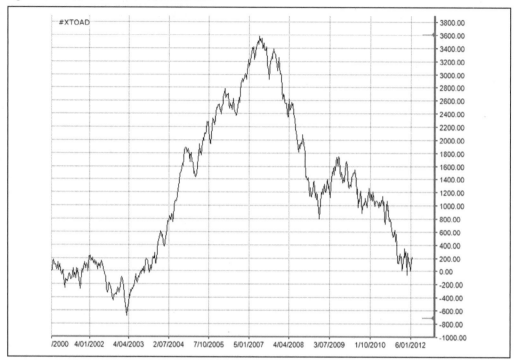

Source: created using Beyond Charts <www.beyondcharts.com>.

Ideally, a bull market will be characterised by more shares increasing than decreasing in value. However, it doesn't always happen this way. The situation can arise when, although the index is climbing, it can be made up of more declining shares than advancing shares. It can still be a rising index because the accumulated value of the declining shares is less than the accumulated value of the fewer advancing shares. The shares with a higher percentage of market capitalisation may also exert a powerful influence over an index. For example, if the market leaders are bullish, then the index will be trending up, even if every other share is displaying bearish characteristics.

Very few data suppliers provide A/D line data. Even fewer suppliers provide separate A/D data based on sub-sections of the sharemarket, such as the Top 100, or separate industry sectors. One data supplier that provides this information is <www.tradinggame. com.au>.

Some traders refuse to trade unless both the index and the A/D line are pointing skyward. Unfortunately, they would have missed out in participating in much of the greatest bull run in history, prior to the year 2000, as there was a negative A/D status present for long periods. Take the A/D line into account, but do not allow this one piece of analysis to outweigh other evidence of bullishness.

Bottom-up analysis

Bottom-up analysis involves searching for shares that have a series of bullish indicators, regardless of which sector they are associated with. Some shares represent an outstanding opportunity, even though the sector of which they are a part is not performing well. The majority of traditional technical analysts seek out opportunities using this method. One interesting alternative with this type of analysis is to search for shares that are outperforming the All Ordinaries index. This can be a novel way of providing an extra piece of bullish evidence, and can work well when run as a search. Once these shares are isolated, they can be analysed to seek entry signals using other technical indicators such as candlesticks, momentum indicators and volume. Another search can be conducted on the basis of this reduced list (which shows all shares outperforming the All Ordinaries) that involves identifying shares trading above their 30-week moving average.

Bottom-up analysis involves searching for shares that have a series of bullish indicators, regardless of which sector they are associated with.

If your software cannot run this type of search, please don't panic! The majority of charting software available cannot delve into this level of detail. Let me assure you that before I used this method to search the market, I was able to still trade profitably—and so can you.

These types of searches are a macro approach to identifying high probability trades. You will still need to observe whether the share fulfils your other criteria before making a decision to buy. If the RSC line is located above its own 30-week moving average, this is a sign that the share has been generally outperforming the All Ordinaries index on a consistent basis (see figure 13.3, overleaf).

Figure 13.3: AMP weekly chart

Source: created using Beyond Charts <www.beyondcharts.com>.

Floats

Initial public offerings are always the flavour of the month when a bull market is surging ahead. Traders tend to beg, borrow or steal money just so they can buy into the latest float. Prices sometimes triple on the day the share lists, much to the glee of the people who have gone to the effort of correctly filling in those annoying IPO forms. Unfortunately, the market most often refuses to continue to react in this manner indefinitely. How very inconsiderate!

In bearish markets, traders of IPOs are not rewarded so handsomely for the particularly gruelling task of accurately filling in paperwork. When markets are downtrending, new IPOs rarely behave with such bullish enthusiasm on the first day of trading. As with every market cycle throughout history — emotional mania becomes depression. Instant millionaires created on the day of listing are an endangered species in bear markets — just ask Big Kev (the enthusiastic Aussie bloke who advertised his own cleaning products and then listed his company). I can bet you he wasn't excited about his results!

There are very few tools that you can use to narrow the list of potential floats into something that resembles a good purchase. Traders with a fundamental mindset analyse the figures that the company presents in its prospectus. For many newly formed companies that float, though, the figures provided often have a 'nudge, nudge, wink, wink' feel to them. 'So, you're going from a situation where you're making a net loss, to making $5 million next year . . . how fascinating. Your net tangible assets at that stage will be more than the gross national product of a small island in the Caribbean! Good for you. I'm really very impressed. Here's $200 000.' Hardly rolls off the tongue, does it?

You may decide that you have no desire to trade floats. As a technical analyst, this is a perfectly valid argument, as there is no price action or volume data to analyse. If you decide that you'd like to try trading a float, as a minimum, check the relative strength of its sector. Although this method does little to ensure the financial security of the company in question, a rising tide tends to lift all ships. If your new IPO is in a favourable sector, there is more of a chance it will begin trading in an upward direction.

If you decide that you'd like to try trading a float, as a minimum, check the relative strength of its sector.

Making a well-timed entry into a position is only part of the story. Now that you've had a look at some of the key trading tools, the next part of this book will cover the essential area of money management. Keep reading to learn all about stop losses and how they can allow you to protect your capital and profits.

Part IV
Trade management secrets

14

GFC victims didn't use stops

In this chapter, you will learn that:

- The goal of a stop loss is to protect your initial equity, and to protect any profits you have derived by retaining that position. Thousands of people halved their superannuation accounts during the GFC. I guarantee that 99 per cent of them didn't use stops. If you're feeling scarred by the past, you'd better switch off the television, silence the phone and lock your door. You need this chapter, or you'll suffer the consequences.

- There are three main types of stops—an initial stop, a break-even stop and a trailing stop.

- Learning how to set a stop loss is one of the main priorities in becoming an effective trader. Without an effective stop loss, your days as a trader will be numbered.

- There are four main ways to set a stop loss—pattern recognition, volatility-based stops, technical-indicator stops and using percentage drawdown.

CHUCK LEBEAU, A WORLD trading authority, tells the story of an eccentric trader who had an incredible track record. Each morning he would put a Coca-Cola bottle up to his ear, nod in a knowing fashion, and then place his orders. (This was before the days of mobile phones.) The other traders were perplexed and asked him what he was doing with the Coke bottle. He said that aliens spoke to him through the bottle and told him which trades to execute! He became the butt of their jokes until they realised that his track record spoke for itself. What do you think was the source of his success?

If your first thought was that aliens have inside information, perhaps you need to avoid Coca-Cola for a little while. However, if you guessed that entry decisions have little to do with your ultimate success in the sharemarket, then you'd be on the right track. It's your exit strategies and your money management skills that will ultimately determine your trading success. When your various entry signals are in agreement, you will have the confidence to pull the trigger and trade.

The golden rule of trading is: 'Keep your losses small and let your profits run.' Stop losses provide a sign that it is time to exit your position as the trade is no longer cooperating with your initial view.

I always remember the first time I lost money in the market. Although I am not proud of it, I actually gave in to the most woeful emotions. I sulked for about two days and complained bitterly to anyone who would listen. This is completely counterproductive behaviour. Any form of negative emotion is self-pity.

...entry decisions have little to do with your ultimate success in the sharemarket...

Watching your hard-earned capital disappear down the drain is never a pleasant experience. Most people actually quit trading after their first four or five losses. That's why this is a game for grown-ups with a high level of emotional maturity. As long as the lessons learned from a losing trade outweigh the emotional torment, it is likely that you will stick around long enough to learn how to trade with skill.

Risk

Trading is not about avoiding risk. It is about managing risk. There are risks that you can control and there are also risks that will catch you completely unprepared. You can avoid some forms of risk by trading only liquid shares, for example. However, there are just some things that you cannot know and therefore cannot plan for. This is why capital allocation, position sizing and stop losses are so important.

Most traders assume that diversification spreads risk. Unfortunately, the equity markets involve many correlations. If you have three banking shares in your portfolio, you actually only have exposure to one sector. This is not diversification. For this reason, as you become a more proficient trader, you may consider diversifying by running a couple of simultaneous trading systems or trading unrelated international markets.

Without a clear idea of how to set a stop loss, your longevity as a trader will be limited. If you deplete your capital to the point when you can no longer trade effectively, you will never know what could have been. Losing large portions of capital takes a horrible emotional toll. Your first aim must be capital preservation. Making money is a by-product of following your trading rules.

Imagine that you have $5000 to trade with, and you lose 50 per cent (or $2500). In percentage terms, how much money do you have to make to break even on your next trade? If you automatically said 50 per cent, you would be incorrect. You need to make 100 per cent on your remaining $2500 to make an extra $2500, and break-even! Things are never as simple as they first appear. Table 14.1 emphasises the importance of keeping your losses small so that you can recover and continue to trade.

Table 14.1: recovery percentages

Loss of capital (%)	Gain required to recover (%)
5	5.3
10	11.1
15	17.6
20	25.0
25	33.3
30	42.9
35	53.8
40	66.7
45	81.8
50	100.0
55	122.0
60	150.0

Discipline

You must maintain a high level of discipline and exit when your stop loss is hit. Many people set a stop loss, but when it is hit they convince themselves that the trend will reverse and that they just need to give the share more time to prove itself. This is detrimental to your emotional wellbeing as well as your bank balance. Don't be another day trader turned long-term investor with stocks that you bought to trade, but continue to hold on to as investments. Set your stops and follow them. If the share hasn't hit your stop, do not exit on a whim. Let the share price gyrate in whatever way it wants to, but when it hits your stop, exit the position.

Types of stops

Setting a stop loss is an imperfect science. It is, in fact, one of the most frustrating areas of trading. By setting tight stops, without taking into account the natural movements of the stock, you will often exit the trade prematurely, only to see the overall trend resume when you no longer have a position. The solution to this annoying prospect is to follow a sound re-entry strategy.

By setting a loose stop, you may feel that you have lost significant amounts of your trading capital or given back too much profit. An advantage with a loose stop is that the trend is likely to have reversed by the time your stop is hit. This provides you with a chance to employ a stop-and-reverse strategy, where you could immediately short sell the share to benefit from the downtrend. However, in the meantime, your drawdown from the paper profit that was within your grasp at the share's highest price compared with your ultimate exit point, may be quite large.

These are the basic differences between setting a tight and a loose stop. The drawbacks of both techniques are considerations when deciding which method to follow.

There are primarily three types of stop losses:

1   initial stops

2   break-even stops

3   trailing stops.

Once you have absorbed the differences between these stops, you can read about the most effective methods of setting a stop.

Initial stops

An initial stop is designed to protect your capital. Despite all of our efforts in the analysis component of trading, most traders find that they make winning trades less than 50 per cent of the time. Even though this sounds discouraging at first, it is adherence to the adage of keeping your losses small and manageable, and letting your

Your initial stop loss will help to prevent your equity from washing away.

profits run, that will ultimately lead to the possibility of extracting great profits from the markets. If you enter a trade and almost immediately the darned thing heads downward, then you need to exit. Your initial stop loss will help prevent your equity from washing away.

You may also need to consider a time stop. Consider exiting your position if the share hasn't cooperated with your initial view within a particular time frame (for example, five days).

Break-even stops

A break-even stop will help lock in a no-loss trade. This type of stop is implemented once a trade has begun to cooperate and there is now little threat of your initial stop being hit. It's always a great feeling when you can move your stop up to cover the costs of your transaction. At least when you have moved your stop to break-even, there is a chance that you will end up with a profitable trade. The goal transforms from protecting your equity to protecting your profits.

The goal transforms from protecting your equity to protecting your profits.

Trailing stops

Trailing stops are designed to protect your profit. To quote Meyer Rothschild:

> **It requires a great deal of boldness and a great deal of caution to make a great fortune; and when you have got it, it requires ten times as much wit to keep it.**

Once the share has trended strongly in the expected direction, you can follow the trend by moving your stop upward. This will result in you exiting the trade with a profit in your account. Many people don't set a trailing stop and watch their share rocket skyward to an amazing level, only exit their trade when they have incurred a loss. Learn to protect your profits as well as protecting your initial capital and you will be well on the way to trading profitably.

Some of the more popular ways of setting a stop are listed later in this chapter. You may find that one method instantly appeals to you, while others do not. Take your feelings regarding this into account because, if your stop loss has been triggered, you need to be able to follow it without question. If you never really believed in the process that you used to set your stop, you may be tempted to passively ignore it, and not exit your position at the appropriate time. Human nature can sometimes be your own worst enemy with trading. Choose a technique that you feel will suit your trading plan and your personality. Commit to a method and follow it. Write it down in your trading diary.

Once you've reviewed the methods listed here, you will also need to consider when to move your stop from an initial stop to a break-even stop, and then onward to a trailing stop. This is absolutely essential if you want to trade well. Your decision about when to alter your stop needs to be considered prior to entering the actual trade. It's easy to lose all sense of objectivity while you have money in the markets. Maximise your chances of success by considering these concepts before you make your next trade. Let's now look at the main methods that you can use to set a stop loss.

Pattern recognition

This is a very popular way for people to set a stop loss. The most intuitive method of setting a stop is to ascertain when the share is no longer trending upward, then exit. The exit can be made if the share's price closes below a trendline or below a support/resistance line. This makes sense, but unfortunately can lead to traders making excuses for not following the stop on their precious little share. Some of these excuses may include:

- 'Well, the share went ex-dividend. Of course it will drop through support in that situation.'

- 'I'll give the trade just one more day, it's likely to recover tomorrow.'

- 'I knew that it would take a while for this trade to be profitable. I'll just put this one in the bottom drawer and be a long-term holder. Shares like this always ultimately trend upward.'

- 'I can't exit today, there's a candlestick bottom-reversal pattern.'

Now, if any of these excuses sounds familiar, please don't tell me about it, because I'll be forced to hunt you down and throttle you. When your stop is triggered, exit the trade. Refuse to accept any excuses. It is always possible to re-enter at a later date.

The problem with pattern recognition exits is that they are subjective. When the time comes to sell, traders try to convince themselves that they should be loyal to the share. There is no room for loyalty in trading.

Write down your stop price in indelible ink, before you enter the trade. Tattoo it on your forehead so that you can be reminded of it every day. Show dogged determination in following this stop. Don't talk yourself out of your initial plan as the share price gets closer to impending doom. Also remember never to set your stop on a round figure. Set it just below, as prices often rebound from round figures.

When to move your pattern-based stop

Often shares will form a staircase pattern. They will travel in a sideways band, then surge up in price, to form a breakout pattern, then travel sideways again. If you have chosen pattern recognition as your stop method, then you can move your stops upward every time this surge ahead occurs (see figure 14.1).

Figure 14.1: Sons of Gwalia weekly chart showing reset stops

Source: SuperCharts version 4 by Omega Research © 1997.

Alternatively, every time your entry system produces a new buy signal, you could move your stop upward.

Volatility

The best types of stop losses are those that take into account the personality of the share. By setting an arbitrary stop based on your own whims, rather than the past behaviour of the share, it is likely that you will be stopped out of a trade without a logical reason.

The best types of stop losses are the ones that take into account the personality of the share.

Patterns are one method by which you can determine the personality of the share. Another method is looking at the level of volatility. You can then exit your position when the volatility increases dramatically, or beyond a pre-defined level.

To assist in this goal, an indicator called Average True Range (ATR) can be utilised. For an exact definition of the ATR indicator, refer to the glossary. A simple definition is the move in cents that a share could reasonably be expected to make during a particular period. On a daily chart, it shows how much the share price is likely to go up or down in a day. It typically shows a figure compiled from the last 15 to 20 days' price activity.

Volatility has no bias—it can increase whether the price is going up or down, because it is a measure of movement, not a measure of direction. It's important to gain an understanding of this concept as it will also be utilised in chapter 15 when we discuss position sizing and money management. Figure 14.2 shows how ATR may be displayed on a chart. As you can see, the average true range is 24.89¢. This means that, as measured over the previous 15 days, Sons of Gwalia could reasonably be expected to move up or down by nearly 25¢ during a usual trading day.

Figure 14.2: Sons of Gwalia weekly chart showing ATR

Source: SuperCharts version 4 by Omega Research © 1997.

Volatility-based stops

Let's say that you have decided to enter a position and you're ready to set a stop loss based on ATR. You definitely wouldn't want to set a stop within the average daily trading range of the share price, because you would have a high probability of your stop being hit, even if the share just behaved in the way it had been acting in its recent past. It would be preferable to exit the position if the share changed behaviour by a set amount.

Chris Tate (<www.artoftrading.com.au>) is the author of several books and has been largely responsible for the widespread acceptance of the volatility-based position sizing and stop loss model in Australia. His book *The Art of Trading*, 2nd edition, covers the concept of ATR and I highly recommend that you put this on your must read trading-book list.

How to use ATR

There has been considerable back-testing conducted by two great traders called Welles Wilder (the trader who introduced the concept of ATR) and Chuck LeBeau that will help you to utilise ATR effectively. LeBeau's and Wilder's testing suggests that if the share breaks out of a predefined range of between 1.8 and 4.0 ATR, then you should exit your position.

Let's say you choose a 2 ATR level at which to exit your position. If a share was priced at $1.50 and had a 12¢ ATR, you would exit at $1.50 − (2 × 12¢:) = $1.26.

Applying this concept to figure 14.2, using a 2 ATR stop, the exit for a trade on Sons of Gwalia would be calculated as follows:

$$\text{ATR} = 24.89¢ \ (\$0.2489)$$

$$\text{Current share price} = \$8.02$$

$$\text{Stop} = \$8.02 − (2 \times \$0.2489) = \$7.52$$

Even from a pattern-recognition viewpoint, it is clear that the stop in figure 14.2 makes logical sense. It is positioned under a significant support line on the share chart.

This method of using ATR as a stop involves anchoring the calculation to a particular share price. By re-calculating ATR as the share price moves up or down, the share's price action will never reach your new calculated level. This should assist you in reaching your goal of trading shares that are trending, while avoiding being stopped out by small price fluctuations. The ideal situation is to find a non-ambiguous method of setting your initial stop loss, which is individualised for each share based on its behaviour. ATR accomplishes this goal. Use your entry price, the most recent high or the most recent low as your anchor. When starting, I suggest that you use your entry price, and use the ATR as of that day to perform your calculations.

When to move your volatility-based stop

You could choose to move your stop to break-even when the share price has gone up by 2 ATR from your purchase price. Using the example shown in figure 14.2 of an $8.02 share with a $0.2489 ATR, you could move your stop to break-even when the share price increased to $8.02 + (2 × $0.2489) = $8.52. You may decide your break-even is a couple of cents more than $8.02, in order to cover your transaction costs. If you have a good grasp of pattern recognition, you should always double-check that the stop that you have chosen based on your ATR calculation makes sense on the chart. This will provide the best of both worlds (that is, a standard ATR calculation, as well as the logic behind pattern recognition) to guide your decision. When the share moves up by another 2 ATR from your break-even point, you could consider adding to, or pyramiding, your position (chapter 17 discusses how to pyramid effectively).

Trail your stop loss behind the rising share price by 3 or 4 ATR as measured from the new high, but do not lower your stop if there is any price fall. This acts like a mechanical ratchet to protect your profits. As the share trends strongly, you could consider tightening or loosening your stop, based on ATR, to suit the term of your investment horizon. There are a variety of methods that you could use, so have a think about which one appeals the most.

The aim is to place your stop far enough away from the usual share price noise so that you will not be required to exit in the middle of the normal trading range. Setting a stop 3 or 4 ATR away will remove you from this noise and prompt you to exit only after the share has shown a substantial change in behaviour.

A short- to medium-term trader could use the ATR calculation based on a daily chart, whereas long-term traders may choose to utilise a weekly chart. Using a weekly chart will eventuate in a wider stop loss placement, so consider using a level that is 2 ATR from the last high, rather than 3 or 4 ATR.

It is a good idea to back-test in order to establish what ATR multiple will suit your individual trading requirements, as well as the current market conditions. In clearly trending markets, many traders use 2 ATR as calculated from a daily chart. In more volatile conditions, I have found that 3 ATR tends to be more universally effective.

Technical indicators

Traders who fall in love with the power of indicators will often implement a technical stop loss. When a sell signal is generated from their favourite indicators, they'll exit the trade. This makes a lot of sense, and can be conducted with a large degree of success by traders who have developed skill with indicators. However, to fully calculate the risk inherent in a position, I believe that it is important to know your exact point of exit, measured in dollars and cents. For instance, a dead cross of two moving averages will not allow you to know this exact dollar value at the time you exit. Quantification is very important. If you cannot quantify your ultimate loss, or exact exit point, you are at a disadvantage. This is especially true in relation to setting an initial stop loss. As the trade progresses, a technical stop can be quite effective (see figure 14.3).

Figure 14.3: Sons of Gwalia daily chart showing technical stop

Source: SuperCharts version 4 by Omega Research © 1997.

Using an indicator as an exit has the tendency to keep you in the trend until a full trend reversal. This can help those of us who have the emotional need to see a share price plummet as soon as an exit has been executed (even though the goal is to remain detached, I love it when that happens!).

If you have a back-tested system that has a high degree of reliability, or if you are looking to apply a trailing stop, then the method of waiting for a technical indicator-based exit may work well for you. Make sure that you are aware of the risks and can overcome the disadvantage of a lack of quantification.

Percentage drawdown

There is a theory that suggests that shares will decrease by a certain percentage from their highest high, and then miraculously rebound in a skyward direction. Traders often think they should exit their positions if the share pulls back by 5 per cent, or by 10 per cent. Can you spot the flaw in this simplistic technique?

That's right...somebody forgot to tell the share that this is how it should behave. Some shares retreat by 10 per cent, and others by 2 per cent, before they continue their existing trend. Are you willing to gamble that a tight, fixed-percentage drawdown will suit all shares? This is not logical (see figure 14.4).

Figure 14.4: Suncorp Metway daily chart showing percentage drawdown

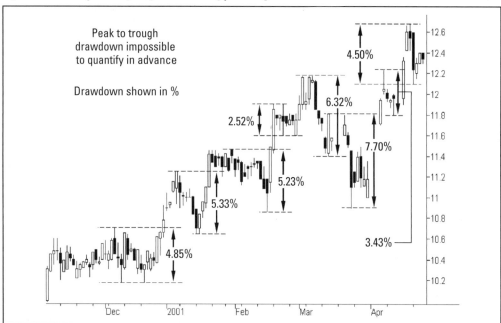

Source: SuperCharts version 4 by Omega Research © 1997.

Suncorp Metway regularly draws down by less than 6 per cent before continuing its upward trend. Compare this with the chart of QBE (see figure 14.5). Applying a blanket ruling based on a tight percentage drawdown to all shares in your portfolio simply does not work.

Figure 14.5: QBE Insurance daily chart showing percentage drawdown

Source: SuperCharts version 4 by Omega Research © 1997.

Use a stop that is based on the personality of the share, tailored to the stock itself. This will lead to an exit based on a sound foundation of logic. The only effective application of a percentage drawdown stop that I have seen is when this is applied as a trailing stop, or as a secondary stop if the primary stop hasn't yet had a chance to respond. For example, some traders use a momentum indicator-based exit on a weekly chart, but if the share drops by a certain percentage from the last high during the week, they will exit their position. This can be an effective method of implementing this type of stop loss.

Partial exits versus full exits

It is possible to designate more than one separate exit level. However, do not use this approach as an excuse for ignoring any of the stop losses that you set. Doing this is not meant to help you avoid discipline. It is a way to maximise or minimise your overall exposure depending on differing market conditions.

Some applications of this method include:

- For very volatile or speculative shares, consider exiting one-third of your position at the appearance of a candlestick top reversal pattern, one-third when the reversal pattern is confirmed by the following candle, and exit the final one-third at a break of support or a breach of a pre-determined level as defined by ATR. This method works very well when trading leveraged instruments such as bought option positions.

- If the percentage of your shareholding in one stock has crept over 20 per cent in comparison with your entire holdings, you could lighten your position in that share by selling a part position at a candlestick top reversal pattern.

- Set your stop two support/resistance levels away from the current price action, and sell half at a breach of the first support/resistance line and half when the price tumbles through the second support/resistance line.

- If the share goes up more than 3 or 4 ATR from the highest high, within a short time frame, you could consider taking a partial profit as this may indicate that the share has become overheated and is therefore due for a correction in the near future.

If you would like to subsequently alter your exit methodology, don't make the change mid-trade.

These concepts form the stop loss procedures and profit-taking methodology components of your trading plan.

Think through the related issues with each of these ideas. Some traders argue against partial entry and exit strategies — so you will need to work out your own personal comfort level with this concept. Whatever you decide, commit it to writing, and stand firm when the time comes to obey your stop. If you would like to subsequently alter your exit methodology, don't make the change mid-trade. Exit, and then write down your alteration in your trading plan. This will provide a level of objectivity, as you will not be making an off-the-cuff decision while experiencing the emotion of having an open position in the market.

Slippage

However you choose to set your stops, the reality of the matter is that you're probably not going to be able to exit at that price. I don't want to burst your bubble, but unless you are selling into an uptrend, or trading an incredibly liquid share, it is likely that you'll always end up exiting at a price lower than you aimed for. Your loss will usually be larger than you first calculated because, when you want to sell, everyone else will probably also want to sell. Therefore, there will not be enough buyers at the price that you have stipulated to absorb the supply. Your losses will usually be larger than you first thought, and your profits will almost always be less than you were hoping for. That's how the sharemarket works.

After-market activity

For the eastern states of Australia, the market officially opens at 10.00 am and closes at 4.00 pm. However, if you have access to a real-time screen, you can see a match price before the open of trade and after the close of trade. At the beginning and the end of the day there is a scramble among the traders as they try to buy and sell. A match price is established where buyers and sellers agree on a price, but these orders cannot be processed because the market is not open. At this time, the market or share is said to be in pre-open.

At 10.00 am, all buyers at the match price or above will buy the share. Once the market closes at 4.00 pm, a similar process occurs and a match price is created. Buyer/seller orders will be matched out at 4.05 pm. This explains why sometimes on your screen, you can see trades go through that are at a much higher or lower price than previous trading, after the market has closed. Options being exercised and off-market orders will also typically be processed after the market has closed.

Sometimes, the final processing of these orders at 4.05 pm will push the share price through your stop. This may complicate things if you are used to exiting close to the end of the day (for example, 3.45 pm). In this situation, you will probably need to exit the next morning.

Setting stop losses is a skill that you will probably continue to refine and perfect throughout your trading life. If you have struggled through this chapter, be patient with yourself. It is one of the more complex areas of trading. Don't be intimidated by the detail. Just choose one method that you understand and relate to, and use it.

I'm providing a review section in this chapter because we have just covered one of the most essential areas of trading effectively. Sure, you could skip over to the next chapter and ignore writing down your thoughts. However, that would put you in the same category as 95 per cent of people who are reading this book for enjoyment, rather than to implement their knowledge. Are you serious about being an effective trader? Then do this review on stops right now. No more excuses.

Setting stop losses is a skill that you will probably continue to refine and perfect throughout your trading life.

Review

1   Define an initial stop, a break-even stop and a trailing stop loss.

    ....

    ....

    ....

2   What are the main ways that you can set a stop loss? Which of these appeals
    most to you? Which do you intend to follow in your trading plan?

    ....

    ....

    ....

3   Do you feel more comfortable with a partial exit strategy or a full exit strategy
    when your stop has been hit? If you want to use a partial exit strategy, which
    method will you follow?

    ....

    ....

    ....

4   Where would you set your stop if you were looking to purchase this share (see
    figure 14.6)?

    ....

    ....

    ....

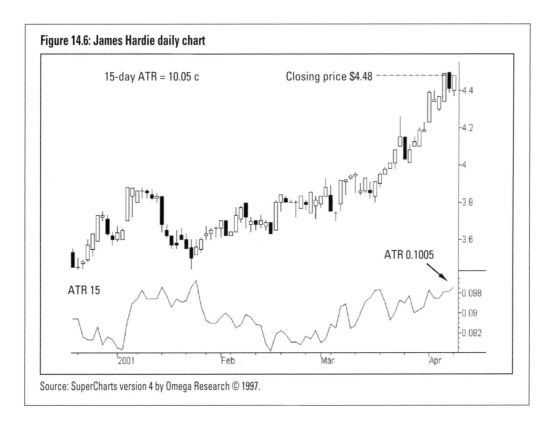

Figure 14.6: James Hardie daily chart

15-day ATR = 10.05 c

Closing price $4.48

ATR 0.1005

ATR 15

Source: SuperCharts version 4 by Omega Research © 1997.

Answers

1 An initial stop is designed to protect your capital. A break-even stop will help lock in a no-loss trade. Trailing stops are designed to protect your profit. Once the share has trended strongly in the expected direction, then you can follow the trend by moving your stop upward.

2 You can set a stop loss using pattern recognition, volatility, technical indicators or percentage drawdown. Think carefully about which type of stop you are attracted to, and which you will use. Make your decision in advance, before you open a position in the market. Don't change your methodology mid-trade.

Stick with your original concept of how to set a stop, and once you have exited your position, refine your methodology. Next time you incur a loss, I dare you to yell 'Next!' at the top of your voice. It may scare the neighbours, but it will do a lot for your attitude.

3   Whether you decide to implement a partial or full exit has a lot to do with your own personality and risk tolerance. This is a personal decision. Consider the pros and cons of each method, and then trade your plan.

4   Setting a stop is a personal issue and you must feel comfortable with the merits of whichever method you choose. Based on pattern recognition, you could position a stop just under a previous low, at the break of a trendline or the break of a support/resistance line (see figure 14.7).

Figure 14.7: James Hardie daily chart showing pattern-based stops

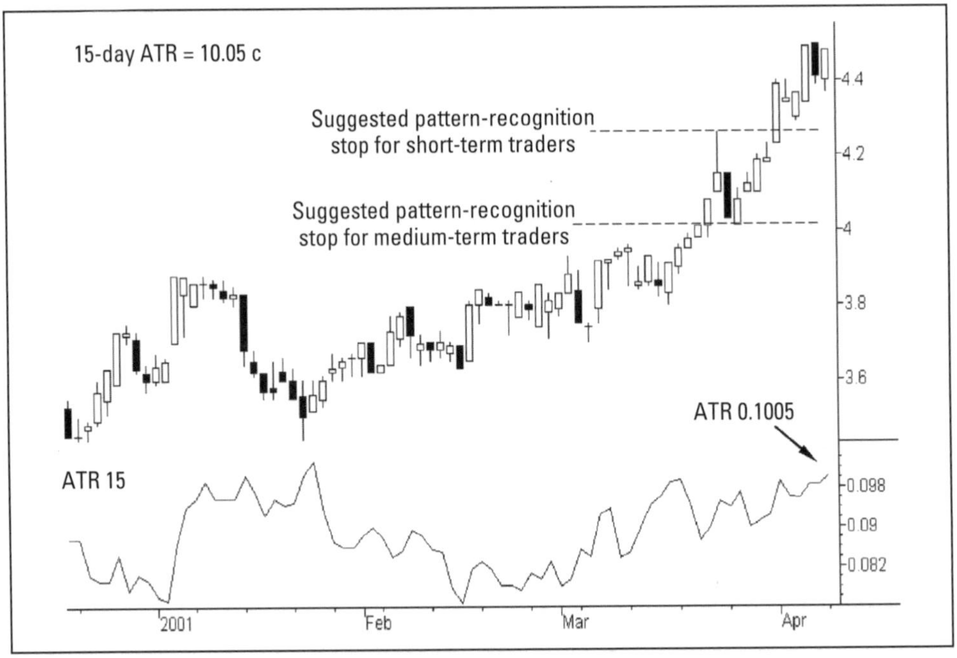

Source: SuperCharts version 4 by Omega Research © 1997.

If you decided to use a volatility-based position-sizing method, you could position your stop at 2 or 3 ATR from the current price. Shorter term traders would consider a stop at $4.48 − (2 × 10¢) = $4.28. Medium-term traders may consider a stop at $4.48 − (3 × 10¢) = $4.18 (see figure 14.8).

Figure 14.8: James Hardie daily showing short-term and medium-term trade options

Source: SuperCharts version 4 by Omega Research © 1997.

Using a technical indicator, you cannot predict the price at which you will exit. You will need to wait for the indicator to produce a signal. The lack of quantification is a significant drawback of using this process for setting a stop.

If you decide to use the percentage drawdown method, what percentage figure will you choose to dictate your ultimate exit? It is impossible to choose one figure to suit all shares.

The next chapter builds on the concept of stop losses and introduces the subject of position sizing.

15

Most people suck at money management

In this chapter, you will learn that:

- Money management is a key skill that separates professional traders from the unprofitable masses. The majority of traders underestimate the importance of this area. They suck at it and they deserve to have money stripped out of their accounts by the markets.

- Money management involves calculating how much money to assign to each position based on your risk assessment.

- There are several ways to establish how much money to devote to each position. The equal-portions model involves dividing your equity by the total number of positions you intend to hold. The market capitalisation model assigns capital on the basis of risk as determined by the market capitalisation of the share you would like to buy. The percentage-risk model assumes you will only lose a set percentage of your equity on any one position. Hybrid methods are also available.

- You must also consider your maximum position size, so that no particular position is too large within your portfolio.

MOST SUCCESSFUL TRADERS SPEND the majority of their time and focus on the areas of money management, stop losses and pyramiding. Novice traders tend to focus on entry methods only.

Money management indicates how many shares to buy and suggests how much of your account to commit to a given market. Studies have shown that even random entry systems can be profitable using effective stop loss procedures and good money management. When people start out in the market they often believe that as long as they hitch a ride with a share that is headed for the moon, they will accumulate untold riches. Very few trades cooperate to this extent (although this mindset does partially explain people's preoccupation with entry signals).

Money management and stop losses will help keep you in the market long enough to experience a few terrific winners, even if you hit a cluster of losers.

Ironically, 90 per cent of the trades that I conduct don't amount to any significant profit. It feels like I'm treading water, waiting for a trend to unfold. The majority of my profits are produced by about 10 per cent of my trades. Trading is often not a consistent income-generating activity. Many people give up or run out of money before they reach that magic upper echelon of very profitable trades. With the law of statistics, it could take you 20 trades in a row of mundane, frustrating, break-even or loss results to hit the one trade that will bring in great profit. It is not a normal distribution of wins to losses in the market when you look at a small sample size. Money management and stop losses will help keep you in the market long enough to experience a few terrific winners, even if you hit a cluster of losers.

There are two types of bites in the market — the piranha bite and the shark bite. The piranha will eventually kill you, but it may take quite a while before you slowly bleed to death. Your initial stop loss will help to protect you from this. The shark bite will kill you with incredible speed. It is equivalent to losing a significant portion of your trading capital, so that you cannot play the game any more. Your methods of capital allocation and position sizing will help to save you from a one-off catastrophic event. As an overriding rule, if you are continually thinking about the performance of your shares, your position size is too large for you to handle.

Money management and capital allocation are often overlooked, much to the detriment of traders who are perfectly capable of detecting a trend. With a bit of extra study of money management, these traders could be transformed from mediocre to proficient. It is important to separate the entry decision from the money management decision. They are two completely different areas.

An essential question that must be asked is: 'How much of my capital should I devote to this trade?' There are several models that perform this task. They each have pros and cons. Ultimately, you need to choose one model, or a hybrid of the available models, prior to buying a stock.

The equal-portions model

When traders begin in the market, they often jump at the first solution that they fully comprehend regarding how much capital to allocate to each trade. The equal-portions model is by far the simplest approach. This does not necessarily mean that it is the most effective method, but it is important to understand it fully in order to build on this concept.

This is a model where your capital is divided into equal amounts. For example, you may have $100000 equity and decide to split it into 10 different parcels of shares worth $10000 each.

There are some inherent difficulties with this concept. It assumes a consistent risk factor across all trades. This is a simplistic assumption. All shares were not created equal. Some are liquid, slow-moving giants, while others are volatile, speculative shares that react with surprising unpredictability. Putting $10000 into CBA has a very different implication to allocating $10000 to a speculative mining company that hasn't yet found gold. CBA is more likely to have high levels of liquidity, a more consistent chart pattern and a less volatile nature. The speculative share has a less predictable nature, so perhaps doesn't deserve the same level of investment.

Most Australian investors hold shares in only one or two companies — you guessed it, Telstra and CBA — because of their successful and highly advertised floats. This is not sophisticated investing. Most people have no idea how to size their positions correctly.

Consider modifying the principles behind the equal-portions model to take into account some of its shortfalls. The next model will assist you in this.

The market capitalisation model

This model divides your capital between areas of risk. Although it can be used in conjunction with other methods of position sizing, it is most often combined with the equal portions model.

One of the underlying principles behind the market is the theory that if a stock has a significant market capitalisation (for example, Top 100 or Top 300), then it is likely to behave in a more predictable fashion. Whether the market capitalisation affects the behaviour of shares is a controversial issue, but it is important that you form a view as to whether you feel this is accurate.

Market capitalisation

Market capitalisation is the total number of shares that have been issued, multiplied by the share price. The market capitalisation will affect, for example, whether a share is included in the All Ordinaries index—Australia's benchmark index. It will also determine whether a share is included in the sector indices: for example, energy, health or materials.

Many fund managers or institutional investors use market capitalisation as an indication of how much of a particular share to include in their portfolio. If a fund manager is trying to outperform the All Ordinaries index, it would seem a good idea to determine which shares make up this index, and what percentage of each share goes toward constructing it. For example, if approximately 30 per cent of the All Ordinaries is made up of News Corp shares, then it would be a good start for fund managers to be aware of this fact. Many fund managers would thus keep their funds in line with the All Ordinaries by maintaining News Corp shares as 30 per cent of their fund. This way, the fund manager gets to approximately replicate the return derived by the All Ordinaries. Not an original concept, but effective nevertheless. It's easy to implement for the fund manager, and allows them to pursue their interest in long lunches relatively unfettered by the demands of their job.

Shares with significant levels of market capitalisation will display changes of trend in a more gradual and predictable fashion than shares with a lower market capitalisation.

Fund managers find that when they try to buy or sell large volumes of shares, they can actually move the market—that is, affect the price activity. If they want to buy $1 million of CBA, they could inadvertently drive the price of the share upward. To overcome this, large players in the market often buy and sell their shares in smaller parcels.

The impact of this behaviour is that there will be large professional players involved in shares with significant market capitalisation. The gradual entry and exit of money from larger market capitalisation shares allows your indicators to react in a more timely fashion and for your technical analysis skills to be implemented with greater accuracy. Shares with significant levels of market capitalisation will display changes of trend in a more gradual and predictable fashion than shares with a lower market capitalisation. This means that any of the Top 100 or Top 300 may deserve a larger percentage of your capital than a speculative share. If you follow and agree with these arguments, then you could be a candidate for using a capital-allocation position-sizing model.

How to use this model

The maximum number of shares that most people can handle at one time with a larger portfolio (for example, $300 000 and above), is approximately 15 separate positions. People with a smaller portfolio often feel more comfortable holding six to 10 shares. This is largely anecdotal evidence because, according to my knowledge, there is no current reliable data regarding the ideal number of positions to hold. As a guideline, the minimum number of positions in a portfolio should be at least three, in order to give you a chance to learn how to trade well. Hopefully, out of those three shares, at least one will be trending in the right direction, although there is no guarantee.

As a suggestion, it may be best to allocate more money to the Top 100 shares (lower risk): for example, 50 per cent of your capital. You could allocate a moderate amount to the bottom 200 shares of the Top 300 (moderate risk): for example, 30 per cent. The least amount of money would then be allocated to all other shares under the Top 300 (higher risk): for example, 20 per cent. This would mean that with an initial starting equity of $100 000, you could allocate $50 000 to lower risk shares, $30 000 to moderate-risk shares and $20 000 to higher risk shares.

Make your capital-allocation rules to high-risk areas explicit. You may decide to commit a maximum of only 15 per cent or 10 per cent of your total equity to higher risk sectors of the market, depending on your risk profile. This will still provide exposure to potential high returns, without bursting the seams of good judgement.

For the sake of simplification, let's say that you're happy with holding 10 positions. This could be split into the equivalent of three separate portfolios defined by the risk inherent within the market capitalisation level. Your low-risk portfolio of Top 100 shares could contain three shares with a position size of $16 666 each. Your moderate-risk portfolio could contain three shares with a position size of $10 000 each. Your high-risk portfolio could contain four shares with a position size of $5000 each.

There are refinements to this method, but if you relate to the concept, then this can be a simple way to position size with a higher degree of sophistication than the equal portions model.

The percentage-risk model

The percentage-risk model suggests that you should only ever lose a maximum of a certain percentage of your total equity with any given trade. This idea has implications with regard to position sizing, or how many of a particular share to buy. The full implication will become clearer by the end of this chapter.

The 2 per cent rule

The 2 per cent rule suggests that you should not lose more than 2 per cent of your total trading capital on any one position you have in the market. For example, with $100 000 of trading equity, you should not lose more than $2000 on any particular trade: $2000 is the maximum amount that you would be willing to put at risk. Risk is directly related to your chances of survival in the market.

... first determine your stop loss exit point, based on your method of choice, then work out the number of shares this allows you to buy to ensure you don't risk more than 2 per cent of your equity.

Some traders take the 2 per cent rule to mean that when a share decreases by 2 per cent in value, they should exit—for example, if a $10.00 share decreases to $9.80, the position should be closed out. This is a complete misinterpretation of the 2 per cent rule. This may mean that you are exiting the trade in the middle of a trading range. For a stop loss to work effectively, it must be based on the previous behaviour of the share price action, not by choosing an arbitrary exit point. Another common misconception is that you should only buy shares to the value of 2 per cent of your total equity. This means that you would end up with 50 positions! That's far too many to manage effectively.

For any share purchase, you must first determine your stop loss exit point, based on your method of choice, then work out the number of shares this allows you to buy to ensure you don't risk more than 2 per cent of your equity.

Daryl Guppy <www.guppytraders.com> is the author of several books, including *Share Trading*. He has been a key promoter of the 2 per cent method in Australia.

When to modify the 2 per cent rule

The 2 per cent rule is suitable for smaller portfolios (for example, less than $100 000), but for larger portfolios a 1 per cent or 0.5 per cent level may be more appropriate. Ironically, the more money that traders have, the less risk they need to incur per position in order to multiply their money. Traders with smaller amounts of capital often have to indulge in very high levels of risk. This is counterproductive and often increases the probability that they will financially blow themselves up.

How to position size

Assume that you have $300 000 in trading equity. Once you have decided where to set your stop loss, you can work out how many shares you can buy. Let's imagine that you are prepared to accept 0.5 per cent risk, as this suits your conservative risk profile. This means that you are prepared to risk $1500 per trade. Imagine that you had decided to purchase BHP and the current price was $20.00. You may decide that an appropriate exit is at the point where the share price drops to $18.98. The basis for your stop could be any of the quantifiable methods described in the previous chapter (for example, pattern-recognition or volatility-based stop losses).

To decide how many BHP shares to purchase, divide the amount to be risked ($1500) by the loss resulting from a presumed exit at $18.98 ($20.00 − $18.98 = $1.02). The number of BHP shares that can be purchased is $1500 ÷ $1.02 = 1470 shares, at the purchase price of $20.00, which equates to $29 400 or 9.8 per cent of trading funds (see figure 15.1).

Figure 15.1: BHP daily chart showing stop loss at $18.98

Source: SuperCharts version 4 by Omega Research © 1997.

Your risk is held at a constant level

By using a per cent based method of position sizing, you can accept and cap the risk at a percentage of your overall equity. The use of the percentage-risk model implies that the wider your stop, the fewer shares you can buy, which is the key to this method. When using the volatility-based stop loss method (as discussed from page 169), the more volatile the instrument, the fewer shares that you can buy. This is because more volatile instruments generate higher average true range figures. Using pattern recognition to set a stop loss, let's say that you were aiming to set your stop underneath a major support/ resistance line. The further away the level of support/resistance, the fewer shares you would end up buying.

... the wider your stop, the fewer shares you can buy, which is the key to this method.

Imagine that you were willing to lose or risk a maximum of $2000. If you decided to position your stop 3 ATR away from the current price, you would buy fewer shares than if you had set your stop at 2 ATR away from the current price. Your risk is held constant, at $2000, regardless of where you set your stop. This is the advantage of using the 2 per cent rule to position size. You can set a very wide stop and still participate in the trade, but hold your risk at a constant level. Your risk remains at $2000, whether your position size is $10 000 or $100 000.

Many traders find that they become gun-shy when their portfolios grow in size. When you begin trading, you may only have a few thousand dollars to manage. In a few years, it is feasible that you will be managing hundreds of thousands of dollars. Keep the concept of the percentage risk clear in your mind, and you won't back away from buying a larger parcel of shares.

Keep your losses small as a percentage of your overall equity, and you will never be afraid to trade.

Maximum position size

There is an efficient threshold regarding your maximum position size as a percentage of your overall equity. At all stages, ensure that any one position contains no more than 25 per cent of your total equity. For larger portfolios, consider dropping this back to 15 per cent or 20 per cent.

Calculate your position size based on the level of risk that you're prepared to accept, but double-check that this will mean you'll be buying shares to the value of 25 per cent or less of your overall equity. For example, if the 2 per cent rule dictates that you should buy $30 000 of shares and your overall equity is $80 000, only buy a maximum of $20 000 of shares. The 25 per cent is the overrider.

Please do not read these next few paragraphs if you are struggling with the position-sizing concepts discussed so far. You have enough knowledge by now to protect yourself. However, if you are open to listening to another concept, then continue reading.

An advanced view

Some traders modify the 2 per cent rule on the basis of volatility.

Particularly volatile shares will show a high ATR in relation to their share price. For example, imagine you are looking at a share with an ATR of 20¢ per day as measured over the past 15 days. If the share price is $2.00, the implication is very different than if the share price is $10.00.

If the ATR is 4.6¢ and the share price is 42¢, it could reasonably be expected that the share will go up or down in value by nearly 5¢ per day (that is, approximately 10 per cent of its overall value). A price variation of 10 per cent per day means that it is quite a volatile share, and needs to be treated in a different manner to a less volatile instrument (see figure 15.2, overleaf).

The concept of defining volatility on the basis of ATR as a function of the share price has been explored by Gary Stone, the director of Share Wealth Systems <www.sharewealthsystems.com.au>. Gary's medium-term trading system usually suggests that a technical momentum indicator called the Smoothed Indexed Rate of Change (SIROC) be used as a stop loss. However, for shares with a volatility of greater than 5 per cent, he suggests that a volatility-based stop loss method be utilised.

When you are starting in the trading arena, it may be wise to trade less volatile instruments, at least initially. This will give you a chance to develop your skills prior to moving into the fast lane. Shares that go up quickly are likely to come down quickly.

As a minimum, make a decision to assign less capital toward extremely volatile shares until you gain the confidence required to trade these shares well. For example, if you are currently using a 2 per cent position-sizing model, you could use a 1 per cent model for shares with a volatility percentage of greater than 7 per cent. This means that you can still enter the position, but you will allocate less capital to shares that have high levels of volatility. It does not imply that you will operate a tighter stop. You need to give shares a bit of room to move or you'll be stopped out prematurely.

Figure 15.2: Amcom daily chart showing volatility percentage

Source: SuperCharts version 4 by Omega Research © 1997.

Determine the level of risk and loss that you're prepared to accept before entering a new position. Assign less capital to higher risk trades. Vow that you will not be oblivious to the risks. Be proactive with your money management and you'll dramatically improve the returns from your trading.

How much money do I need to start trading?

Traders often run out of money before they learn how to trade well. Many are undercapitalised and seem to want to know the answer to the question, 'How can I make bucket-loads of money from trading if I don't have any to start with?' The brutal truth is that you won't—the world doesn't work that way.

Some analysts suggest that you only invest the amount you are prepared to lose in the sharemarket. I vehemently disagree. This uneducated mindset is setting you up for failure before you even begin.

You need to have at least enough money to suffer a string of losses, without wiping out your equity. If you forced me to choose a figure, I would suggest at least $15 000 as a minimum. However, you should be aware that the less capital you have to trade with, the greater the impact of transaction costs such as brokerage will be as a percentage of your position sizes. It is close to impossible to pluck out of thin air a minimum amount that would be widely appropriate. By committing more money than this, you are more likely to stay loyal to efficient money-management methods. You can start with less, but you really aren't giving yourself a fighting chance. Keep reading and investigating the market, but perhaps don't start trading until you have built up a reasonable pool of equity.

So many people remain completely oblivious to the dangers that lurk in the sharemarket. They feel all the emotions of a fun park, without any idea about how to approach trading professionally. This is not like a game of Monopoly: there are no 'Get out of the sharemarket free' cards given to you when you sign your broker's agreement. Through ignorance, you could lose everything that you have invested.

How much money will I make?

If making money is your focus, you'll probably be a net loser in the markets. Most people are. I honestly have no idea how much money you will make. Your skill and discipline will dictate this. Once you've started the ball rolling by trading over a variety of different market conditions, you will have a much clearer idea about how much money you will make. Chapter 18 provides some clues about how you can measure your performance and project the type of results that you can expect in the future.

Summary

My preferred methods for setting a stop are pattern-recognition-based stops and volatility-based stops. Here is a formula to help you calculate your position size based on where you set your stop loss using either of these methods.

Step 1

How much money in total do you have to invest in the market? Note that when building a portfolio, it is advisable that you never place more than 25 per cent of this in a single position. Traders with larger portfolios (for example, more than $100 000) could use a 15 per cent or 20 per cent maximum position size.

Step 2

How much money are you prepared to lose in each position? Make this 2 per cent or less of your total capital available on any one position: for example, $2000 total loss per position on a $100 000 portfolio.

Step 3

Look at the chart to find a logical stop loss point: for example, just under a support line or a trendline, or at 2 or 3 ATR from entry price.

Step 4

a) Current price − stop price = risk amount (that is, the drop in share price that you are prepared to risk). If you are using a volatility-based stop loss, the amount you are risking will be equal to 2 or 3 ATR.

b) $\dfrac{\text{Total acceptable risk \$}}{\text{Risk amount}} = \text{no. of shares you can purchase}$

c) No. of shares × share price = total investment

Let's say that figure 15.3 shows a share that you have already decided to purchase. Assuming a $100 000 capital base, and a 2 per cent risk level, the position size for the proposed purchase can be calculated. For the sake of simplification, rather than discussing the impact of various stop loss methods on the ultimate position sizing, I have used a 2 ATR stop loss level:

a) Current price − stop price = risk amount (that is, the drop in share price that you are prepared to risk)

Amount that you are prepared to risk = 2 ATR = 2 × 4.82¢ = 9.64¢ (that is, 10¢, rounded)

$2.20 − $2.10 = 10¢

b) $\dfrac{\text{Total acceptable risk \$}}{\text{Risk amount}} = \text{no. of shares you can purchase}$

$\dfrac{\$2000}{0.10} = 20\,000 \text{ shares}$

c) No. of shares × share price = total investment

20 000 × $2.20 = $44 000 (which exceeds the maximum position size — in this case we will use 15 per cent)

Therefore: 15 per cent × $100 000 = $15 000

$\dfrac{\$15\,000}{\$2.20} = 6818 \text{ shares}$

It is always a good idea to round this figure down to make an allowance for brokerage, so buy 6800 shares.

Figure 15.3: Futuris daily chart

15-day ATR = 4.82 cents
Current price = $2.20

ATR 15

ATR 0.0482

Source: SuperCharts version 4 by Omega Research © 1997.

As discussed in chapter 10, a reliable technical indicator can also be used to define a stop loss, but you will be unable to quantify your exit point in advance. Another technique is the percentage drawdown method. This is not an effective way to set a stop loss if you use a tight, fixed-percentage drawdown.

Trading insights

Watch your thoughts, they become your words. Watch your words, they become your actions. Watch your actions, they become your habits. Watch your habits, they become your destiny.

With trading, you can't leave your choices to guesswork. If you do, you will fail. You've got to challenge common assumptions about trading, your mindset and your progress. Understand this—people generally don't question. They meekly accept their miserable fates. Rarely do they strive to achieve. Rarely do they stand up and shout, 'Over here, Success. Pick me! Pick me!'

Review

Imagine that you have $100 000 to trade on the sharemarket. Have a look at the chart in figure 15.4. It is within the top 100 market-capitalisation level. Try not to get hung up on whether or not to buy the share — entry decisions are separate to position-sizing decisions. Assume that you have already made the decision to buy the share and that you are trying to work out how many to buy.

Figure 15.4: Santos daily chart

15-day ATR = 15.34 cents
Current price = $6.78

ATR 0.1534

ATR 15

Source: SuperCharts version 4 by Omega Research © 1997.

1   How would you set your stop? Which method would you use?

....
....
....
....
....

2 How would you decide on the number of shares to buy using the equal-portions model?

....

....

....

....

3 How would you decide on the number of shares to buy using a market-capitalisation model?

....

....

....

....

4 How many shares would you buy using the percentage-risk model?

....

....

....

....

5 Which method of setting a stop feels the most comfortable?

....

....

....

....

6   Which method of position sizing did you find the easiest and most effective?

....

....

....

....

Answers

1   You could choose either a pattern-based, a volatility-based or a technical indicator-based method to set your stop loss. The percentage drawdown stop is another method, but it is not recommended.

2   Using the equal-portions model, you could assign 10 per cent of your trading equity to this position (that is, $10 000). This would result in the purchase of 1474 shares at $6.78 ($10 000 ÷ $6.78). Round this figure down to make an allowance for brokerage, so buy 1470 shares.

3   Using the market-capitalisation model, you could assign $16 666 of your trading equity to this position, as it is in the top 100 of market capitalisation. This would result in the purchase of 2458 shares at $6.78 ($16 666 ÷ $6.78). When you round this figure down to make an allowance for brokerage, you could buy 2450 shares. There is no need to cap this figure at 15 per cent of your total equity, as the market capitalisation model allows for some positions to be significantly larger than others within the portfolio. A cap of 25 per cent would be more appropriate when using this model.

4   The percentage risk model suggests that you are prepared to risk only 2 per cent of your total equity in a single position. Assuming a 2 ATR stop loss procedure, your stop loss would be at $6.47 ($6.78 − [2 × 15.34¢]).

   a)   Current price − stop price = risk amount
         (that is, the drop in share price that you are prepared to risk)
         $6.78 − $6.47 = 31¢ = amount that you are prepared to risk
         (that is, 2 ATR = 2 × 15.34 = 31¢ when rounded)

b) $\dfrac{\text{Total acceptable risk \$}}{\text{Risk amount}} = \text{no. of shares you can purchase}$

$\dfrac{\$2000}{0.31} = 6451 \text{ shares}$

c) No. of shares × share price = total investment

6451 shares × $6.78 = $43 737.78

This is too great a proportion of your total trading capital, so cap this figure at 15 per cent to invest $15 000 or 2212 shares.

Answers to questions 5 and 6 will be unique to your own situation.

The next chapter discusses ways you can capitalise on a winning position to make your profits even greater.

16

More bang for your buck

In this chapter, you will learn that:

- Pyramiding is a strategy where you add money to a winning position. When carried out correctly, it maximises your profit and gives you more bang for your buck.

- You don't need to pyramid to trade effectively. Use this strategy only if you are comfortable with the concept, and perhaps have a little experience under your belt.

- Buy your largest position first, monitor your risk levels, and reset your stops every time you add money to the position.

- Setting profit targets is rarely an effective strategy.

- An anti-martingale strategy increases your position sizes when you are on a winning streak and decreases your position sizes when you are encountering losses. It is a key principle that the majority of profitable traders adhere to, in order to ensure success.

- As your overall equity grows, the size of your individual share trades can increase. This is a perfect application of an anti-martingale system and will have the benefit of multiplying your trading results.

Half the failures in life arise from pulling in one's horse as he is leaping.

—Julius Chares Hare and Augustus William Hare

YOU MAY OFTEN HEAR THE misleading saying, 'You'll never go broke taking a profit.' When faced with a profit, traders will often become risk-averse and are tempted to take the profit and run. This is exactly the time that you need to defy your own feelings — rather than running away from risk, you should actively seek it when you are profitable by adding money to your original position. Given that only a minor percentage of your trades will actually be spectacular winners, it sounds logical to multiply your profits when you have detected an enduring trend. The trick lies in doing this effectively while monitoring your risk levels. This is called pyramiding. It is important that you pyramid correctly if you are intending to try this method.

If you are just starting out in the trading arena, it may be wise to shy away from pyramiding, until you have developed confidence and refined your trading system. I have reviewed hundreds of share trades, both profitable and unprofitable, conducted by traders with varying levels of experience. There are often many profitable trades converted into break-even positions, or even losses caused by ineffective pyramiding. Once you've been trading successfully with a simple, uncluttered system for six months or so, you'll probably be ready to consider pyramiding. Most experienced traders swear by it.

This type of strategy tends to work best in a clearly trending market. Without the benefit of a trend, markets that whipsaw can send traders who are learning about pyramiding a little batty.

There seems to be some unseen pressure on people who learn about trading to conquer everything in a day. If you are working to an effective trading plan, you can stick to trading equities and avoid pyramiding, yet still come out net profitable. You don't need to trade contracts for difference (CFDs), options, futures, and, in your spare time, juggle warrants and the foreign exchange (FX) market. Keep things simple and you can gradually work your way through other more complicated strategies at a later date.

Pyramids and inverted pyramids

It often helps to express our share purchases in units. For example, your usual position size could be considered as one unit. Future purchases should be a fraction of this unit (for example, 50 per cent or 25 per cent of one unit). Every time the share trends significantly in the expected direction as defined by your trading rules, you could add more money to your position, using a decreasing increment of your original unit purchase.

To pyramid correctly, it is essential to buy your largest position first. Every subsequent purchase should be smaller in size than this first position. Hit the share with your biggest position size when your risk/reward is at the best level. As the trend unfolds, buy smaller parcels. That's why this method is called pyramiding.

Experienced traders could try pyramiding positions as a decreasing percentage of risk in comparison with total equity. For example, for your first entry, you could position size based on a 2 per cent risk level. When subsequent entries are added, you could position size based on 1 per cent risk and then 0.5 per cent risk. This would have the effect of ensuring that your largest position was at the first entry.

To trade effectively, you often have to go against your gut feelings. It would probably feel more comfortable to buy only a small amount of a particular share and then, as it performs, buy larger amounts.

Can you see the problem with this inverted pyramid concept? If you have bought larger amounts of shares with each subsequent purchase and the share price drops quickly, you will lose more money than you would by following the pyramid model. An inverted pyramid system would ensure that your biggest position, rather than your smallest position, would suffer the greatest loss.

Staged entry

Beginners in the market, or perhaps traders recovering from a series of losses who need to regain confidence, could use a staged entry method. Once you have decided on the share that you would like to buy, you could buy 50 per cent of your usual position size. As the share trends in the expected direction, confirming your analysis, you could make subsequent purchases. Make sure that each subsequent purchase is of a smaller size than the initial entry. For example, you could buy an extra 30 per cent of your usual purchase as the next tranche, then a final 20 per cent, to push your position size up to the full amount that you are used to buying.

To trade effectively, you often have to go against your gut feelings.

The staged entry method has a similar result to toning down your risk level from 2 per cent to 1 per cent when you are using a percentage-based position-sizing model.

Resetting stops

Every time you add money to any position, you should reset your stop loss level. You need to protect your existing position, as well as the new vulnerable money that you have just added to the market, by adjusting your stop in the direction of the trend.

Average up, never average down

As a share trends in the direction that you were expecting, you should get used to adding to your position. (For some ideas about timing the addition of new capital, review page 167 for pattern-based methods and page 170 for volatility-based methods.) If the share trends against your initial expectations and you buy more (that is, average down), you are committing one of the cardinal sins of trading. You are throwing good money after bad, and not trading in the direction of the trend.

> If the share trends against your initial expectations and you buy more (that is, average down), you are committing one of the cardinal sins of trading.

By deciding to ignore your stop, and buying more of a downtrending share, your average purchase price may be lower, but the amount of capital that you have in the trade would have increased. Following this strategy, you may be ultimately holding a large parcel of downtrending shares that are draining your trading equity. Often, people follow this course of action in the doomed attempt to turn a losing trade into a winning one.

An example

Let's say that you decided to buy 500 shares at $15.00. Imagine that the share price drops, so in your infinite wisdom you decide to buy another 500 shares at $12.00 and an extra 500 shares at $10.00. After all of this, your average price would be $12.33. Now you own 1500 shares in a stock that is downtrending (congratulations, you must feel very proud).

Instead of buying more of this downtrending share, it would have made more sense to exit at an initial stop loss of, say, $14.00, and capped your loss at $500 ($15.00 − $14.00 × 500 shares). To contain your loss to only $500 after you have averaged down, the share has to trend from $10.00 up to $12.00. How likely is a share price increase of $2.00, or 20 per cent, when the share is already in a confirmed downtrend? It is a very unlikely event in the near future. This is why averaging down doesn't work. The more times you average down, the greater the commensurate increase by the share price required in order for your total position to break-even. Find a share to buy that is trending up or suffer the consequences.

Now that you know this, don't let me ever catch you averaging down — or else!

You may get away with averaging down once or twice, and make a profit. Eventually though, probability will catch up with you, and the depletion of your trading account won't be too far away. For a high probability trade, you must always trade in the direction of the trend.

Setting profit targets

Some traders in the sharemarket limit themselves unnecessarily by exiting their positions when they have hit some predetermined, superstitious level of profit. For example, you may be happy with a 30 per cent profit from a particular trade, and exit your position once this target has been reached. What a shame the share wasn't aware that it should have stopped at a 30 per cent increase, instead of going up an extra 250 per cent!

Have you heard about how they train fleas to perform in a flea circus? They keep the poor little guys in a shoebox for a couple of days. Every time they hit their head on the top of the box, it hurts, so they learn to jump to a height just under the lid. As a result, when the box is opened, the fleas never again try to jump any higher than the rim of the box. Callous, yet effective. They really need to form some sort of union, don't they?

You are capping your profits by setting profit targets. Your share may have had the ability to jump higher, dragging your capital with it, but you have put a false cap on your potential (just like the performing fleas). To survive all of the nasty small losses in the market, you need to make the occasional windfall profit. If you cap your profit potential, you may just end up a net loser. Ride the trend until it reverses, or until your money management rules suggest you should exit from your position.

Martingale versus anti-martingale systems

For a few years I traded from a small office. I found the monotony and boredom of staying home to trade at that time a bit of a drudge, so being surrounded with some other human beings suited my purpose. The office building where I traded was shared with a group of horse-mad professional gamblers. Some of these guys bet on horseracing using a system that resembles a robust trading system. They're the most successful type of gamblers. The ones that use gut feel are always net losers at the track. There's even a name for them — omen gamblers. A very sombre professional gambler told me, 'There is no such thing as a successful omen gambler.'

If you cap your profit potential, you may just end up a net loser.

Interestingly, the most effective gamblers follow the same laws that govern the sharemarket. When they are on a winning streak, they allocate more capital to subsequent bets. However, when they hit a cluster of losses, they lower their bet size accordingly — that is, they use an anti-martingale system. Martingale systems are where you increase your bet size if you've suffered a string of losses, or a drawdown, hoping that your luck will change. They do not work.

Ed Seykota's achievements rank him as one of the best traders of all time. In times of trading pressure, I find it useful to remember some of Seykota's wise thoughts. When asked for some of the main contributors toward his success, he stated:

> **I handle losing streaks by trimming down my activity. Trying to trade during a losing streak is emotionally devastating. Trying to play 'catch up' is lethal.**

You can apply the same anti-martingale logic to your share trading. As your trading account increases with your successful trades, start increasing your position size. According to Dr Van K. Tharp, author of *Trade Your Way to Financial Freedom*, this is the best way to multiply your trading results quickly.

A simple way to implement this knowledge is to recalculate your level of equity on a regular basis. Add your paper profits into your calculation. Short-term traders could conduct this exercise on a monthly basis. For medium-term traders, recalculate your equity every three months or so. Feed your overall equity, including your unrealised paper profits, into your position-sizing calculation if you are using a percentage-based method. This will ensure that your position sizing will grow as you make money in the market. Clever, isn't it?

Review

1   Define an anti-martingale system. Why is it considered to be the best method of trading?

    ....

    ....

    ....

    ....

    ....

....

....

....

....

....

....

....

....

2   Do you intend to pyramid your positions? What trigger do you intend to use, and why?

....

....

....

....

....

....

....

....

....

....

3   Do you intend to implement a staged entry method, or to enter your trade
    completely from day one? Why have you chosen this method?

    ....

    ....

    ....

    ....

    ....

    ....

    ....

    ....

    ....

4   Explain why it is important to never average down.

    ....

    ....

    ....

    ....

    ....

    ....

    ....

    ....

    ....

Answers

1   An anti-martingale system provides the most bang for your buck. By increasing your position sizing while you are winning, your profits will be multiplied accordingly.

2 and 3 Answers to questions 2 and 3 are strictly personal matters for you to decide. It is essential that you come to a conclusion about the triggers you intend to use to pyramid, as well as your view toward staged entry methods. These decisions will need to be made prior to engaging with the market.

4   Losers average down—their egos stand in the way of their profitability. Always trade in the direction of the trend, which means never buying more of a share that is going against your initial view.

As you gain more experience with trading, you will occasionally find that you are faced with an incredibly juicy profit from a particular trade. The best traders have considered in advance how to handle this situation. The next chapter will show you some of the main things you need to contemplate in relation to handling a windfall profit.

17
It's TattsLotto time

Sharemarket novice: I just made a zillion per cent on the new float 'Dot Gone Pty Ltd' and I'm so excited!

Me: Oh.

Sharemarket novice: I'm going to become a full-time trader!

Me: Oh.

Sharemarket novice: I'm going to resign from my job on Monday morning.

Me: Do you realise that fewer than 10 per cent of traders make enough money to support themselves?

Sharemarket novice: Oh.

In this chapter, you will learn that:

- It is essential to plan in advance how you will define and handle a windfall profit situation.

- You must make sure you reward yourself by taking part of your winning position and doing something nice to spoil yourself. Ensure your reward is proportionate to the size of your profit.

- Guarding yourself against the dreaded ego bug is very important. One sting from this nasty creature can ruin a very promising trading career with lethal speed.

WHENEVER I HEAR ABOUT A NEW TRADER being very profitable within their first few months of trading, my heart skips a beat. Instant success breeds complacency. Often, a very profitable entry into the sharemarket makes it seem as if money can be easily made, with little or no skill. Mark Cook, a well-known US-based trader, says in his interview in *The Long-Term Daytrader*, 'I always tell people, I hope you lose money on your first trade, because anyone can handle winners; few can handle losers.' Despite Mark's thoughts on winning trades, handling an unexpected windfall profit that exceeds your initial expectations can be quite tricky. Plan in advance how you will manage this. If you have not yet been in that position, it is only a matter of time before you will be (if, of course, you are sticking to a written trading plan and devoting your attention to improving your trading methods). When an unexpected windfall profit happens, it is important to know now to react.

Firstly, if you have just made a windfall profit, what makes you certain that you were the cause, and it was not just the hand of Lady Luck? Without a written trading plan, I can guarantee you that your win was a total chance occurrence. Unless you have defined rules you will lose in the markets over the long term.

Mania

From time to time in the markets, you will hook onto the right side of a trade that goes absolutely ballistic. Sometimes, if the uptrend has caught the attention of the relevant authorities, the share will be issued with a speeding ticket, and be placed on suspension. This means that you will not be able to buy or sell the instrument, pending some significant announcement. This is by far one of the most horrid things that can happen to a trader. With bated breath you wait eagerly for the announcement. If you're lucky, it will only take a day or two. Sometimes, shares on suspension end up being out of action for months!

Unless you have defined rules you will lose in the markets over the long term.

There is no rule of thumb to assist in determining whether the announcement will be positive or negative. Often, however, when the share trades again after its period of suspension, the result will be dramatic and the share price will react with incredible bullishness or bearishness. You need to consider in advance how to handle this event.

On returning from suspension, the share may trade well above the last close. For example, a surge of 15 per cent may occur. In this situation, it may be prudent to exit your position, and re-enter if you receive a signal that the share is likely to continue in a bullish direction.

Selling into mania allows you to protect your profits, and let the emotion wash out of the existing shareholders. Once comparative calm has been re-established, you will be in a better position to react with cool detachment.

Sometimes the share price falls rapidly when it trades after the suspension. Always exit your position if your stop has been breached. You can always re-enter at a later date if the uptrend that was in place prior to the suspension continues. Alternatively, you could decide in advance to exit part of your position, and let the other part run. The choice is up to you, but if you ignore your stop loss at any stage of your trading career, it is a sign of poor discipline. Plan how you will respond beforehand and stick to your plan.

Reward yourself

Reminiscences of a Stock Operator has been a very influential book for me. First published in 1923, it is a biography of terrific trader, Jesse Livermore, who built his fortune and lost it several times. Jesse stated:

> **There isn't a man in Wall Street who has not lost money trying to make the market pay for an automobile or a motor boat. I think the resolve to induce the stock market to act as a fairy godmother is the busiest and most persistent.**

When trading in this deprived/depraved state of mind, we hope, we gamble and we run much greater risks than if we were speculating dispassionately. This certainly echoes my own experiences.

However, if you follow your trading rules and experience a windfall profit but do not reward yourself, you are setting yourself up for failure in the future. Our unconscious is responsible for many aspects of our success, so if you do not reward your own good behaviour, you could very well sabotage your future trading. As with a child, you need to be rewarded when you do things well, or you will be less likely to repeat that good behaviour.

Take a small percentage of your winnings and buy something for yourself and your family. Whenever you look at that asset, or remember that holiday, then you will create a feedback loop where your subconscious will seek further rewards. This is one of the reasons why winners in the markets go on to create even bigger wins in the future, and losers continue to lose money.

Interestingly, some people have no trouble with the idea of rewarding themselves for a job well done. They will take their $600 profit, add a little more to it, and then buy themselves a Ferrari! This is not appropriate at all. The idea is to buy something commensurate with the size of the win, preferably something tangible, or an experience that you can remind yourself about when the going gets tough. The more you reinforce your winning behaviour, the more likely your unconscious will seek out ways to duplicate your efforts.

Beware of overconfidence

Feel free to beat your hairy chests, men — your testosterone levels helped get us out of caves and into centrally heated houses. Unfortunately, primal urges now have to be disguised as more sophisticated behaviour — such as bragging to your golfing partners. It can be difficult to remember to be humble when everything that you've recently touched has turned to gold.

Some people feel the need to gloat after a big win. This is definitely a sign of the evil ego bug! If you feel the need for external validation, tell your dog or your teddy bear. Resist the urge to brag. It won't assist your trading in the long run. Give yourself a pat on the back, but don't expect others to share your enthusiasm — jealousy is a terrible thing.

When I started trading, after almost every major sharemarket win that I made, I experienced a losing streak. I am not ashamed to say that the main reason this happened was due to an inflated ego. Jesse Livermore said:

> A great many smashes by brilliant men can be traced directly to the swelled head — an expensive disease everywhere to everybody, but particularly in Wall Street to a speculator.

Eventually, I became determined not to judge my next trade on the basis of the last trade that I made.

The past's grip is firm and its reach is long. Do whatever you can to focus on the present, rather than dwelling on the past. Smash your rear-view mirrors.

When our self-worth is attached to whether we are making or losing money, it is a symptom of a very shallow inner life. The best traders stay loyal to their trading plan, take entry and exit signals without question, and have a money management system that minimises the risk of taking any particular individual trade. There is no room for the luxury of ego.

The sharemarket has nothing in common with a TattsLotto ticket. With trading, you can attribute a windfall profit to a back-tested system, and therefore ultimately duplicate your results in the future.

Trading insights

Many years ago I read a terrific little book called *The Forgotten Secret to Phenomenal Success*. The premise of this book is that the real secret in life is to do what you set out to do. Simple? Have you seen how many things get started but never finished by your friends, neighbours, and work mates … even you? So few people finish what they begin. Sure, they start with remarkable enthusiasm, but then they fizzle.

If you're still waiting for the profits to come pouring in, it may all be just around the corner. My advice? Devote yourself to your education, be determined to make your mark in the trading world, and stick at it. Remember the importance of persistence. Refuse to give up, smash your rear-view mirrors and forgive yourself for your past mistakes. The wealthiest, happiest and most effective traders on the planet rely on a support mechanism. Don't try to do this on your own.

The next chapter will discuss some objective ways to measure your performance in the sharemarket.

18

Warning! Measure or go broke

In this chapter, you will learn that:

- Measuring your performance is an essential component of effective trading. The best traders track their key performance indicators each month. The rest go broke.

- One of the most important measurements to conduct on a monthly basis is charting your equity curve. This is one of the purest ways to show whether you are making a profit or a loss over time.

- Other more advanced measurements involve calculating your expectancy. You will need at least three to six months of trading results to complete this calculation with any reliability.

Now, I know that you probably expect me to tell you in this chapter that if you're not making 60 per cent per annum, then you're useless and that all decent traders worth their salt make 90 per cent plus per year. I won't tell you this because it is not true. Many full-time traders don't make anywhere near this return on investment. Unfortunately, this very misconception is reinforced in the media by advertisers of online brokerage companies.

Many traders have unrealistic expectations about their potential performance. Most fund managers get to keep their jobs if they make over 12 per cent each year — and they are the professionals in the business. According to Mercer Investment Consulting, the average Australian managed share fund returned 16.1 per cent in the year to the end of

December 2004. Keep in mind, however, that these were the best returns achieved in 10 years, so the fund managers were probably very happy with themselves. In fact, if we fast forward a little, in the 10 years prior to 2011, an APRA survey of the top 200 super funds found that the average return was 3.9 per cent per annum.

Numerous funds make losses, yet the people managing the fund are still gainfully employed. Sometimes the sharemarket does not cooperate with the amount of money you feel it should provide you with. More often than not, beginners imagine a life of luxury, where positive returns are generated every month, based on a trading base of less than $100 000 in equity. This does not reflect reality. Even professional traders have losing months and, sometimes, losing years!

Traders often underestimate the importance of compound returns of even 10 per cent each year on a regular basis. If you are making approximately 14 per cent or greater per year, then you are matching the longer term rate of return of the All Ordinaries index prior to the GFC, so you are doing very well indeed. Anything greater than this amount on a consistent basis and you are beating the professionals at their own game.

... in the 10 years prior to 2011, an APRA survey of the top 200 super funds found that the average return was 3.9 per cent per annum.

Rather than discussing percentage returns, there is a better way of evaluating your performance. Would you like to discover a method where you can diagnose and detect flaws within your own trading system with precision? Just as a doctor diagnoses a patient after giving him or her a thorough examination, you also need to consider how to examine your own performance in order to prescribe the appropriate medicine. The market is the best source of education, so by tracking your own results, you have the power to alter the way you trade. By the end of this chapter you will be able to work out the exact areas that require your focus in order to improve your overall results.

Beginners in the market won't yet have a track record to measure performance. When you've been actively trading for three to six months, come back to this chapter so that you can fully understand the implications of these concepts. It's very difficult to steer a parked car, and until you've already started moving or trading, as the case may be, it is almost impossible to make improvements to your methods. Traders with more than three months of experience should look back over their trading results and record important information regarding their performance. You may choose to perform these measurement calculations once a month, to track your ongoing performance. Anything more frequent than this time interval probably won't reveal any further meaningful information, and will just create unnecessary work. The best traders review their performance regularly because, without measurement, there can be no improvement.

Almost every job has some form of system for tracking key performance indicators. These indicators provide information for the company's managers about productivity and goal achievement. Specific areas for improvement can then be targeted to lift overall performance. If you apply the same discipline to your trading as you would at your job, you'll be more likely to achieve consistent results. Measure the key indicators of your trading success and you will start to drive improvements into your trading methods.

Win to loss probabilities

Record how many times you made money on a trade, compared with how many losses you made, in absolute numbers. This will enable you to calculate a probability percentage of your wins to losses.

Let's say you have traded 20 times, and eight of these were wins and 12 were losses. What would be your win to loss ratio? It would be 2:3, where, for every two wins that you made, you made three losses (or 1 win to 1.5 losses). Your probability of making a winning trade would be 0.40 (or 40 per cent) and your probability of making a loss would be 0.60 (or 60 per cent).

Dollars made compared with dollars lost

Once you have calculated your probability of making a win, you must then calculate how much you win on average, in comparison with how much you lose. Imagine that you make two wins for every one loss. This may make you feel warm and secure, until you calculate how much profit you make on average per win, compared with your losses per losing trade. For example, if you lose $1500 on average when you make a loss, and you only make $300 on average when you make a profit, your system is in serious need of improvement. Alternatively, if you make $1500 on average, but you lose $300 on average — your system is probably robust.

If you are losing more dollars than you are making, you need to address your position-sizing rules. Your stop loss methods also require review.

Let's say that your stops, position-sizing rules, and entry/exit procedures are exemplary, yet you still lose more on the average trade than you make. This means that you are lacking discipline when you trade. Even though your system is telling you to behave in a particular manner, you are obstinately ignoring it. That's fine if you're trading for fun, but if your aim is to do well from this endeavour in the long run, you're kidding yourself.

Frequency of trades

Record the average amount of time that you hold each share for your winning trades and also for your losing trades. This will confirm whether you are genuinely maintaining a short-term, a medium-term or a long-term perspective. You may consider yourself to be a longer term player, yet discover that your average hold time when you combine your winning and losing trades is three weeks. Provide a touch of reality to your trading by measuring your actual results.

If you can safely figure out how to get each little dollar of capital panting with exhaustion by the end of the year, then this will have dramatic effect on your overall returns, assuming that your system has a positive expectancy (the concept of expectancy is discussed next). Hopefully you can see now why just looking at the percentage return that a trading system can produce is fruitless. You need to know the ratio of wins to losses, the average win compared with the average loss per dollar invested, and the frequency of trades, in order to gain a full picture.

...get each little dollar of capital panting with exhaustion by the end of the year...

By looking at the impact of the frequency of trades on your expectancy, you will see the importance of taking every signal that your trading system produces, provided you have capital available.

Expectancy

Expectancy shows you how many cents you make or lose every time you invest one dollar in the market. The number that you calculate must be a positive figure, otherwise it's costing you money every time you trade.

The expectancy for your system usually alters over time. That's why you need to keep recalculating this on a regular basis: to ensure that you are fully aware about how you are performing in the market. For most active traders, a recalculation every three months, based on the last six months of activity, is suggested.

To calculate expectancy, you'll need to calculate your probability of winning trades, your probability of losing trades, your average win per dollar invested and the average loss per dollar invested.

Here's the formula:

$$\textbf{Expectancy} = \textbf{(probability of winning} \times \textbf{average win)} - \textbf{(probability of losing} \times \textbf{average loss)}$$

An example of positive expectancy

The first pieces of information required to calculate expectancy are the average gain per dollar invested on your winning trades and the average loss per dollar invested on your losing trades. Table 18.1 shows an example.

Table 18.1: average win/loss per dollar invested

Position size	Wins		Losses	
	Gain	Gain per $1*	Loss	Loss per $1*
$7000	$4550	$0.65	–	–
$7500	–	–	$1575	$0.21
$9000	–	–	$1170	$0.13
$8500	$8925	$1.05	–	–
$8000	–	–	$4480	$0.56
	Average gain/$1 = $0.85		Average loss/$1 = $0.30	

*The gain per $1 is the gain divided by the position size; the loss per $1 is the loss divided by the position size.

Table 18.1 shows that the probability of winning is 0.40 (or 40 per cent) and the probability of losing is 0.60 (or 60 per cent). Your expectancy using this trading system would be as follows:

$$(0.40 \times 0.85) - (0.60 \times 0.30) = 0.34 - 0.18 = 0.16$$

For every dollar that you invested in the market, you would expect to make 16¢. That is, for every initial dollar that you had invested, you would expect to have $1.16 in your trading account, after closing out your positions. There is no time component in the formula for expectancy. Based on your results, the frequency of your trades within set time frames can be utilised to calculate your overall return on investment per annum. Let's run some numbers and look at the impact of this.

The more frequently you can turn over every dollar in your portfolio, the more you can multiply your results. Of course, you must be acting on the basis of valid entry and exit signals with a system that produces positive expectancy for this method to positively impact your bank account.

As an extreme example, let's say that you manage to turn over your $100 000 five times in a year. Every dollar that you have in your portfolio has the power of a five-dollar note, if you look at it throughout the course of a year. You have effectively managed to make your $100 000 do the work of $500 000. This shows the inherent advantage of maintaining a medium-term perspective, rather than a longer term perspective.

The more frequently your trading system produces effective buy and sell signals, the more often you can turn over your available equity. Your average hold-time will enable you to factor in how often you turn over your available equity within the course of one year, so you can calculate these figures on your own performance in the markets.

The frequency with which your system produces tradeable opportunities becomes of paramount importance, if your system is producing figures with this level of reliability.

Also implied is the importance of being fully invested at all times. From your records, if you are, on average, 75 per cent invested in the markets, you will need to factor this into your calculation.

Negative expectancy

Imagine that, for every dollar you placed into the market, you lost 30¢ (that is, you had a negative expectancy) — my goodness! You'd stop trading immediately to revise your system, wouldn't you? Unfortunately, this is exactly what some traders discover, after they've calculated their expectancy. Systems with a negative expectancy mean that you are losing money every time you trade. The speed with which you deplete your equity will be in proportion to the number of times that you turn over your trading capital.

Equity curve

Whenever your capital has reduced from its initial size, or has reduced from a previous equity peak, you are said to be in drawdown. Being in drawdown is a situation all traders will experience from time to time and will have to learn to handle psychologically.

To track your overall profit or drawdown, it is a great idea to plot an equity curve each month. Add up all of your money at the bank as well as the closing value of all of your open positions. This will give you a figure. Record this figure on a monthly basis and plot it on a graph. You will be able to clearly recognise whether you are increasing or decreasing your overall equity. It is one of the most potent measurements a trader can perform.

There is a slight variation for conservative traders calculating their equity curve. Rather than basing the overall equity on the value of the open positions, if you are using a stop loss system that provides a defined exit price, use these values instead. The amount of your open positions if they hit your stop, in addition to your cash at the bank, will provide a more accurate reflection of your equity if you are stopped out of all of your positions at once. Some people are more comfortable with this concept, as opposed to accepting the closing values as the basis for this calculation.

Record-keeping

Without accurate records, you'll never manage to work out all of these figures. The easiest way is to keep a trading diary. Chapter 23 provides suggestions regarding how to set up a trading diary.

This chapter is by no means meant to be definitive in its suggestions on how you should measure your performance. I suggest that you continue your education in this arena by reading *Trade Your Way to Financial Freedom* by Dr Van K. Tharp.

This part of the book has been mainly concerned with money management principles, which are essential to master in order to be profitable. In addition to learning about these principles, if you're aiming to trade over the long haul, you'll need to work out how to make money regardless of differing market conditions. The next part of this book will show you how to do this and introduce you to some excellent instruments (such as CFDs, options and foreign exchange trading), to help leverage your returns.

Review

1   The majority of robust systems produce wins only 50 per cent of the time. A key component of your success will be the size of your wins compared with the size of your losses. If you can win twice as much as you lose, this would be fantastic.

Take the following system, and calculate the expectancy:

Probability of a win: 0.50

Probability of a loss: 0.50

Average win per dollar invested: 80¢

Average loss per dollar invested: 30¢

....

....

....

2   Once you have completed this, put the answer to your calculation in a sentence.

....

....

....

3   Why is frequency of trading such an important factor to consider?

....

....

....

4   Explain why it is an advantage to have a system that provides enough signals so that you can be fully invested in the markets.

....

....

....

Answers

1 Expectancy = (probability of winning × average win per dollar invested) − (probability of losing × average loss per dollar invested)

$$(0.50 \times 0.80) - (0.50 \times 0.30) = 0.40 - 0.15 = 0.25$$

2 The key is to ensure that you are making more than you lose on a consistent basis, with a system that produces a reasonable percentage of winners. With a system that produces an expectancy of 0.25, for every dollar that you have invested in the market, you will make 25¢. Another way of describing this is to say that you will have $1.25 in your trading account for every dollar you had invested.

3 The harder you can get your money to work for you, the better. By making each dollar of your equity turn over two or three times in a year, you have effectively doubled or tripled your results.

4 If your system is 100 per cent accurate (keep on dreaming...) and only produces one signal per year, you will not be able to turn over your equity frequently. It may take you 10 years to turn over your $100 000 once. You would derive a return on your investment of the same magnitude in 10 years as another system could produce in six months, for example (assuming that this latter system turned over your equity twice a year). By investing a greater proportion of your equity in the market and using a system with a positive expectancy, each dollar that you own will multiply more rapidly. If you are only 50 per cent invested on average, then your system will take you twice as long to derive the same returns as a system where you are 100 per cent invested. Having said this, it is important that you don't try to create trades out of thin air. If your system is not producing enough signals, then you need to consider using it in conjunction with another reliable system, or altering some of its parameters.

The next part of this book will help you profit in a downtrend. Keep reading to expand on your skills and ensure your longevity as a trader.

Part V
Recession-smashing strategies

19

Make the bear your friend

In this chapter, you will learn that:

- When the market becomes volatile, it is essential that you act on your stops, follow your trading plan, don't guess at the next market leaders, and learn how to use strategies appropriate to the market conditions.

- Short selling allows you to profit from a downtrend. You can short sell using the services of a broker, or by using CFDs. CFDs are covered in chapter 21. Most traders use CFDs rather than short selling directly.

- You need to carefully define your set-ups and triggers into a short position before engaging the market. Also, ensure you understand the implications of dividends prior to short selling, as they can give novice traders a nasty kick if not treated with respect.

THERE IS NO SUCH THING as a born trader. Every principle of trading is learned. Most people know how to make money in a bull market, but few know how to profit from a bear market. Professionals make money regardless of the market direction. This chapter and the next will provide you with strategies to make money whether the market is trending up, down or sideways. This is your key to longevity as a trader. Let's have a look at some of the methods that you can use if you've identified that the market is trending downward.

Act on your stops

If you recognise that a bear market is in place, the first step is to review your existing portfolio. Take a close look at where you have set your stop losses, and make sure that these levels are consistent with your trading plan. If your stop is hit, exit immediately. Do not hope that your shares will recover. Traders tend to hold on to shares that are trending down, yet prematurely sell shares that are trending up. This trait will ensure that you stay among the mediocre masses and never fight your way to the top of the class.

Unfortunately, most traders skipped over this step and this created the devastation of many super funds during the GFC. There's a tendency to be optimistic and believe everything will be OK in the long run. However, there really is no space for this type of view when it comes to trading.

Learn how to handle volatility

Often a bear market will produce an increase in volatility. Trading ranges may swing wildly in both directions. Contrary to popular opinion, in volatile market conditions, I suggest that you do not set tighter stops. The key is to manage risk by position sizing correctly. Buy fewer shares and allow the share room to move if conditions have become lumpy. An effective strategy would be to alter your acceptable percentage risk factor from 2 per cent to 1 per cent. A good alternative could be to set your stop at 3 ATR rather than 2 ATR away from the current price, or use a weekly chart's ATR figure instead of the ATR calculated using a daily chart. If you prefer pattern recognition to set a stop loss, try setting your stop two support/resistance levels away, instead of one support/resistance level away from your purchase price.

Don't guess at the next market leaders

During a bear market, it's important to realise that if you want to buy shares, you are trading against the trend. In this situation, it makes sense to apply a more stringent set of entry rules, rather than expecting every breakout to lead to blue sky. Also be aware that the leaders in the previous bull market probably won't lead again. The leaders of the technology market during the bullish rally experienced by this sector up to April 2000 weren't the ones to lead the next bull run. A bear market is not the time to guess when shares have bottomed. Find a share in a confirmed uptrend before you decide to buy it. Plus, it would be my advice that you implement a macro filter to tell you when to trade long. Buying shares while the overall market is trending down is a very painful experience. Sure some shares will be trending up during a bear market, but why not stack the odds in your favour and only short sell? That way you're trading in line with the overall market conditions.

Traders tend to hold on to shares that are trending down, yet prematurely sell shares that are trending up.

Short selling

A very effective technique that few Australian traders utilise is short selling. Because a large number of traders are unfamiliar with the concept, less than 1 per cent of transactions in Australia are executed utilising this method. Step aside from the crowd and develop an understanding of this interesting strategy.

Short selling is similar to buying a share, only the buying/selling order is reversed. Instead of buying a stock and then selling it, you sell the stock first and then buy it back at a later time. In effect, you borrow shares that you do not own (your full-service broker will organise this for you), sell them with the expectation that the share price will drop, then buy them back at a later date. Your profit or loss is the difference between your sell price and your buy price—so if the share price drops, you make a profit. If the price increases, you will incur a loss (so make sure you have a stop loss in place). It is actually quite a simple concept.

A significant benefit with short selling is that, unlike the options and warrants markets, there is no time decay issue (bought options and warrants decrease in value as they approach their expiration date). If you would like to read more about some terrific short-selling tactics, you can order my *Special Report—Successful Short Selling*, which is available via <www.tradingsecrets.com.au>.

The US market versus the Australian market

Many of the texts available on short selling originate from the US market. There are a few differences between the Australian market and the US market. The good news is that, in many ways, these differences serve to improve rather than detract from the efficiency of Australian-based traders. Although you cannot short sell online in Australia at this stage without using CFDs, you at least don't have to wait for an uptick in price to short a stock. The uptick rule means that, in the US, you have to place an order one tick above the last sale. US traders are more likely to have the trade trend against their initial view, prior to it cooperating and ultimately dropping in price. It is likely that in the near future, an online shorting facility will be introduced in Australia, but, for now, you must use a full-service broker to short the market.

Contrary to the views of some journalists, you cannot drive the share price downward by short selling. You are not legally allowed to short sell at a price below the previously recorded last sale price. This is one of the main execution differences between short selling and the usual method of merely buying a share. It is also one of the likely reasons why there has been a delay in establishing short selling as an online facility. Complications such as this tend to delay programming. From my understanding, there is no real legal reason as to why an online facility could not be introduced.

Broker considerations

Some old-fashioned brokers may lead you to believe that you are required to pay a daily fee to cover their costs, but this practice is largely being phased out of the industry. Other brokers purport to allow short-sold positions to be active for only a limited time period (for example, three days), before they will close your position. This is not an ideal situation, and I would question this rule with your broker. It is becoming a more common practice for brokers to enforce deadlines of three or six months. Unless you can be convinced otherwise, it is likely that time limits are negotiable. Alternatively, you could close out your initial position and then re-open it. Unfortunately, you will incur additional brokerage fees, but if your system suggests that you re-enter your position, you should follow it.

When you place your order with your broker, make sure that you stipulate that you want to short sell. By just asking your broker to sell, it could appear that you are requesting the sale of an existing share position.

Not all Australian shares can be short sold. A complete list can be obtained from your broker. There are approximately 200 shares that can be short sold on the Australian market, so the field is wide open for you to make money from a downtrending share. This list varies only to a minor degree on a month-to-month basis. You cannot short sell any shares involved in a takeover bid and, if you're in a current position with a share involved in a takeover, you'll probably be instructed to close out.

Smaller brokerage firms, especially, may have difficulty borrowing the scrip required for you to open a short position, and they're more likely to enforce a maximum time limit for the position to be active. Dealing with one of the larger brokers for this type of transaction will help you to avoid a multitude of problems that smaller brokers are likely to experience. A large brokerage firm should be able to borrow any scrip on its short-sell list to enable you to perform your transaction, and there are fewer limitations on the minimum position sizing and time limits. Some firms require a minimum position of $10 000 for you to execute a short-sold position, although this varies according to company policy and your relationship with your broker. You may in fact have to shop around to find a broker who will short sell for you. Many full-service brokers will offer you this service, but smaller firms often do not.

In the majority of cases, a leverage of 5:1 applies, as brokerage firms usually require you to lodge 20 per cent of the value of the initial share price in a cash-management account. When you're starting, however, it's astute to consider that you have short sold the entire value of the share, so that you will not be margin called. Being margin called means that you will be required to place more money into this account if the share price trends upward (against your initial view) to maintain the original leverage ratio. Convince yourself that you don't have this advantage of leverage and that you are responsible for the entire value of your position (that is, the total number of shares that you have sold,

A large brokerage firm should be able to borrow any scrip on its short-sell list to enable you to perform your transaction…

multiplied by their share price). By doing this, it's unlikely that you will run into difficulties with margin calls. It's important to know how to trade successfully before you apply any form of leverage, as leverage will multiply your results, whether they are positive or negative.

Remember that a short-selling strategy must be used with shares that have sufficient liquidity, or you will have trouble extricating yourself from the position if the market suddenly turns bullish. You'll need to arrive at your own rule for liquidity, but as a guide, you should not open a position in a stock where you are short selling more than one-fifth of the average daily volume over the last three months. There is nothing worse than being trapped in a trade due to a lack of volume.

CFDs

CFDs are contracts for difference. They have caused a trading revolution. Traders have flocked to this relatively new tool to gain access to leverage, and develop the ability to go long and short on a variety of instruments. The main tool utilised is the ASX Top 200. Other possibilities include CFDs on sharemarket indices, foreign exchange and metals.

CFDs allow you to deal on share prices without having to physically settle on the trade. With CFDs, you are trading a contract that represents the share. This has many advantages. One of the main tangible benefits is that there is often minimal brokerage charged for these types of transactions. Other fees may be charged (such as a holding fee for keeping the trade open for longer than one day), however, this cost is usually quite low in comparison to the full-service fees charged by some brokers. The benefit of not paying full brokerage is, of course, immediately apparent. One of the side benefits is that you can test out your theories in real-time and real life, without being penalised for gaining this knowledge (apart from a genuine market move against you). This is one way to gain trading experience when using a new system or just regaining some confidence. It can also allow you to implement short-selling strategies with ease. For a suggestion regarding the most appropriate CFD provider for you, have a look at the 'Support' section at <www.tradingsecrets.com.au>. Chapter 21 covers CFDs in more detail.

Sometimes the best way to learn about short selling is to try it and see how you go (ideally with a small position size when you begin). This will teach you the lessons that the sharemarket is seeking to reveal to you with amazing clarity. As Marie de Vichy-Chamrond (1697–1780) said, 'The distance is nothing; it is only the first step that is difficult.'

Entry strategies

To some extent, to enter a short position in the market, all you need to do is to reverse the entry signals that you would usually use for a long position. This certainly simplifies your search routines. Here are some of the signals that you could look for:

- a share trading below its 30-week moving average that has just dropped through support on a bearish black candle

- a gap downward during an existing downtrend

- a top reversal pattern of a temporary uptrend during an existing, overall downtrend

- divergence in a momentum indicator to show a sign of weakness, prior to entering a short position on a black candlestick that has punctured an uptrend line

- a share that bearishly trades below a candlestick bottom reversal pattern, without responding to its potential to reverse the trend

- the sector to which the share belongs. A share that has been underperforming its sector, in a sector that has been underperforming the All Ordinaries index, is preferable. A discussion of how to find these shares is detailed in chapter 13.

There are many other patterns that assist in identifying a profitable entry into a short-sold position. The list is only limited by the extent of your familiarity with technical analysis.

Volume

There is an important difference between my assessment of a high probability uptrend and a high probability entry into a short-sold position. For an uptrend to commence, I place significant emphasis on the importance of heavy relative-volume levels. Contrary to this view, if other set-up signals are present but volume is not increasing during downticks in share price, I am still likely to short sell the share. It becomes a higher probability trade if increased volume levels are evident as the share drops in price, but it is not an essential prerequisite.

The emotion of fear is much more pervasive than the emotions of greed or hope. A ripple of fear will spread very quickly throughout a market. It really only takes one small stone to begin an avalanche. It only takes one seller at a price below the current market value to create a selling frenzy.

Exit strategies

Consider the term of your view regarding the strength of the downtrend prior to determining an effective exit strategy. Traders with a medium-term view can allocate a wider stop to their positions and be prepared to weather the discomfort of several periods of countertrend reversal. Shorter term traders may find that their short-sold positions are closed out within just a few days. Stops can be set utilising any of the same methods used to exit a long position, only in reverse. Examples of stops may include:

Traders with a medium-term view can allocate a wider stop to their positions and be prepared to weather the discomfort of several periods of countertrend reversal.

- a break upward past a resistance level

- a top reversal pattern of a temporary uptrend within an existing downtrend, that fails

- at 2 or 3 ATR above the point of entry

- a technical indicator that has provided a bullish signal.

Position sizing

Position sizing for a short sale can follow the same principles that you apply to your long positions. You will also need to decide whether you are comfortable pyramiding into your position if it continues trending downward. Some traders take full advantage of their leveraged situation to pyramid very aggressively into short-sold positions.

An example

Say that you have identified a share that is trending down, and you would like to short sell it. Let's have a look at an example regarding where to set your stop. Using pattern recognition or a volatility-based stop, you could position your stop above a line of resistance or at 2 ATR above the current price. In this example, both methods of setting a stop would eventuate in an exit point at approximately the same price (see figure 19.1).

Figure 19.1: ResMed daily chart showing two methods of setting a stop

Source: SuperCharts version 4 by Omega Research © 1997.

The implications of dividends

Understanding the implications of dividends while short selling is essential. Make sure you check the dividend status of the company that you're trying to short sell, prior to entering a position. Occasionally a brokerage firm will absorb the dividend payment, especially if it is insisting on a daily fee to hold the position open. Most firms will make you pay the dividend out of your account, as well as any franking credit benefit that may be derived, to cover the tax implication. This can be an unexpected shock for the newcomer to the shorting market. As a suggestion, when you are learning to short sell, don't short anything where the underlying share is due to pay a dividend, or you may end up being responsible for the amount of this dividend, plus any associated franking credits.

Have a think about how you could use the guidelines explored from page 227 regarding expected share price behaviour during ex-dividend situations. One strategy that you could consider is short selling a share that is in an existing downtrend after it has gone ex-dividend. This will help you avoid any of the consequences of being ultimately responsible for the dividend, while capitalising on the additional momentum that an ex-dividend gap may provide in favour of the existing downtrend.

For shares in an existing downtrend, a gap downward may act as a trigger to open a short position. A gap that drops through a previously well-established level of support is a particularly bearish signal. Pay close attention to the trend of the share prior to the presence of a gap, and trade in line with the direction of the trend. The lead-up to the gap, and whether it is confirmed by subsequent trading activity, must be taken into account if you are to trade effectively using this method.

The sharemarket will continue to redistribute wealth to the people who are committed to educating themselves. Much of your success will ultimately be determined by the strategies you implement, as well as your discipline and mindset. Knowing how to short the market means that you need never fear a bear market again.

Review

1   Define short selling.

....

....

....

....

....

....

....

2   Describe a signal that would be likely to trigger your entry into a short-sold position.

....

....

....

....

....

....

....

....

....

....

3   How do you plan to exit your short-sale position?

....

....

....

....

....

....

....

....

....

4   How does an ex-dividend situation affect the share price action? If there was a fully franked dividend of 26¢ declared on a share, what would be the likely share price drop when it went ex-dividend?

....

....

....

....

....

....

....

....

....

....

....

....

....

....

....

....

....

....

....

Answers

1   Short selling is similar to buying a share, only the buying/selling order is reversed. Instead of buying a stock and then selling it, you sell the stock first and then buy it back at a later time. Your profit or loss is the difference between your sell price and your buy price — so if the share price drops, you make a profit. If the price increases, you will incur a loss.

2   This is a personal decision, but any bearish chart pattern, preferably within an existing downtrend, could trigger your entry into a short sold position.

3   Exits can be made on the same basis as the signal required to exit a long position, only in reverse. For example, you could use a volatility stop loss, a pattern-recognition stop loss or a bullish technical indicator.

4   An ex-dividend situation will often create a bearish gap in a chart. If a fully franked dividend of 26¢ is declared, the share price is likely to drop approximately 39¢ that is, 26¢ plus (50% of 26¢) or (.50 × 26¢).

Trading insights

Studies have confirmed that people have two beliefs about how intelligence works. Some believe it is fixed and others believe it is more malleable and can alter over time. Students who believe that intelligence is fixed are less resilient.

If you truly don't believe you can learn from your mistakes, you're hardly going to welcome the experience of failure as it seems that it serves no purpose. However, when students are taught that the brain grows when they work hard and make errors, they show a spike in their grades and actually enjoy school more. Because they're less afraid of failure, they succeed more.

You can grow more and learn more than you ever thought possible. There is nothing you can't achieve if you believe in yourself and have the right guidance.

Short selling isn't the only way to make money when the market is downtrending. The next chapter will introduce you to option trading so that you will be equipped with profitable strategies to apply whether the market is trending upward, downward or sideways.

20

Options multiply your results

In this chapter, you will learn that:

- Options are a leveraged tool, designed to be used by traders with previous experience who are trading unleveraged instruments such as equities.

- There are four main strategies you can use when trading options. You can buy a call, write a call, buy a put, or write a put. Trades combining these four separate actions are called spreads.

- If you own shares and write call options over them, you are writing covered calls. Naked calls are written when you don't own the underlying stock.

- If you believe that the share is trending upward, an appropriate strategy would be to buy the stock, buy a call option or write a put option.

- If you believe that the share is trending downward, profitable strategies include short selling the stock, buying put options, or writing call options.

- Trading options is inherently more complex than trading shares. There are many variables that affect the price of an option that you'll need to come to terms with to trade effectively. These variables include liquidity, time decay, volatility and the different types of option strategies available.

MANY NAIVE NOVICES BEGIN trading options prematurely, often to their detriment. Trading a leveraged instrument will multiply your results. If you're not already trading proficiently, options will only speed your demise. However, if you are already a skilled trader, then options may be worth investigating.

Consistent sharemarket winners have a series of strategies for rising markets, but they also know how to benefit from a sideways-trending or downtrending share. There are a variety of instruments available that don't involve the purchase of shares. Learn about options and short selling so that you'll be better placed to make money in all market conditions. For traders interested in further exploring option strategies that will allow you to make a profit regardless of whether the share is in an uptrend, a downtrend or travelling in a sideways band, refer to my book entitled *The Secret of Writing Options*.

Let's define call and put options, and have a look at some of the ways that you can safely begin trading options.

Definition of a call option

In general, there are two types of call option traders. There are traders who write (sell) call options, and traders who buy call options.

Writing options involves collecting a small fixed premium, yet incurring a theoretically unlimited loss. Buying options has a lower probability of success than writing options, yet, due to the leveraged nature of this strategy, the rewards from the 20 per cent of trades that do work may outweigh the losses from the 80 per cent of losing trades. You'll need to make your own assessment regarding whether you should play the options game.

Consistent sharemarket winners have a series of strategies for rising markets, but they also know how to benefit from a sideways-trending or downtrending share.

Call option writers are under obligation to deliver (or sell) a given security at a certain price within a given time, if the call option buyer exercises his or her rights. Traders who write call options seek to locate a share trading in a sideways lateral band or in a downtrend. As with short selling, writing an option involves selling to initiate the transaction. This can sometimes cause confusion, as traders can be more used to buying to initiate transactions.

Buyers of call options have the right, but not the obligation, to buy a given security at a certain price within a given time. Traders who buy call options are hoping that the share price will trend upward strongly.

The following sections will provide you with examples of these strategies.

Writing call options

It's easy to feel daunted when talking about options, but I'll make this as clear as possible for you. Once you've nailed the definitions, you can really make these babies fly.

The covered call

There are two types of written call options—a covered call and a naked call. A covered call is where you own the underlying stock. It's a simple way that you can generate a solid cashflow if you currently own a parcel of shares in the Top 15 category of market capitalisation. Writing covered call options is, in my opinion, the safest way to learn about the options market. To make this strategy worthwhile, you'll probably need to own at least 300 shares of a single stock. In Australia one contract provides exposure to 100 shares, so if you own 300 shares you could write three covered call contracts.

If you are exercised (that is, you are told to sell your shares) and you have written a call with an option strike price greater than your share purchase price, you will realise a capital gain on the share. This is in addition to the premium (for example, 40¢ a share) that you received for writing the call. Only write call options over shares you are willing to sell, or you'll need to take defensive actions to remove yourself from risk before being exercised. By consistently writing calls over shares that you own, you could receive a cashflow similar to receiving a dividend cheque in the mail every month.

> *Writing covered call options is, in my opinion, the safest way to learn about the options market.*

The covered call strategy is suggested for shares that are trending gently upward, moving sideways or trending gently downward. A share with an erratic, volatile trend is not suited to this technique. You will receive more in premium for a share that fits this description, but your risk of being exercised increases.

Be aware that the premium you receive by writing calls will not outweigh the capital loss you will incur by holding on to a downtrending share. Set your stop losses and stick to them, even if you have open written call positions over that particular share.

A valid concern is that you may miss out on the additional capital gain that you could receive if the share trended upward suddenly. Written calls are rarely exercised prior to expiry (in contrast to written puts). It may be best to close out your call option position if the share becomes very bullish. Alternatively, a sound re-entry strategy to repurchase your uptrending shares may be required if you are exercised. For this strategy, always choose options that are liquid (that is, have large open interest that means there are many other buyers and sellers). If you don't deal with liquid options, it may be difficult to close out your position if the share trends against your initial view.

The naked call

You can write a naked call if you don't own shares in a suitable underlying instrument. Writing a call assumes that you have a sideways-trending or downtrending view on the future share price action prior to the expiry date of the option. As long as the share price stays below the strike price of the option, you will get to keep the full premium that the option taker or buyer paid you. If the share price goes above the option strike price, you are likely to be exercised and told to deliver shares for sale to the option taker. Because you don't own shares in the underlying instrument when you're using a naked call strategy, you will be required to buy them at market value, and deliver them to the option taker. This strategy is best reserved for very experienced traders who fully understand the risks involved. Professionals' fortunes are built on the inconsistencies and ignorance of novices.

Buying call options

Options depreciate in value, right up until a defined expiry date. This depreciation of value is called time decay and works against the buyer. Once you have sold another trader an option (that is, written an option), if all other things remain equal, the option will expire worthless. You'll have the money in your bank account and the buyer of the option will be holding a worthless asset. In fact, up to 80 per cent of people lose money when buying options.

Buying options is often similar to having a TattsLotto-ticket mentality. Novice buyers of options are particularly attracted to cheap options, which ironically have very little probability of appreciating in value. Although there is a very slim chance that you will win TattsLotto, many families still gamble on this small probability of winning a fortune. The slight probability that you will actually win is overcome by the small amount of money required for a TattsLotto ticket, which makes it seem irresistible and worth a punt. These reasons assist in explaining why the vast majority of option buyers end up net losers in the market. Buyers of low-priced options enter a trade with a low probability of success where the rewards are potentially high.

> *Professionals' fortunes are built on the inconsistencies and ignorance of novices.*

If the call option buyer's view is correct and the share increases in value, he or she can either sell the option at a profit or choose to exercise his or her rights. The call option buyer has the right to purchase the writer's shares at the strike price (which will be lower than the current market value).

Most players in the options market do not exercise their rights. They sell their options if their position has cooperated, to experience a capital gain. An overwhelming majority of options are only ever traded once and then left to expire worthless.

If you're looking to buy an option, there are a few simple rules to follow:

- Buy an option with a significant time until expiry. This will assist in minimising the negative effects of time decay.

- Always exit your bought position before the final stages of expiry. An option close to expiry will incur exponential time decay, sweeping away your capital at an alarming rate.

- Buy an option that is in-the-money, which by definition will not be the cheapest option available. Betting that BHP will go up by $10.00 within two weeks is not a high probability trade. Buy an option that gives the share a bit of room to move, just in case it doesn't cooperate immediately. If you don't fully understand the implications of in-the-money, at-the-money and out-of-the-money options, don't buy options.

- Do not buy options if you don't understand the impact of delta and volatility on option prices.

- Only buy options if short-term trading suits your trading style.

- Only trade options that have sufficient levels of liquidity.

Definition of a put option

There are two types of put option traders—traders who write put options and traders who buy put options.

As with call options, writing means selling to initiate the transaction. Put option writers are under obligation to buy a given security at a certain price within a given time, if the put option buyer exercises his or her rights. Traders who write put options are usually hoping for the share to be trading in a sideways lateral band, or they are bullish in their view.

The buyer of a put option has the right, but not the obligation, to sell a given security at a certain price within a given time. Traders who buy put options are generally hoping that the share price will trend downward very strongly. Alternatively, they are using the bought put option as a form of portfolio insurance — this is known as a hedging strategy.

Writing put options

Put option writers are of the opinion that a share will be trading in a sideways band, or they are bullish in their view. They are under obligation to buy the shares from a put option taker at the strike price should they be exercised. You could implement this strategy if you were happy to buy the share at a certain value below the current market price.

There are defensive actions available if the trade does not trend in the expected direction. However, as an option writer, your loss is technically unlimited. It is for this reason that monitoring is an essential component of trading options, particularly for written put strategies. Never write a put if you have concerns that the share will trend downward, or if you have reason to believe that the market is due for a correction. If you don't have a clear view regarding the direction of the share and the effects of volatility, you shouldn't write or buy options. Don't write more puts than you can cover if the market suddenly trends downward sharply. Keep in mind that it is prudent to have enough cash or shares at hand to cover your level of exposure.

Never write a put if you have concerns that the share will trend downward, or if you have reason to believe that the market is due for a correction.

Buying put options

As the share price drops, the prices of put options increase, often very dramatically. When volatility increases, the prices of both put and call options increase. Time decay will erode your profit if you buy a short-dated option. For this reason, it is preferable to buy an option that expires in at least four months or more, and exit before the final month. The guidelines in the section on buying call options are also applicable when looking to buy a put option.

Some traders hedge their portfolios by buying put options as a form of insurance. They are willing to pay a premium in order to be able to sell their shares at a predetermined price if their shares decrease in value.

Option strategies

Every option strategy available will be one, or a combination, of the four strategies outlined in this chapter. You can either buy a call, or write a call. You can either buy a put, or write a put. When you combine these four separate actions, you can create a variety of further strategies. These are called spreads. Even if your broker suggests that you try a spread, make sure that you have a clear idea about the desired share price action before automatically agreeing to the option trade. Many spreads incur vast amounts of brokerage, so they may benefit your broker more than they will benefit you.

Have a clear exit strategy in mind before you enter into any position in the sharemarket. Unless you are trading shares successfully, it would be foolhardy to move into a leveraged area such as options, warrants or the futures market. For experienced traders, however, options can multiply the available rewards.

Many traders mistakenly believe that a Utopian risk-free trade exists—and they spend their lives searching for this elusive goal. Options do not represent a shortcut to untold profits. Even if on paper an options spread appears to have no downside but significant upside, in practice, life is never as clear-cut. As with any leveraged instrument, options will escalate your speed of failure if you do not fully understand the inherent principles of successful trading.

This chapter was designed just to give you a brief overview of the options market. I realise they're complicated, twitchy little things, but if you're keen on learning more and you feel you have the necessary level of sophistication, then you're welcome to read my book *The Secret of Writing Options*. Otherwise, frankly, leave these instruments alone for the time being. There are lots of other things to conquer before you need to learn how to trade options effectively.

Review

1   Imagine that you have identified a share trending strongly upward. What is a suitable options strategy that you could employ? What else could you do to make money from this share?

....

....

....

....

....

....

....

2   If you have identified a share trending downward strongly, what is a suitable options strategy that you could use? What is another strategy that you could implement to make money from a downtrending share?

....

....

....

....

....

....

....

3   Why is liquidity important when trading options and short selling?

....

....

....

....

....

....

....

....

....

4   How would you decide whether to short sell, or use an option to benefit from a downtrend?

....

....

....

....

....

....

....

....

....

5   If you have located a share in a downtrend, how would you decide whether to write a call option or buy a put option?

....

....

....

....

....

....

....

....

....

Answers

1   If you have located a share in a strong uptrend, you could buy the physical share, write a put option or buy a call option.

2   For shares trending downward, you could write a call option, buy a put option or short sell the physical share.

3   Unless you are trading options or short selling shares that have significant levels of liquidity, you may find yourself unable to exit a losing position.

4   You can choose whether you would like to short sell or trade options with any of the shares with significant market capitalisation; for example, usually the Top 200. However, only trade options on the shares with the highest levels of market capitalisation, such as the Top 15. Option trades tend to be quite short term due to the issue of time decay. If you feel that you have identified a medium-term downtrend, it may be more effective to short sell the instrument, rather than buy a put option or write a call option.

5   If you have detected a share that is likely to decrease in price very quickly, it would be more beneficial to buy a put option. This will provide a greater return on your investment. However, if you have reason to argue that a share is likely to drift in a sideways to downward direction, without an explosive break to the downside, you might as well collect the small fixed-premium income that writing a call option would provide. The question of whether to write or buy an option depends on your view regarding the strength of the trend.

Besides share price direction, there are several other issues to consider before entering into an options trade. These include:

a)   liquidity

b)   time decay implications

c)   the effect of volatility

d)   the choice of option strategy; that is, call versus put, and writing versus buying.

If you take the time to learn about the impact of these concepts, you will be in a better position to trade options profitably.

Whichever instrument you choose to trade, it is essential that you follow a sound written trading plan. The next chapter will help you to formulate an effective trading plan based on your individual requirements.

21

New trading products

In this chapter, you will learn that:

- CFDs allow you to trade a vast array of different instruments, long and short, all from the one contact point, using the one account, without having to talk to a broker. They increase the flexibility available to traders, so they can focus on their trading system, rather than spending so much time on execution of their orders.

- Foreign exchange trading involves trading currencies that are among the most liquid markets in the world. Suitable for intermediate to advanced traders, this type of trading can provide diversification, additional trading opportunities and ease of entry and exit.

CHRIS TATE HAS A LEGENDARY REPUTATION as a great trader. He began his career as a research scientist, but quickly realised that money was limited in that field. His quiet, logical approach and mathematical ability stood him in good stead to trade. For over 30 years, Chris has traded almost every instrument available, and has become one of the more colourful characters on the Australian sharemarket scene. Known for his gruff, almost dogmatic approach, as well as his successful application of principles derived from his study of various martial arts, Chris is a force to be reckoned with. Standing at over six feet and looking more like a weightlifter than a trader, his presence commands respect. He is the author of the best-selling books *Art of Trading* and *The Art of Options Trading.*

Chris and I have been friends for many years, so I was very pleased when he agreed to provide his thoughts on CFDs and foreign exchange trading for this edition of *Trading Secrets.* Here is what Chris has to say about these remarkable tools.

So, what are CFDs and how did they evolve?

A CFD is best explained by reference to its full name; it is a contract for difference. You have a contract with a market maker whereby you agree to settle, in cash, the difference between the price at which you open the contract and the price at which you close it. So, in effect, it's like a virtual share.

There is no physical delivery of a CFD contract, so they cannot be exercised in the same manner as an options contract. Also, you don't have any of the ancillary benefits of owning a share, such as attending the annual general meeting. However, you do participate in dividends, by way of a cash adjustment to your account, as well as any corporate actions such as bonuses.

All CFD trading is settled in cash. Money either flows into or out of your account depending upon the success of your trading. Let's have a look at an example of a CFD trade. Imagine I am bearish ABC and wish to short sell it. I could use my CFD account to place a trade to short sell ABC at $10.00. To establish this trade I pay a small margin. The trade can remain open as long as I continue to hold my bearish view on ABC, with the proviso that I can continue to meet any margin payments that may be levied against me. Margin payments are usually about 10 per cent to 20 per cent of the trade. This is held in trust until the trade is closed out and adjusted to reflect any changes in the value of the share during the course of the trade.

Let's assume that, two months down the track, ABC has fallen to $9.00, so I decide to close out the trade. My profit is the difference between the price at which I opened the position ($10.00) minus the price at which I closed the trade ($9.00). This yields me a profit of $1.00 per contract. It is important to note that I would also be liable for any losses that are incurred during the life of my trade.

CFDs evolved into the rather sophisticated instrument used today by traders as a result of the difficulty with international share trading. Before the advent of internet-based trading and settlement facilities, all share trading was a nightmare of paperwork and complex back-office procedures.

These procedures became even more complex and labyrinthine when trading offshore instruments. To avoid unnecessary delay, dealers would enter into simple contracts that facilitated the quick buying and selling of shares across differing borders, currencies and legislative requirements. In addition to this, what is known as the spot foreign exchange market has always operated on a basis of simple contracts for difference, albeit on a vast scale.

From a trading perspective Chris, can you give us an idea about your experiences? What exactly can be traded using CFDs and what has been the impact on you as a trader?

Virtually any instrument can be traded using CFDs. To give you a sense of the range of markets covered, the following are the most widely known instruments:

→ ASX 200 or ASX 300 shares, depending on the provider
→ S&P 500 and Nasdaq 100 shares
→ UK FTSE 350 and constituents of all major European indices
→ foreign exchange, including all major cross rates and a selection of minor and exotic cross rates
→ all major share indices
→ options on major share indices
→ gold and silver along with oil and most other commodities.

Some CFD providers will even allow you to trade CFDs against house prices.

My experience with CFDs has been so positive that they have replaced all the other instruments that I trade on a regular basis. I can honestly see no need to have separate accounts to trade domestic shares, foreign shares, commodities, options or currencies when I can perform all these transactions from a single point using a single account. The other major benefit has been the introduction of the guaranteed stop, also known as a guaranteed stop loss order (GSLO). This has allowed me to explore some extremely interesting forms of money management and to control risk in ways I never thought possible even a few years ago.

Do you think CFDs are only for experienced traders? What are some of the things people should be aware of?

The most important thing to be aware of when dealing with CFDs is the impact of leverage. Novice traders are often seduced by the prospect of very high leverage. For example, it is possible to gear up your investment tenfold; you can open a CFD account with $100 and then purchase $1000 worth of shares.

The mindset behind this type of thinking generally revolves around windfall scenarios. Traders may think, 'If I have $1000 and I buy $10 000 worth of shares and they go up by 20 per cent, I make $2000 and double my investment'.

Such strategies are generally the product of wishful thinking and completely neglect the fact that, if your shares go down 10 per cent, you lose your entire investment, or the possibility of your shares having a catastrophic fall and creating a situation whereby you not only lose all your investment but also end up owing the CFD provider money.

My feeling is that traders should learn their craft in an unleveraged environment. The most important aspect of a trading system is how you react to the natural ebbs and flows of the market. Novice traders enter the market excited about the prospect of making lots of money. They often give no thought to the possibility of losing money, even though losing money is one of the realities of trading. All traders have losing streaks and, when first encountered, these losing streaks can be extremely distressing. In their distress, novice traders will opt for emotionally easy but completely incorrect actions, such as ignoring stops or worse still, averaging down. In an unleveraged account, such behaviours can have extremely serious consequences. Even worse, when using leverage, such conduct can endanger your financial future.

Why would someone trade CFDs in preference to other instruments such as options and futures?

Different traders could nominate several different reasons. For me it is the ease of risk management and the convenience of dealing in multiple markets through a single account.

Where can people go to get more information about how to trade these tools and the best trading strategies to utilise?

There are heaps of tools available to help you begin trading CFDs with confidence. Some of the CFD providers hold free seminars on the topic. Also, I have written a manual called *CFDs—A Complete Guide* and created a CD about CFDs called *Power Trading*. For information about these products, refer to my websites <www.artoftrading.com.au> or <www.tradinggame.com.au>.

It's worth getting out of your comfort zone to try some new instruments from time to time. A lot of people feel a bit nervous before they trade a new trading instrument, but once they've had some experience, they grow to love it. Start with a small position and test it out for yourself before putting your usual position size into the market.

Now let's have a look at FX trading.

Can you define FX trading and list some of the benefits and disadvantages?

FX is literally dealing in differing currencies. Instead of taking a view on an instrument such as a share or an option, a trader will take a view on a certain currency. The FX market is by far the world's largest market, with a daily turnover in excess of US$1.5 trillion. This is a staggering amount of money. The scale of trading comes into true focus when you consider that the entire market capitalisation of the Australian sharemarket is approximately A$800 billion. So in a single trading session, you could drop every listed Australian company into the FX market and it would sink without a trace. This massive liquidity is obviously attractive to traders since there is never a problem with either price discovery or the setting of a position. Price discovery is apparent when there are enough buyers and sellers in a market to create a consistent level of demand and supply. Share price charts are much simpler to interpret with sufficient liquidity, and it is also much easier to exit from positions.

Dealing in FX is somewhat different to dealing in shares or indices. Firstly, there is no physical location or major exchange where currency trading takes place. Trading takes place courtesy of a vast network of large banks and dealers who deal directly with one another with no need to deal via an exchange or use brokers. In addition to this there is a second tier of market participants who offer FX trading to retail clients. Such retail operations are often offshoots of large banks and trading institutions.

Secondly, all FX contracts are traded in pairs such as A$/US$ or US$/¥. This means that, when you go long one currency, you are automatically going short its counterpart. For example, if I thought that the Australian dollar was going to strengthen against the US dollar, I would buy the A$/US$ pair. So my instruction would be to buy x number of contracts of the A$/US$ pair (or 'the Aussie', as it is sometimes referred to).

Conversely, if I thought the A$ was going to weaken against the US$, my instruction would be to sell x contracts of A$/US$. It is impossible to trade currencies without reference to another currency. The first currency in the pair is referred to as the base currency and is the currency you are either buying or selling. The second is known as the counter or quote currency. So, in this example, the Australian dollar is the base currency and the US dollar is the counter, or quote, currency. A quote of 0.7100 for this pair means that A$1 is worth US$0.71.

It's this difference in terminology that provides the first hurdle for new entrants into the FX market. In share trading, if I wanted to buy BHP, I simply place an order to buy BHP. I don't have to state that I am buying BHP with reference to another stock. However, in FX, this is the norm.

It is extremely important to make certain you understand the quoting conventions of FX trading before you place an order. A failure to understand how quotes are structured could lead you to either buy or sell the wrong currency. And in the financial world, there is no sympathy for such mistakes.

The second major difficulty is in understanding how values are calculated within the FX arena. Traders also have to come to terms with the value of each FX contract that they trade. Traditionally, contracts for each of the quoted pairs come in two types, mini and standard contracts. A standard contract traditionally refers to 100 000 units of currency. For example, the A$/US$ standard contract refers to A$100 000. So if I bought a single A$/US$ contract at a quote of 0.7100, this would give me a contract size in US dollars of $100 000 × 0.7100, or US$71 000.

A mini contract refers to 10 000 units of currency. For example, if I were to trade a single mini contract of A$/¥, I would have control over A$10 000 worth of Japanese yen. Mini contracts are a valuable tool for traders who are new to FX trading and/ or who have smaller account sizes that might preclude them from trading full-size contracts.

Do people combine trading FX with other instruments (for example, equities) or do most FX traders focus on the FX market exclusively?

This becomes a question of diversification. If you asked a broker to define diversification he or she would simply tell you that you should hold shares with different names. In a small equities market such as the Australian market, it is very difficult to attain true diversification. To circumvent this issue, more mature traders seek out markets that are not correlated, such as combining FX and share trading. Not only does this bring a much-needed element of diversification to most portfolios, but it also enhances the number of potential trading opportunities.

Is this something that a beginner trader should try, or is it more for people who have developed skill in trading equities, but are looking for more leverage?

Once again, whenever large amounts of leverage are possible, I would recommend that traders develop their skills in an unleveraged arena. FX is not something traders with no experience should be trading.

I really appreciate Chris providing his views on these great tools. If you ever get the chance to see Chris in action by attending one of his seminars, I highly recommend it. He also runs the advanced component of our Mentor Program. The Mentor Program will provide you with the ability to turn your trading around, and give you everything you need to be a superb trader, across every time frame, and with every instrument. For more information, have a look at his websites <www.artoftrading.com.au> and <www.tradinggame.com.au>.

Trading insights

People often underestimate the power of focused attention over the long term. They flit from activity to activity—never landing for any significant period of time. Earl Nightingale said, 'One hour per day of study will put you at the top of your field within three years. Within five years you'll be a national authority. In seven years, you can be one of the best people in the world at what you do.'

One of the hidden keys to happiness is simply to focus on doing what you love and what you do best. Aim to aggressively and systematically divest yourself of all activities that you don't do well, happily, or that you find boring. Invest your energy, time and talents into things you do extraordinarily well, enjoy doing or find stimulating. I'll bet you'll be amazed at what you can achieve.

Now that you've had a look at some of the specifics related to profitable trading, let's have a look at some of the people who could end up sabotaging your success…

Part VI
Words of wisdom

22

Associate with success

In this chapter, you will learn that:

- If you don't associate with success, you'll fail. When developing a new skill, you can be vulnerable to a variety of people who do not necessarily have your best interests at heart. Alternatively, sometimes those closest to you can inadvertently curtail the learning curve you need to experience to succeed.

- It's important to be respectful of others' needs as you learn about the sharemarket; you may be shaking their level of security without really meaning to.

- Sometimes those we respect and admire most do not have any idea about what it takes to become a successful trader.

- In any group situation, such as forums or share-trading clubs, it is advisable to be aware of the effect of group dynamics.

IN THE COURSE OF ACHIEVING your aim of developing skills in the market, you may find yourself becoming a magnet for a variety of shady characters who want to 'help' you (and I use that term loosely). They may speak with the voice of vested interest and perhaps they genuinely mean well. However, they often set about sabotaging your trading efforts with military precision.

In his book *Winning Through Intimidation*, Robert Ringer states that when it comes to people who can sabotage you, there are three kinds of people: those who know they are out to get you and say so (for example, an enemy you actively avoid); nice people who, through their ineptitude, victimise or restrict you in some way (for example, a relative);

and those who act as though they are nice people but are actually ruthless and cunning (this could be your best friend!). Not everyone is as sweet as they appear. Be careful who you talk to and who you trust.

Your friends

Have you ever seen live crabs in a basket? When there is only one crab in the basket it will soon work out how to escape. If you put a whole bunch of these cunning crustaceans into a basket, they will actually hold each other within the confines of their prison — any critter that tries to climb out will be dragged back in with all of the others.

Sometimes your friends may be happy that you are succeeding, just as long as you don't achieve more than they have. Don't get mad at them — it's human nature. Be aware of this phenomenon, be strong enough to not brag to them, and don't ask for sympathy if the markets haven't been cooperative.

Trainers

Some sharemarket trainers fall into the category of people who should arouse your suspicions. To maintain integrity, trainers need to practise what they preach. The formula should be 'learn, do, teach', not 'learn, teach and then never do'. Ideally, ensure that someone you trust has referred the trainer to you. Take steps to make sure that the trainer you have chosen has the runs on the board.

As a guideline, if your chosen trainer is unnecessarily arrogant and acts as though his or her way of trading the market is the only method that will bring about success, you should be wary. The market has a way of humbling its players through losses, which are a common occurrence for traders. Arrogance suggests that the trainer hasn't traded in a long, long time.

The formula should be 'learn, do, teach', not 'learn, teach and then never do'.

Keep in mind that almost every elite level individual was encouraged by at least one mentor, or a group of supporters, to excel. This made the difference between whether the individual achieved brilliance, or whether their raw talent withered on the vine like an unripened fruit.

Practice and encouragement to continue seems to lead to great skill by developing the cognitive construct of chunking. This is the ability to group details into easily remembered patterns that ultimately require less brain activity to be expended. People with the ability to chunk in their chosen field are able to spend more energy looking for subtle dynamics, as the basics are already truly mastered.

You don't have to conquer it all in one day. It's okay to make mistakes, and to feel your way slowly. This isn't a race. The best traders often started in a very humble way.

Corporate professionals

Many successful professionals have established an enviable level of success in their corporate roles. Often they feel that the sharemarket should recognise that they are about to trade and roll out the red carpet of profits. Some seem to have an unfailing belief that they are bulletproof.

There is a psychological phenomenon called the halo effect, which causes its sufferers to oversimplify events in the world in order for their psyches to cope better with getting through life. The halo effect suggests that, if someone has developed knowledge and skill in one area of life, then this should radiate to a totally unrelated area. This is why Kieran Perkins advertised milk. 'Well, if he can swim like a champion, then he must know the best type of milk for me to drink!' It also explains why Buzz Aldrin recommends fitness products, and bikini-clad beauties sell spanners. ('Well, if those girls recommend that I should buy that brand of spanner, maybe I will find that beautiful women will throw themselves at me as soon as I leave the hardware store...') It is a simple leap of logic designed to line the pockets of clever marketers.

It is tempting to feel that, if you have been successful in one area of your life, this should spell automatic success in the sharemarket. This is simply not the case. There are few similarities between the backgrounds of great traders. Some terrific traders used to be garbage collectors, others doctors. Your past profession has very little to do with your future as a trader.

This is also one area where IQ does not guarantee your success. Some of the dumbest people make great traders because they follow their trading rules without question. As Peter Lynch, a very successful trader, states in *The Book of Business Wisdom*:

> **In terms of IQ, probably the best investors fall somewhere above the bottom 10 per cent but also below the top 3 per cent. The true geniuses, it seems to me, get too enamoured of theoretical cogitations and are forever betrayed by the actual behaviour of stocks, which is more simple-minded than they can imagine.**

He goes on to say:

> It's also important to be able to make decisions without complete or perfect information. Things are almost never clear on Wall Street, or when they are, then it's too late to profit from them.

In many ways, the highly paid corporate professionals who begin trading are at a psychological disadvantage. Due to their above-average incomes, the losses they make can often be mitigated if they take on one extra patient or see one extra client. Trading from this perspective negates the importance of discipline. It's far better to trade as if your very life depended on it, even if it doesn't.

If your dentist tells you that XYZ is a good share to buy, don't be fooled by the halo effect and attribute to this professional a generalised sense of good judgement. Do your own research.

Authority figures

Many traders are beginning to make their first trades at a fairly young age. Some even begin to paper trade while they are teenagers. If this describes your situation, I applaud you. You will have years ahead to perfect your trading system, and to spend the money that you'll make. To quote Jim Jorgensen:

> If you want to build a realistic retirement nest egg, you have to marry the stock market as soon as you can and stick with it for the rest of your life.

If you tend to respect authority figures, you may feel susceptible to the views of your parents. They would like to have you believe that they know more than you do due to the longer time they have spent on this planet. However, this is one area where you should probably make your own decisions and do your own research. Your parents may have good intentions, but if they have your best interests at heart, they will let you make your own mistakes within the guidelines of effective money management. Hopefully, you will be able to rely on their encouragement to learn from books and seminars to shorten the yellow brick road to trading success.

One of the great parts about starting to trade while you have relative youth on your side is that, often, you will not mind as much if you are wrong. It seems that, as you get older, you become more intent on maintaining appearances. In the markets, the impulse to always be right can be incredibly damaging to your bank account. 'The greater our knowledge increases, the greater our ignorance unfolds,' stated John F. Kennedy. Don't let anyone tell you that you're too young to learn how to trade. The sharemarket has no inherent respect for status, age or life experience; it only respects careful analysis, strategy and discipline.

Forums and chat rooms

Many people like to big-note themselves, but ironically, they are often not the genuine article. They can tell you the exact formula for the Stochastic Indicator, but if you asked them to show you their last contract note, they'd run a mile. This type of person is often too scared to test his or her theories in real life on the current markets. In fact, these people tend to know more and more about less and less, until eventually they know everything about practically nothing!

By making your knowledge seem puny and inferior, these egotistical rocket scientists are doing nothing to improve your financial situation. They are probably deriving personal benefit from your feelings of ineptitude. Unfortunately, these types of people have found a high-technology area to spread their sophisticated concepts far and wide. It's called the chat room or the trading forum.

Forums and chat rooms allow traders to share their ideas about the sharemarket, online. They appeal to the gossipmonger in all of us. Traders love to listen to gossip and rumour. It helps them feel that they are accessing some form of inside information. This type of behaviour is not productive; it effectively works against us.

The majority of good traders will agree that trading is a largely solitary occupation. If a trader has internalised a decision, this is the only guarantee that he or she will follow these rules. A forum may alter your perception regarding the correctness of your view, and cause you to suffer self-doubt. Traders who are easily swayed by others' views may experience an instant decline in profitability.

Traders who are easily swayed by others' views may experience an instant decline in profitability.

On a positive note, chat rooms can serve as a place for intellectual exchange about the pros and cons of different trading methods. Some are real-time, so if you have a question to ask, then you will receive an answer within a few seconds. That's not to say that the answer is correct or will suit your trading style, but at least you'll receive an answer. This may at least inspire you to seek your own solutions.

Trading chat rooms can be a valuable source of information about how to trade, but there are drawbacks involved in this type of research that could work against you. At the risk of you thinking that I am totally against this method for training traders, let me tell you that I actually write for a couple of forums in the interests of helping new players become profitable. So, if you are aware of the dangers and you feel that you can overcome the disadvantages of forums, then by all means, log on and ask some like-minded people about their approaches to trading.

Your partner/spouse

Sometimes, the ones we love hurt us the most. At other times, they are our strongest supporters.

Trading is a peculiar business. The majority of the time you feel like you're getting nowhere. Profits may appear to be elusive and losses frequent. Even though you may understand that this can happen in the world of trading, your spouse may not be as sanguine about the situation.

If you are the main breadwinner in the family, you should realise that your actions may shake your partner/spouse's level of security. Your partner may not understand why money is continually being spent on buying software, data, books and courses. Your purchases and study may not be seen as an investment. You know that such expenditure is necessary for you to be able to provide a better life for your loved ones in the future, but are you sure that they know that? The outgoing of money, especially when you are starting to trade, may seem like it will never be replaced. Tell your partner your reasons for getting involved in the sharemarket. Share your vision.

It is possible that he or she may be jealous of the amount of time you spend with your computer and feel like a jilted lover. Even though you are excited about shares, it doesn't mean that those around you feel the same level of enthusiasm. Your partner may feel a sudden impulse to send you the latest virus by email, in an attempt to prove that your computer is inferior and not to be trusted. Try to see the situation from your partner's perspective.

Your partner could surreptitiously sabotage your results. It's unlikely that this would be done on purpose, but the results of repressed annoyance can be damaging to your trading account. It could be that your partner will let the children into the room during the times you need to analyse the market. Perhaps he or she could talk you out of taking a stop that you needed to follow in order to stay loyal to your trading system.

Should you blame your partner for any of this? Let me give you a clue: the correct answer is a resounding *no!* If you are the one with the vision for your family, then it is up to you to shoulder the burden of responsibility. Life isn't fair — deal with it.

Do your best not to whinge about the markets to your partner. You should approach trading with the calmness of a professional, and not the crazed, erratic zeal of the village idiot. Stay positive, even when facing a loss. However, if you are facing a large potential loss, then let your partner know calmly and objectively, as quickly as possible. If you're after sympathy regarding how hard you've been working and how little you're making, go and tell your psychologist. At least you are paying your shrink to listen; your partner has to do this on a voluntary basis. Don't make your partner suffer the effects of your self-pity.

If you happen to have an understanding and supportive partner, then you're very lucky. This is not a prerequisite for trading success, but at least it's one aspect of life that won't hinder you. Where possible, encourage your partner's participation. Being invited to seminars, or receiving a present as a surprise when you have derived a profit from the markets, are two ways of involving your partner. Make sure that your partner feels included in this part of your life if he or she wants to be.

Tell your partner your reasons for getting involved in the sharemarket. Share your vision.

If you have the type of partner who just leaves you to your own devices with trading, then you are likely to be in a very good position to get on with the business of making money. You have managed to avoid the potential relationship issues which other traders sometimes face.

If I haven't yet met you personally, hang around this industry for long enough and I bet we'll get a chance to have a chat eventually.

After years of watching thousands of traders progress and grow, I've found that the best traders are the ones who maintain an objective mindset. They examine their results with realistic honesty—not overrating their abilities, yet not overemphasising their flaws. They are stable and balanced in their approach and self-evaluation. They also don't rely on others for external confirmation or flattery.

The best traders are self-reliant, and detached when it comes to reviewing their trading results and personal abilities. Because you're reading this book, I know that these are the qualities you're aiming to emulate, regardless of whether you use candlesticks or Gann (goodness gracious!) to help you make your trading decisions.

I can also tell that you're more likely to be financially savvy in comparison with those out there in 'non-*Trading Secrets* land'. However, when did you last make a budget or seriously talk about your spending habits with those you love?

Census information from the US has come in and, as always, it's sent the researchers scurrying away to find side spin-off projects to investigate. Did you know that four in 10 married couples have serious, recurring arguments about money? Those who have a written budget are 30 per cent less likely to argue on a recurring basis than those without. Of the battles, 49 per cent argue about what to buy or not buy and at what price, 33 per cent fight about debt, and 26 per cent about savings (Matt Bell, author *Planning for Fewer Financial Fights with Your Spouse*).

My advice? Next time you have a chat with your partner about the latest chart that has caught your eye, open up the discussion a little. Have a talk about your budget and jot down a few notes. You'll fight less and have more time for the fun things in life.

Singles, don't let your eyes glaze over and think that I'm leaving you out of this discussion. For traders currently between partners (a phrase coined by a single girlfriend of mine), or if you have made a lifestyle choice in this area — then you only have yourself to argue with, and we all know how frustrating and unnerving that can be. Especially when you start to answer back!

Share-trading clubs

Trading clubs pool the money and resources of their members. Joint decisions are made regarding which shares to buy and sell. These groups usually require a unanimous consensus to trade any share. This sounds so nice and comfortable, doesn't it? The warmth and closeness of a group of like-minded people may even make the activity of trading feel less lonely. (Time to gather around and have a big group hug. There, feel better?)

Have you heard of The Beardstown Ladies' Investment Club? It was a lovable, but arithmetically challenged, gaggle of 14 stock-picking old dears. They wrote five books, delivered hundreds of speeches and made dozens of TV appearances based on their claim of earning compound annual average returns of 23.4 per cent in the 10 years leading up to 1993. The *Chicago Magazine* challenged their results, so with the appropriate level of indignation, the ladies went to Price Waterhouse for an audit. Much to the surprise of the group of grandmas, they discovered that their actual return was only 9.1 per cent!

What was the reason for the discrepancy? The ladies, evidently, were making incorrect entries into their computer. Nobody double-checked the maths. This is an example of wishful thinking personified.

Even if you do manage to keep accurate records, trading via share clubs does not usually produce optimal results. Brad Barber and Terrance Odean studied the investments that 166 clubs made over a six-year period. About 60 per cent of the clubs analysed underperformed the index. Disturbingly, 'The stocks the clubs bought produced lower returns than the stocks they sold,' Odean says.

There are some inherent difficulties with the club mentality. Often, consensus can be difficult to attain. It's hard enough working out your own trading plan, let alone trying to correlate your ideas with those of 20 of your friends. A potential issue is the amount of time taken to gain consensus. By the time everyone in the group has been consulted, the ideal opportunity for entry or exit may have long since passed. Systems must be put in place to avoid this drawback if the group is to be successful in the long term.

It's hard enough working out your own trading plan, let alone trying to correlate your ideas with those of 20 of your friends.

In many groups, a domineering figure will emerge, often with the people skills and social conscience of a praying mantis. The person who dominates the decision-making will often have the least knowledge, but will have the biggest mouth (empty vessels make the most noise). Less vocal participants often feel obligated to keep the peace, and go along with the group's decision.

In psychology circles, this process is called group think. This is the same impulse that lemmings feel, just before the herd stampedes over the cliff to plummet to the jagged rocks below, when they commit mass suicide.

While we're talking about psychological principles, there is another concept called division of responsibility. This is where a group of people watch a house burn down, or a murder take place, yet no-one thinks to call the police or fire department. This isn't only because of the appalling recent decay in social order: it is because everyone assumes that someone else has already phoned the authorities.

When trading in a group situation, members will often suffer a division of responsibility effect, where no-one actually makes a decision to buy or sell. The members feel a cosy warm glow due to the group dynamics, but nothing is ever actually achieved.

If you can overcome these deficiencies and would still like to trade in a group format, then go ahead. Just make sure that your own growth as a trader is encouraged, not stifled. And for goodness' sake, keep accurate records!

So who should you hang out with?

If you don't associate with successful people who have achieved what you want to achieve — you will fail. I've seen it too many times to think it's a coincidence. Imagine for a moment that you've just come back from meeting a trader with the latest techniques, who has introduced you to a group of other like-minded experienced traders. These people are committed to their goals, and realise that, by helping you, they are gaining. Imagine you'd found a community that understood what you're going through and that it felt like home. Pretty soon, the mindset of these exceptional people would start to rub off on you, wouldn't it? The way they handled losses, profits and thought about money would begin to sink in.

- What difference would this make to your trading?

- What changes would this make to your life?

- Would being involved with this place fulfil you as a trader and give you the support you've been craving?

- If you had the chance to get involved, would you?

If you haven't found a group of people like this yet, you really need to. It's an under-valued, overlooked secret to phenomenal success.

Are you ready to take charge?

A lot of us who are full-time traders tend to be quite hard on ourselves. We demand more from ourselves than a boss would ever dare demand, and we tend to beat ourselves up whenever our grasp falls short of our reach.

We set arbitrary deadlines for ourselves, and work mightily to meet them. We strive to keep our lives in balance and aim for excellence.

Still, I ask you, if you're not being hard on yourself and demanding substantial achievement, then what's the point? If you don't learn to discipline yourself in pursuit of your own trading goals and life desires, then I guarantee there will be someone willing to discipline you so they can achieve what they value most in life.

I've been exactly where you are now — filled with hope and determination, but unsure about the best way to unlock the money vault. I can tell you one thing, until I committed to my own trading education, I was stuck. Stuck doing exactly what I had been doing, year after boring year. The monotony was half killing me. By reading this book you're saying: 'I refuse to stand for it any more!'

I'd love to hear your success story as you take charge of your own financial destiny. If you feel this book has egged you one step closer toward trading success, and you'd like to appear on one of my Rave Reviews pages, I'd love to hear from you. Just email me at <louise@tradingsecrets.com.au> and tell me what you've been up to.

Trading insights

If you're feeling fear about your future, you're in the best possible position to make changes to your life. If you numb that fear, your drive to act to get yourself out of where you are now is also dulled. By not stepping up and taking responsibility for your own future, you become needy and dependent, and the real you is diminished. Instead of being larger than life, you are left vulnerable and small.

Work on yourself as hard as you work on your trading system and rewards will be closer than you think.

The next chapter will help you detail everything that you have learned about trading so far into a magnificent document — your trading plan.

23

Write it down or suffer the consequences

In this chapter, you will learn that:

- Trading plans and trading diaries are essential tools used by every profitable trader.

- Your trading diary should include your thoughts and feelings about the trade, not just the mechanical details of entry and exit.

- Your trading plan is a master blueprint of your goals and objectives, procedures, performance measurement and trading system.

- Effective trading requires excellent planning and discipline. Trading favours those who follow a consistent plan.

BOTH WINNING AND LOSING TRADES teach us important lessons. Losing trades often provide the greatest opportunities for personal growth as traders. As an aerobics instructor of mine once yelled in the middle of a class, 'That which does not kill us, strengthens us.'

Over time, a robust trading plan will produce greater profits than losses. A good trade is made when you follow your trading plan to the letter, regardless of a profit or loss result.

Writing a trading plan is a sign of a disciplined trader. If you are having trouble developing your own plan, I suggest that you utilise the ideas of other traders/authors who you relate to. After you have tried out their concepts, you can make alterations to suit your situation — duplicate before you innovate.

During my university days, I was told of a study of Harvard business graduates. The study was designed to establish the common factors that lead graduates to ultimately succeed financially. Interestingly, 20 or so years after their degrees, 5 per cent of the graduates were earning 95 per cent of the total money earned by all graduates. It was the same 5 per cent who had written down their goals and dreams all those years ago. The maintenance of a written life plan somehow helped these graduates to attain their goals. Some even carried their personal mission statements in their wallets.

> *...duplicate before you innovate.*

Do you want to be in the top 5 per cent of investors? Quick — grab a pen and paper and get writing. Fill in this section of the book before you continue reading any subsequent chapters. It is essential! Take heart from the words of Warren Buffett:

> **To invest successfully over a lifetime does not require a stratospheric IQ, unusual business insights, or inside information. What's needed is a sound framework for making decisions and the ability to keep emotions from corroding that framework.**

A trading plan can provide you with the framework that you need to succeed in the sharemarket. To help you draw up your trading plan, let's have a look at three essential areas — keeping a trading diary, monitoring your active positions, and developing a trading system.

Keep a trading diary

If we all had a personal trading coach, I'm sure that we would detect our own flaws and strengths, and improve our strategies, with overwhelming speed. Because trading is largely a solitary occupation, you will need to be responsible for your own trading development. Achieving objectivity is a difficult prospect. You will accomplish trading excellence by regularly analysing your own strengths and weaknesses.

My key to maintaining objectivity is to keep a trading diary. I keep an A4 ringbinder folder, and assign one page to each share that I buy. All of the most successful traders use some form of recording their trading history. Before entering a trade, I record all of my thoughts and analysis. Unless I can justify my trade on paper, I will not enter the position. Imagine that you were trying to convince another person, who is incredibly sceptical about shares, to buy a particular share. If you could win such an argument, go ahead and buy the share.

It is essential to keep your records in date order and to separate your completed transactions for each trading month. After each trade has been completed, write down your profit, your loss, the amount of time that you held the share and the main lessons that you have learned. After making a profit or a loss, I record my answers to the following questions:

- What did I do well?

- What would I do differently if I repeated this trade?

Unfortunately, some traders must go through some sort of catastrophe to finally get their own attention, and make an effort to improve their system. Psychologists call this one-trial learning. The one experience is so excruciatingly devastating that it results in an instant change in behaviour—painful, yet effective. A quick whack to the side of the head can sometimes be the best thing to ever happen to you, as long as your head doesn't get completely knocked off in the process. By following the guidelines set out in this book, it is unlikely that you will need to go through such an experience in order to learn how to trade effectively. However, unless you have written down your trading plan by the end of this chapter, put on your crash helmet when you next feel the urge to trade.

A quick whack to the side of the head can sometimes be the best thing to ever happen to you, as long as your head doesn't get completely knocked off in the process.

Monitoring your positions

For short-term traders there are some systems that will allow you to register alarms once a share has moved above or below a predetermined price level. As an alternative, some brokers are willing to place for you a buy stop or an automatic stop loss. A buy stop involves an immediate purchase of an instrument as soon as it goes above a set price. It will often trigger an early entry into a breakout trade. Some providers allow for these stops to activate only after a certain volume of shares has been bought or sold at the price that you stipulate. This automation may assist if you do not have the facility to closely watch the market. If you are utilising CFDs or futures, these automatic stops are fairly common practice. However, they are rare in the equities market.

In many cases, a human broker's idea of an automatic stop loss is to write your order down on a sticky note and stick it to the side of his or her computer. Very few brokers have access to an alert facility that will tell them when your predetermined price has been hit. Your broker is under no official obligation to sell your position should your stop be hit, so you may incur quite substantial slippage. It is really up to you to monitor your open positions in the market.

I have organised for my mobile phone to alert me with an SMS when the shares on my watch list have penetrated or fallen through certain price levels. Perhaps you could ask whether your mobile phone service provider is capable of providing the same service. Be aware, however, that there are drawbacks with using this system. To quote James Coffey from the forum on <www.tradinggame.com.au>:

> I can remember using SMS alerts while I was at work to inform me when a security had traded at a certain price. The problem I then had was what I was going to do next with this information. I'd worry for the rest of the day until I got home that night to see how bad things were. Write down specifically what you are going to do with your alert once you receive it. This will at least give you some consistency and certainty about the approach you are taking.

Paging systems are available that display price, volume and chart activity. In the majority of cases, pagers have been surpassed by the appropriate app on your mobile phone.

The flexibility of automatic stop losses and mobile phones has meant that traders no longer have to be obsessed screen watchers to trade effectively. You need to decide the value you place on personal freedom. Personally, I prefer to invest in an effective service that provides me with the flexibility to leave the computer screen for the day, without fear of suffering a substantial loss. Our success as traders depends, to a large degree, on the tools we use to conduct business.

Developing a trading system

A trading system typically includes three components: the entry/exit methodology, risk management and money management.

1   The entry/exit methodology deals with the techniques you will employ to enter/ exit your trades.

2   Risk management deals with your risk profile. Your risk profile takes into consideration how much you are prepared to lose on a trade before you can no longer hold on, or how much of your portfolio you are prepared to lose before

you stop trading altogether (that is, maximum portfolio drawdown). How much financial pain can you bear before you throw in the towel? The idea is to establish your trading approach so that you have very little chance of reaching such a point.

3   Money management deals with how much capital you invest in each trade as your portfolio value fluctuates. You must calculate how much of your capital to invest in each position. This is called position size and was dealt with previously in chapter 15.

We will discuss each of these components in turn.

Often traders aspire to being discretionary. These traders are successful when they use discretion consistently. Those who do not master consistency remain in the trading wilderness for years until, eventually, they give up because of a lack of trading funds or too many emotionally painful experiences. Rather than seeking the freedom or confusion of trading on a whim, a good goal is to become a mechanical trader. Mechanical traders apply a strict set of trading rules and never deviate from them. This is an effective way to ensure consistency and become profitable. Relying on a set of unambiguous rules will also keep your trading unemotional, which is essential to your wellbeing.

Entry/exit methodology
Mechanical traders implement rules based on entry/exit signals, risk management and money management. Every detail of the trade has been planned in advance.

Entry signals
In part III of this book we discussed the entry signals that you could use when trading shares, as well as leveraged instruments. As already mentioned, entry signals will only help you to engage trades with a high probability of success. They will not tell you how to exit or how much money to place into a trade.

Exit signals
In *24 Essential Lessons for Investment Success*, William J. O'Neill states:

Investors spend most of their time deciding what stock to buy. They spend little if any time thinking about when and under what circumstances their stock should be sold. This is a serious mistake.

Before you place your order, you must decide on where you will exit. I advocate that you use a stop loss to capture your profits and avoid large losses. Refer to chapter 14 for a comprehensive look at the various types of stop losses and how to use them.

Successful technical traders have a defined set of rules to enter a position, to exit from the market promptly at the first sign of a downtrend, or to preserve their capital after the share or derivative has retraced in value.

Risk management

Risk management is about limiting the size of loss trades. It also has to do with limiting the amount of drawdown that may result from a portfolio of open positions in the market and from recently closed trades.

Your risk management rules and processes should be closely aligned with the entry/exit methodology you design. Obviously, there will be less risk if you take medium- to long-term non-leveraged positions rather than short-term leveraged positions. Rules need to be customised accordingly.

> Your risk management rules should not only match your entry/exit methodology, they should also match your risk profile.

Your risk management rules should not only match your entry/exit methodology, they should also match your risk profile. Are you a risk taker or are you more risk averse? A good methodology should allow risk to be customised to reflect a trader's risk appetite, which will change over time.

The sorts of indicators that can be used to assess risk include overall market direction, sector direction, liquidity, traded volume, market volatility, stock volatility, stock direction and market capitalisation. Using these tools, you can construct unambiguous rules that assess the level of risk as high, medium, low or even, according to a scale of one to 10.

Risk management rules should also determine how much risk you can take with your overall portfolio funds. This involves determining how much drawdown you can expect in certain market conditions in the future. Compiling portfolios of historical trades will give you an excellent idea of what drawdowns are likely.

Money management

Once risk is assessed it can be managed by adjusting the amount of capital you commit to each trade and/or to the market.

Your trade size should be determined by how much risk you are prepared to take. Your portfolio value and other factors will also come into the position-sizing calculation, such as the amount of leverage you are trading with and the risk assessment for each individual trade.

As a rule, when your portfolio value increases, so do your position sizes. If your portfolio value decreases into drawdown, your position sizes should also decrease. Also, the higher the risk assessment, the smaller your position size should be.

The objective of money management is to define how much capital you should commit to each trade to consistently generate portfolio profits.

Your trading plan

Wayne Goldsmith <www.moregold.com.au> is a sports scientist and consultant. He says the first step toward achieving sporting success is to:

> …define specific goals to accomplish within set time limits. Wanting to 'win' is not sufficient. The daily process of moving toward that goal must be mapped out to ensure success.

Treat the business of trading as seriously as if you were preparing to represent your country at the Olympics. Define your personal level of aggression, estimate the returns for different strategies and be realistic about your own capabilities. Consider every conceivable occurrence in advance.

Goldsmith goes on to state:

> Evaluating an athlete's fitness, speed, skills and mental abilities is essential. Specific aspects of performance to improve during training must be identified. This process is called performance needs analysis (PNA).

Athletes and share traders ultimately succeed because of their strengths, and fail because of their weaknesses. An objective personal assessment of your own situation may be painful, but it is necessary in order to improve your trading skills. Perform your own PNA by writing down your strengths and weaknesses as a trader.

Suppose you were planning to purchase a business that had the potential to create an unsurpassed lifestyle for you and your family. Would you spend some time discovering the critical components necessary for success? Of course you would. You'd also work your tail off to develop a business plan that would set you up for the future.

The sharemarket has the potential to change your lifestyle forever. It's up to you to lay out a road map that will take you from where you are now to where you want to be. That's where a trading plan will assist.

You will derive the most benefit if you spend at least half a day considering the issues described in this chapter. The time that you invest in considering all of these possibilities will set you apart from the majority of traders.

Trading plan questions

1   Clearly write out your objectives. Are you trading for wealth creation, income or for fun? Your objectives should be as specific as possible. Exactly what are you hoping to achieve?

....

....

....

....

....

....

....

....

....

....

....

....

....

2 What are your psychological strengths and weaknesses in relation to trading? What steps are you taking to overcome your weaknesses and maximise your strengths?

....

....

....

....

....

3 What structure will you trade under (for example, partnership, trust, or company)? If you are uncertain, visit your accountant or tax agent to ensure that you are setting up with the best structure for your individual situation.

....

....

....

....

....

4 How much time per day/per week will you devote to trading? How many distractions do you face while you are trading? Is there any way to overcome these distractions?

....

....

....

....

....

....

....

5   What size of percentage returns are you expecting per annum? This will have an impact on the types of markets that you trade. For example, if you are expecting a 60 per cent average return on investment, then it is likely that you will need to investigate derivatives or futures. A 10–20 per cent return would be more suited to trading shares.

....

....

....

....

6   How much capital do you have to devote to your trading system? Will you use only one trading system, or several?

....

....

....

7   Which markets will you focus on (for example, futures, managed funds, equities, warrants or options)? Will you trade Australian shares, or overseas markets? How will you allocate capital between these areas?

....

....

....

8   If you experience a consecutive string of losses, how will you react? What percentage of your initial capital can you tolerate losing before you will stop trading temporarily/permanently?

....

....

....

9   What procedures will you follow on a day-to-day basis, week-to-week basis, etc. to search for opportunities, monitor your existing positions and review your performance?

....

....

....

....

....

10   Over what time frame will you trade (for example, intraday, daily or weekly)? What is the average time that you envisage holding each position? If you are already trading, how long is your average hold time? Does this fit in with your psychological profile and goals?

....

....

....

....

....

11   What percentage of your capital are you willing to risk on each trade? When, if ever, will you alter this percentage?

....

....

....

....

....

12 How will you determine how much money to commit to each position? When will you increase or decrease your position size?

....

....

....

....

13 How will you set your initial stop, your break-even stop and your trailing stops?

....

....

....

....

14 What are your entry triggers?

....

....

....

....

15 Will you pyramid into your long positions? Will you pyramid into your short sold and/or bought option positions? Describe the method you will use.

....

....

....

....

....

16 How will you keep a record of your transactions?

....

....

....

....

17 How will you measure your performance? How often will you review your
    existing portfolio? How will you know when you have done well or poorly?

....

....

....

....

18 How will you define/handle a windfall profit?

....

....

....

....

19 What will you do with your open positions when you go on holidays?

....

....

....

....

....

20 How do you plan to deduct money from your trading account (for example, your salary)? When will this be conducted? How will this affect your position sizing, etc.?

....

....

....

....

....

The questions outlined here are designed to get you thinking in the right direction. You may find that they raise other questions that you need to address.

Your trading plan should be reviewed on a frequent basis to ensure that it is in line with your current objectives. Short-term traders should review this process every month. If you are a medium-term or longer term trader, every three to six months should suffice.

Once you have considered all of the issues outlined, there are three components that you need to record in your trading diary, prior to entering a new position:

• entry and exit (stop loss) requirements and procedures (entry/exit methodology)

• level of risk/amount to be risked (risk management)

• position sizing (money management).

I have a standard challenge that I issue to the attendees of the seminars that I run. I ask for the course participants to email me once they have completed their trading plan. I don't actually ask for their plan to be emailed, as the information in your trading plan is usually quite personal. I only want to know that the attendees have completed writing down their plan. When I suggest this in the course, they all nod in agreement, and provide me with knowing smiles and assurances that they will email me when they have written down their plans. So I wait, and I wait, and I continue waiting for the influx of emails. Usually only about 1 per cent of seminar attendees actually email me to tell me that they have written down their plan. No wonder there are so few winners in the sharemarket! People who treat trading as a business will receive business-like results. Effective business plans amplify your chances of success. If you approach trading haphazardly it is unlikely that you will ever earn a significant income from the markets.

I am predicting in advance that I am likely to get emails from readers of this book, demanding answers to all of the questions listed in this chapter. They will say that this text is incomplete, as I have not provided them with the preferred responses. I must say, if this does happen, I will be incredibly amused. There is no one correct answer to all of the questions listed. The process of trading involves self-directed discipline.

It is essential that your plan blends in with your lifestyle and personality, and it is impossible for me to fully understand your own private situation. No two traders, and therefore trading plans, are the same. This is your blueprint for success—no-one else's.

Develop urgency

Many, many years ago Charles Schwab, president of US Steel, told an efficiency expert that he didn't have time to listen to his full presentation, but asked the man for his top suggestion for him. The expert said, 'Every morning, make a list of the things you have to do that day in order of importance. Concentrate on the first task until it is finished, without diverting your attention to anything else. Then go onto the second task, and so on, completing as much as you comfortably can in the course of the day. Try it for one month and then pay me what you think it is worth to you.'

Thirty days later, Schwab sent the man a cheque for $25 000.

If it's good advice for Schwab, it's good advice for all of us. Give your top priority for the day your top priority. Refuse to let yourself get sidetracked. I bet you'll be amazed at what you have achieved in just one week.

We all need to be hungry, no matter how much cash we've got in the bank.

Many of the effective traders who have done my Mentor Program have told me that they've never lost their drive to improve. Urgency is important. And here is the big lesson. You want to know what it takes to be ludicrously productive and achieve more, not just in trading, but in every part of your life? Then … *Cut down on the time you take between learning something and implementing it!*

We all know that post seminar feeling. You've sat there, all weekend, absorbing the wisdom of the presenters, and determined to put it all into action on Monday morning. However, when Monday ticks around, you realise you're behind with your emails, the dishes have piled up, and you have to attend a meeting. Monday blends into Tuesday, and then Friday … without your having taken any action to apply your new-found knowledge.

Before long, that urgency you felt has been converted into sloth and the attitude that, 'One day I'll get around to it.'

In 10 years time, you'll be in exactly the same place you are now, (or worse off), *unless* you start taking action. Take all knowledge you gain. Implement it straight away. Even if you mess it up, you'll still be much further along than if you procrastinate and do not act on it.

Mike Vance, formerly from Disney, asks: 'Do you have a method to achieve continuous breakthroughs?'

Sure, a big part of your success depends on the quality of the information you're absorbing, but frankly, unless you DO, rather than just READ, you'll never fulfil your destiny.

Move fast. Be urgent. Do: don't just sit. You'll be propelled forward with a momentum you never knew existed. Gallop toward the finish line — don't dawdle!

The next chapter discusses the key habits to develop that will boost your profitability in the sharemarket.

24

Habits determine your success

In this chapter, you will learn that:

- Good traders are made, not born. They follow distinct behaviour patterns that increase their probability for success.

- The development of good habits provides a framework for your trading activities and can help you to persist, even when the going gets tough.

- The main habits to cultivate are:

  – trading with the trend

  – setting stop losses

  – utilising a written trading plan

  – developing money management skills

  – remaining detached

  – using an appropriate instrument

  – persisting in the face of adversity

  – standing on your own two feet.

People sometimes ask me if they can watch me work. I always decline because they'd shrivel up with boredom. I work in rushes. Most of the day I goof around with my kids, talking about their hopes and dreams, immersing myself in their worlds, full of jealousies and fears. I'm with them 100 per cent, total eye contact and attention, making sure their needs are number one.

Then, I trade. No interruptions. No phone calls. No-one asking for my opinions. I trade with total focus and silence.

Then I look after my traders. I point out more profitable ways of approaching the markets. I write articles, get interviewed by journalists, and create resources that I feel will help people reach their potential as a trader. I help them run on my belief for their futures, when they're stumbling in the dark.

And ... I play and do things just for me — just for fun. I go to the gym, have a wine with friends, and laugh so loudly people turn around and stare at me in cafes.

I'm not a circus performer. There's little to see. One thing that you will notice though is that I'm completely focused on what I'm doing during that particular time. I work to a written list. I'm a meticulous planner. I take pride in being productive and achieving, as well as being a caring mum and an excellent trader.

My life is just like yours. I juggle. I rush. I get out of breath. However, I find a plan of action dissolves the stress. Plus, it helps me achieve more than the average person. (Not trying to make this into a commercial message — just reporting the fact.)

Everything I've said here is available to you. The only person standing in your way is ... *you*. You can achieve more, do more and have more fun. You just need to *make* it happen.

Most people put more effort into planning their next holiday than their long-term financial future. The bleak truth is that the only way to live well tomorrow is to begin planning today. If you have chosen the sharemarket as the vehicle via which you will attain financial freedom, there are eight habits that you must develop, which we will go through in this chapter. This will act as a summary of the main points already covered in this book. If you find that any of these concepts are a little confusing, I suggest you go back and re-read the relevant chapter.

Trading with the trend

Would you like to make money in the sharemarket beyond your wildest dreams? Trade in direction of the overall trend and you'll be amazed at the results. This sounds obvious, but in reality you will probably spend the rest of your trading life trying to achieve this goal.

Whether you decide to pursue fundamental or technical analysis techniques, work on developing your skills. Aim for perfection, but be aware that there is no particular technique or method that will work in all circumstances. Be rule-oriented, but maintain a degree of flexibility and adapt to changing market conditions.

Setting stop losses

If you do not know how to set a stop loss, then for goodness' sake, stop trading immediately! An initial stop loss is designed to preserve your trading capital. A break-even stop will help lock in a no-loss trade. A trailing stop loss will assist in preserving your profits. Learn how to set a stop and then follow it. Contrary to popular belief, if you exit on the basis of a stop loss, the world will not abruptly stop spinning, flinging you into space, but you will live to trade another day. If you can keep investing in the markets for long enough, you are bound to learn the secrets about how to succeed.

Most people put more effort into planning their next holiday than their long-term financial future.

Develop a ruthless quality when it comes to taking a loss. To quote Chin-Ning Chu, 'The killer instinct is not solely reserved for the vicious and cunning; it can benefit the virtuous and righteous as well.'

Utilising a written trading plan

Detail your position-sizing rules, entry and exit triggers, and list the markets that you will participate in. Complete all of the questions in chapter 23 on how to write a trading plan. This small display of discipline is one of the keys that separate professional traders from unprofitable try-hards.

Developing money management skills

Money management is the part of your trading system that tells you how many of a particular share you are going to buy or how much of your account will be committed to a given market. The most effective traders have a method of attributing a greater percentage of their capital to low-risk, high-probability trades. Higher risk trades are still entered into, but a smaller position is taken. John Train says:

> **In all games, the difference between the amateur and the professional is that the professional plays the odds, while the amateur, whether he realises it or not, is among other things a thrillseeker.**

Remaining detached

The only way to trade well is to aim to be a good trader, rather than to make money. I have personally found that every time I demanded that the market provide me with a certain monetary return, then profits became ridiculously elusive. However, when I aim to trade well and to follow my trading rules, money easily flows into my account. Frustrating darned game, this! Successful traders have had to learn how to handle the inevitable losses that will ensue from investing. The 13th century Hindu philosopher Shankaracharya said:

> Even the greatest warrior sweats with fear while standing in a battlefield. Even though his body is fearful, his spirit is fearless.

He is able to detach himself from the fear and act with a clinical decisiveness in order to accomplish the task at hand.

Using an appropriate instrument

For some reason, novices seem attracted to the futures market like beetles to a bug zapper. 'The more volatile the better!' they cry as they launch themselves headlong into financial oblivion. Begin with shares, and trade them successfully for at least a year. Once you've proven yourself in this less volatile arena, then you can move on to leveraged instruments such as options, CFDs, warrants and futures.

Learn how to take advantage of a bear market. By using short selling, CFDs and options as part of your strategy, you can make money whatever the market is doing.

Persisting in the face of adversity

The only way to pass Share Trading 101 is by attending the school of hard knocks and staying in the trading arena, even when you feel like quitting.

Standing on your own two feet

Take responsibility for your own financial future. You are perfectly capable of learning how to trade. You can do this. You will ultimately be successful if you put in the effort and learn from your past mistakes. There are others who may have more knowledge than you at this very moment, but you have the resources necessary to develop your own strategies. Any negative people that doubt your skills have really underestimated your tenacity. Stay committed and focused and you will achieve your objectives.

You are worthy of success

A lot of people amputate their own success because they feel unworthy — unworthy of the rewards of trading, unworthy of being happy and definitely unworthy of greatness.

This is why we must continually find people to boost us and see the best in us. Without support, our mind gets claustrophobic and we never see how incredible we can be. Just like Vitamin C, it seems our body can't store these positive thoughts easily. Unless we get continual shots of positive, our minds drift toward the negative.

You need to register to get my free monthly email newsletter on <www.tradingsecrets. com.au>. Each month, I strive to bring you your 'fix', your shot in the arm, your boost so that you will not only be the best trader you can be, but also so you can be the best person you can be.

The way we approach one thing in life, is the way we approach everything in life. It's impossible to achieve success as a trader unless you have made some substantial steps forward in self-development. So, get my newsletter — stand tall, claim your place at the victory table, and be proud of your achievements.

The next chapter will make this whole book fall into context for you. Keep reading to learn the real secret of trading success!

25
The real secret

If you have turned to this page without reading the rest of the book, shame on you ... go back and begin at chapter 1! Once you've read through the other chapters, you are welcome to keep reading ...

Traders are a predictable bunch. The majority seem obsessed with finding the magic indicator/software/set-up that will help them to become a monumental success. The irony of this does not escape professional traders who have learned the real secret of trading. The secret is … there is no secret!

The markets reward traders who work to a written trading plan and are willing to put in the hard work and discipline required to trade effectively. Those who follow sound trading rules will capture monetary rewards. There is no specific secret that will guarantee your success. Effective trading is a reflection of emotional maturity. Your level of financial success will rarely exceed your level of self-development. Good traders work as hard on themselves as they do on their trading plan.

Effective trading is a reflection of emotional maturity.

Some people investigate the sharemarket and then ultimately decide that they do not have the temperament to trade. If you have reached this conclusion, based on the information that you have assimilated, this is perfectly valid. There is no harm in investigating an area and then deciding not to pursue a particular activity.

However, if you have decided that you would like to trade, and you haven't put any money into the market yet, what's stopping you? You've got far more information at your fingertips than I ever did when I first started trading. Assuming that you have completed all of the exercises in this book, you have all that you need to know in order to begin trading. If you haven't completed the written sections, then go back and finish them off now. This will be your best preparation for the battlefield.

The only way to truly test your knowledge is to put money into the market and see how you go. Set yourself a deadline to execute your first trade. Start with a small amount. Unless you are willing to take a risk, it is unlikely that your skill as a trader will develop. To quote Kahlil Gibran, 'A little knowledge that acts is worth infinitely more than much knowledge that is idle.'

Unless you begin to trade, you have cultivated a hobby that actually costs you money, rather than developing an income-generating business. There is simply no better time to start than now. To know and not to do, is not to know.

Your carrot and your stick

Have you seen the movie *Mao's Last Dancer*? It tells the story of Li Cunxin who defected from communist China and became one of the greatest dancers in the whole world. It's such a stirring story, I'm sure you'd love it. If you have seen it, you may remember the two teachers who were instrumental in Li's development both emotionally and physically. There are some primary lessons in this movie from a trading perspective.

One of Li's teachers gave him a dream. He taught him about passion, and he believed in him. He trusted him and nurtured him. He taught him to feel the music with his soul, and to listen to his heart. Think back to your school days. (Yes, that may be quite a while ago, but indulge me). Did you ever have a teacher that brought out the best in you, and that made you strive to be a better 'you'? I certainly did. Sometimes we need to be inspired, and to be guided by someone who can see the seeds of greatness within our hearts.

Li's other teacher challenged him and made him want to get stronger to earn his respect. He expected perfection and pushed Li almost beyond his limits. No excuse would be tolerated. No weakness would be indulged. This man drove Li to define himself as not only a dancer but as an athlete. He set the bar high and demanded the very best.

This got me thinking about my own life, and what I am running toward, as well as what I am running away from. In your own life, what is your carrot and what is your stick? Are these images fleshed out in your mind's eye so that these are real and vivid? Can you see the colours, and smell the fragrance of what success means to you? Inspiration and discipline. These are the two pillars by which all achievement is supported.

This is what it takes to become exceptional — and not just in the trading arena. If you're caught up in the drudgery of life and you've lost your spark, I can bet that one of two things in your life is taking a back seat. Either you're lacking inspiration, or you're avoiding the discipline it takes to get ahead. If you can't do this for yourself, seek out teachers with the qualities that you are lacking and draw your strength from them, just as Li did. I'm hoping that you'll choose me to be one of your teachers and mentors. We've come a long way together in this book. If you choose, this could just be the beginning of the journey.

Until our paths cross in the future, happy trading!

Further reading

Introductory

- Bedford, Louise, *Charting Secrets,* Wrightbooks, 2004

- Bedford, Louise, *The Secret of Candlestick Charting,* Wrightbooks, 2004

- Bedford, Louise, *The Secret of Candlestick Charting Poster* and *The Secret of Pattern Detection Poster,* available via <www.tradingsecrets.com.au>

- Bedford, Louise, *The Secret of Candlestick Charting — Video Program,* available on DVD at <www. tradingsecrets.com.au>

- Bedford, Louise, Tate, Chris and Cunningham, Jason, *Trading and Tax* (CD or cassette), available via <www.tradingsecrets.com.au>

- Bedford, Louise and Tate, Chris, *ShareTrading 101 and Leverage 101 — CD Programs,* available via <www. tradingsecrets.com.au>

- Darvas, Nicolas, *How I Made $2 000 000 in the Stockmarket,* Lyle Stuart Inc., 1986

- Tate, Chris, *The Art of Trading,* Wrightbooks, 1997

- Weinstein, Stan, *Secrets for Profiting in Bull and Bear Markets,* Irwin Professional Publishing, 1988

Intermediate – advanced

- Bedford, Louise, *The Secret of Writing Options,* Wrightbooks, 2005

- Bedford, Louise, *Candlestick Charting Home Study Course* and *Trading Psychology Home Study Course,* available at <www.tradingsecrets.com.au>

- Bedford, Louise, Tate, Chris and Stanton, Dr Harry, *Psychology Secrets — Peak Performance for Traders — CD Program* and *Relaxation for Traders — CD,* available at <www.tradingsecrets.com.au>

- Bedford, Louise, Tate, Chris and Wilson, Matthew, *Power Trading — Trade CFDs Like a Professional — CD Program,* available at <www.tradingsecrets.com.au>

- Seligman, Martin E.P., *Learned Optimism,* Random House Australia, 1992

- Tate, Chris, *The Art of Options Trading,* 2nd edition, Wrightbooks, 2002

- Tharp, Van K., *Trade Your Way to Financial Freedom,* McGraw Hill, 1999

- Tvede, Lars, *The Psychology of Finance,* John Wiley & Sons, 1999

Glossary

ask   *see* bid.

at-market or at-the-market   An order to buy or sell an option or a share at the prevailing market price.

at-the-money   When the exercise price of the option is close, or equal, to the current market price.

average down   To buy more of a security that is not cooperating with your initial view; for example, buying more of a downtrending share. You are trading against the trend. Only ever buy more of uptrending shares.

average true range (ATR)   The average of the true ranges over the past x periods (where x is specified by the user). *See also* true range.

average up   To buy more of a share that is cooperating with your initial view.

back-test   A method of testing an indicator's performance by applying it to historical data.

bar chart   This is the standard form of chart utilised in Western technical analysis. A single bar consists of an open price, a high, a low and a close price for a particular session.

bear/bearish   A trader with a negative expectation of the market or share. Some texts use this phrase to signify a sideways-trending market as well as a downtrending market. For the sake of simplicity, this text refers to bearish as representing a downtrending market or share.

bid   The price at which buyers have registered their interest in a share. A real-time screen will show the buyers who are queuing to buy the share as bids, and the sellers who are queuing to sell their shares as asks.

black box system   A trading system that generates buy and sell signals, yet the calculation or rationale for these signals is not disclosed.

black candle   A bearish session showing that the close was lower than the opening price.

breakaway gap   *see* gaps.

breakout trade   An entry into a long position in an instrument in an existing uptrend after a significant level of resistance has been bullishly transcended.

bull/bullish   A trader with a positive expectation that prices will rise in the market or for a particular share.

call option   A call option gives the buyer the right, but not the obligation, to buy a given security at a particular price up to and including the day of expiry.

candle body size   The height of the real body of a candle can provide a clue to the level of conviction of either the bulls or the bears. The presence of a long candle in relation to the most recent candles of previous sessions holds special significance.

candle range   The range from the high to the low, or the peak of the upper shadow to the base of the lower shadow, is a general indicator of the level of volatility for that period.

candlesticks   A seventeenth-century Japanese technique that uses the same information as contained in a Western bar chart, but provides a different graphic representation. Candlestick patterns of one, two, three or more candles (bars) provide an excellent timing/confirmation tool when used in conjunction with other indicators.

capital   The amount of equity, or money, that you have set aside to begin trading with.

capitalisation   *see* market capitalisation.

CFDs   *see* contracts for difference.

confirmation   The activity of the share price that confirms a trend after the appearance of a trigger pattern. Some patterns require greater levels of confirmation than others.

continuation gap   *see* gaps.

continuation pattern   After the appearance of this pattern, a share is likely to continue in the direction of the predominant, established trend. These patterns imply a pause or consolidation within the prevailing trend.

contracts   Options are sold by the contract. One option contract usually controls 100 shares in Australia. For example, five BHP options contracts would control 500 BHP shares.

contracts for difference (CFDs)   CFDs allow you to deal on share prices without having to physically settle on the trade. With CFDs you are trading a contract that represents the share. Benefits include low brokerage, the ability to trade online, and leverage.

consolidation   *see* sideways trend.

correction   A movement in prices against the general trend that typically occurs with little or no warning. For instance, the market periodically loses value as many of the underlying securities drop in price by several per cent.

defensive actions   These act as a last resort when the share goes against the view you had when initially writing the option. Defensive actions are a way of removing yourself from risk and minimising your potential loss if the trade goes against you.

delta   The sensitivity of the option price to a change in the share price.

derivatives   A derivative is a financial instrument that has another asset as its underlying base; for example, options, warrants.

dividend   This periodic payment is a part of a company's net profit that is paid to shareholders as a cash reward for investing in the company's shares.

double top   This pattern is where price action on a chart displays that the price has rallied twice in quick succession and stopped at or near the same high. This pattern forms two prominent peaks in the share price action and often signifies that a downtrend is imminent.

downtick   Any downward movement in price action. This downward movement can even be by the smallest price increment available (for example, 1¢).

downtrend   Where prices are making consistently lower highs and lower lows.

downtrend line   A straight line is drawn at a downward right-slanting angle connecting the peaks of the share price action. Once the prices show evidence of rising above this line in a sustainable manner, it is likely that the downtrend has been broken. Ideally, this should be accompanied by a simultaneous increase in volume.

drawdown   The amount of dollars lost at a particular point in time compared with the previous overall gain. An alternative meaning is a retracement in equity from a previous equity high. On a share chart, the drawdown from the previous high to the current share price will show the amount by which the share price has fallen.

EMA   *see* exponential moving average.

equities   Another term for shares.

exchange traded options   The options traded over shares in Australia are called exchange traded options or American-style options. This type of option allows the option holder to exercise the option at any time during the life of the contract.

ex-dividend   The day after the shareholders have taken the dividend. This typically results in a share price drop.

exercise   To exercise your rights as an option buyer means that you may choose to buy or sell the shares covered by the option. Generally, this occurs when the option has reached, or is close to, its strike price. You can do this at or before expiration. It is likely, however, that you will exercise your rights only after the share price has transcended the strike price of the option, or if there is a vested interest to exercise due to the effect of an ex-dividend scenario.

exhaustion gap   *see* gaps.

expectancy   This is a mathematical calculation that will provide a measure to show, for every dollar that you have invested in the market, how many dollars you will extract.

$$\text{Expectancy} = (\text{probability of winning} \times \text{average win})$$
$$- (\text{probability of losing} \times \text{average loss})$$

expiration date   The final date of the option contract. The duration of each option contract will often be 12 months or more. As a writer, you can choose to write contracts on options with six months to expiry, or one month to expiry — the choice of time frame is up to you.

exponential moving average (EMA)   The Exponential Moving Average places more emphasis (on an exponential basis) on the most recent prices and forms a moving average line. A moving average takes the closes of several periods and plots a point. When several of these points are connected, a moving average line is formed. Moving averages are most effective as trend-following tools. They smooth out the price action but incorporate a time lag. A moving average in a sideways-moving market is less effective.

exposure   As a writer of options, this is the total possible amount of money that you would be liable for, if the options were to be exercised.

foreign exchange (FX)   Foreign exchange is the worldwide currency market. It is one of the most liquid markets available.

formation   *see* pattern.

fundamentals   Fundamental analysis assists in detecting which shares have a probability of increasing or decreasing in value, based on the company balance sheet and profit/loss details. Economic supply and demand information is analysed rather than the market activity of price and volume action on a share chart.

futures   Agreements that are legally binding to buy and sell specific quantities of specified commodities or financial instruments at a particular date in the future.

FX   *see* foreign exchange.

gaps   Gaps show that the price activity of the preceding period is completely above or below the next candlestick or bar apparent on the chart. The gaps are spaces or holes left on the share chart when viewing candlestick charts or bar charts. In Western analysis, there are three main types of real gaps: continuation, breakaway and exhaustion. A continuation gap suggests that the prevailing trend direction is likely to continue. An exhaustion gap is a gap that occurs toward the end of a trend and signals that the trend direction is likely to end. Such a gap can often be observed prior to a reversal trigger candlestick pattern. A breakaway gap usually signals the beginning of a new trend. Such a gap can often confirm the new trend direction after a reversal trigger candle pattern. There are also false gaps (gaps that occur on low volume) and sucker's gaps (gaps that occur because of an ex-dividend situation).

illiquid   Instruments with low levels of trading are considered illiquid and are best avoided. By trading in illiquid options/shares, if the trade goes against you, exiting from your open positions will be considerably more difficult.

in-the-money   A call option that has the current share price above the strike price, or a put option that has the current share price below the strike price.

line chart   This type of chart connects the closing prices for each period to provide a continuous line that depicts share price action.

liquid   Shares or options with a significant number of buyers and sellers already participating in actively trading this instrument.

long candle   A candle showing a larger real body range than those of previous candles on the chart.

long or going long   This implies a bullish view of the market and describes the situation when a trader purchases an instrument to initiate a transaction. When buying shares, traders have a long view of the market.

macro filter   A condition formed on the basis of the chart of the predominant index that when met will tell a trader when to go long, when to go short, or when not to trade.

managed fund   A pool of money over which investors relinquish power to a fund manager, or a so-called professional trader, regarding buy and sell decisions.

margin   The amount of money retained in trust by the options clearing house or your broker while you have an open written options position, a futures contract, or a short-sold position. This partially insures your broker or the clearing house against a loss on your open positions.

margin call   When the share price trends against your initial expectation, your broker will require a further amount of money to be deposited, often within 24 hours, in order to maintain the margin ratio of the original leveraged position.

margin loan   A sum of money that is available for you to borrow in order to purchase a select group of stocks (for example, the Top 100). Although allocations for specific firms will vary, you may be able to borrow up to 70 per cent of the value of the shares that you would like to purchase.

market capitalisation   The total number of shares that have been issued, multiplied by the share price.

Mentor Program   A six-month course run by Chris Tate and Louise Bedford to give you everything you need to trade every instrument across every time frame, confidently and safely. Full details can be found at <www.tradinggame.com.au>.

momentum   The velocity of a price trend. Momentum indicators show whether prices are declining at a faster or slower pace.

moving average   *see* exponential moving average.

naked calls   Writing call options when you do not own the underlying security.

open interest   The number of outstanding option contracts at a particular strike price. This is a concept comparable with volume.

open market risk   When you combine all of your active positions and calculate the exposure from the current share price to the stop price that you have stipulated, you have calculated your open market risk.

out-of-the-money   When the share price is below the strike price of the call option, or when the share price is above the strike price of a put option. Writing out-of-the-money call and put options is the most conservative and safest method of writing options.

overbought   This term and the following term are generally used in relation to momentum indicators. An overbought line may be constructed manually by looking at the historical high points on a momentum indicator, or it may be an integral part of the indicator and shown as an indexed number from zero to 100. When a momentum indicator has risen to a historical or indexed high, it implies an overbought condition where the instrument may be vulnerable to a sell-off.

oversold   An oversold line may be constructed manually by looking at the historical low points on a momentum indicator, or it may be an integral part of the indicator and shown as an indexed number from zero to 100. When a momentum indicator has dropped to a historical or indexed low, it implies an oversold condition where the instrument may be likely to rally.

pattern   A single period or a number of separate trading periods that form the data for a defined candlestick formation, or another pattern based on technical analysis.

period   The time increment on a share chart. For example, a daily chart would show each candlestick to be composed of the open, high, low and close price for a day. The terms session and period are interchangeable.

position   Holding, or intending to hold, equity in the market.

position size   This shows you how many of a particular instrument to buy or sell, according to your risk profile, and the capital you have available for trading. There are several methods to assist in this goal, including the equal-portions model, the market capitalisation model and the volatility-based model.

pullback   *see* retracement.

put option   A put option gives the buyer the right, but not the obligation, to sell a given security at a certain price within a given time.

pyramid   To add more to your position as an instrument trends in the expected direction; for example, to buy more of an uptrending share. To do this effectively, you should buy the largest parcel of shares first, and then add increasingly smaller positions to your initial position.

rally   An upward movement of prices.

rate of change (ROC)   A momentum indicator with manually derived overbought and oversold conditions.

real body   The thick part of the candle representing the range between the opening price and the closing price. This is considered to be of more importance than the high and low prices for the period.

relative strength comparison (RSC)   The Relative Strength Comparison takes the progression in price of one instrument and compares it with another. It is often displayed as an indicator in many of the more popular charting packages.

resistance   A price level at which sellers are expected to enter. It appears above the current price action and suggests that the price becomes resistant to making a higher high.

retracement   A less significant version of a correction.

retracement trade   This is where an entry into a position is made, preferably on a candlestick bottom reversal, after the share price has made a counter-trend reversal.

scrip   Shares borrowed by a brokerage firm for use in a short-sold position as security.

selling options   *see* writing options.

session   *see* period.

shadow   Shadows are the thin lines above and below the candlestick real body, representing the extreme high and low for that session. The shadow provides an indication of buyer or seller strength. Tails, wicks and shadows are interchangeable terms.

shadow location   If there are long upper shadows at the top of an uptrend, this implies that the buyers have weakened and the sellers have begun to move in. If there are long lower shadows at the bottom of a downtrend, the price has dropped to a low enough level to encourage buyers to purchase the share.

short or going short   This implies a bearish view and describes the situation when a trader short sells the market, or sells to initiate a transaction. Selling shares and then purchasing them at a later date and a lower price can generate substantial profits. Approximately 200 Australian shares can be short sold.

short candle   A candle showing a shorter real body range than those of previous candles on the chart.

sideways trend   A period of lateral price movement within a relatively narrow price band between a level of support and a level of resistance.

strike price   The price at which you can buy or sell the underlying security as an option buyer.

support   A price level at which buyers are expected to enter. It appears beneath the current market price and signifies that the price is resistant to making a lower low.

system design   Your entry, stop loss procedures, profit-taking methodology and position-sizing methods, which should appear in a written trading plan.

tail   *see* shadow.

technical analysis   The use of price and volume action on a share chart to reach conclusions about the likely direction of future price activity.

trading plan   Your personalised business plan that outlines how you will go about trading the market. Goals and objectives, procedures, performance measurement and trading-system details should be explicitly addressed and written down before you initiate your first trade.

trigger candle   This is the actual appearance of a reversal or continuation pattern. For a one-line candle, the trigger will be represented by one session only. For more complex two-line patterns, the trigger will comprise two sessions.

true range (TR)   This indicator was defined by Welles Wilder as being the biggest of the following for each period:

- the distance from today's high to today's low

- the distance from yesterday's close to today's high

- the distance from yesterday's close to today's low.

uptick   Any upward movement in price action. This upward movement can even be by the smallest price increment available (for example, 1¢).

uptrend   Where prices are making consistently higher highs and higher lows.

uptrend line   A straight line is drawn in an upward left-slanting angle connecting the troughs of the share price action. Once the prices show evidence of dropping below this line in a sustainable manner, it is likely that the uptrend has been broken.

volatility   Choppy shares with greater distances from the peak to the trough of the share price are more volatile and will produce a greater candle range. For shares with a lower volatility level, the option premiums will also be lower. Shares that are illiquid will usually show heightened levels of volatility.

volume   The level of trading in a particular instrument. If volume increases in the direction of the trend or breakout, this adds to the weight of evidence that the share price movement is sustainable. A volume increase to confirm an uptrend is very important.

warrant   A certificate that gives the holder the right, though not the obligation, to buy or sell securities as a stipulated price within a specified time limit.

weight of evidence   Using more than one indicator on which to base your decision regarding the likely share direction. When several chart patterns and indicators point in the same direction, their signals are reinforced. If the weight of evidence of several indicators suggests that the share is uptrending, then the bulls have probably taken control of the market.

white candle   This candle shows a session where the closing price was higher than the opening price. This is inherently bullish.

wick   *see* shadow.

writing options   Option writers collect a premium or fee from an option buyer and subsequently they are obligated to fulfil the demands of the option buyer. In relation to call options, the writer must sell their shares or have their shares called away from them, if the buyer decides to exercise his or her right. A put option writer is under obligation to buy the shares from a put option taker should he or she be exercised; that is, have the shares put to them.

Testimonials

Confused by the markets? Here is your solution...

I read tons of trading books for five years and I felt like they were all speaking Martian. Only after reading your books, Louise, I finally got my questions answered. You speak in a language that I understand and your wit shines through. Now I know precisely how to pick a share and how much to invest.

Vera Cvetkovik, business analyst, NSW

Brian is now a full-time trader

Some years ago I was lucky enough to read *Trading Secrets*. Now, as a professional trader, I am pleased to have access to the revised edition. Anyone seeking trading success should read this book.

Brian Carpenter, full-time trader, QLD

Matt is sleeping soundly now

This book is not only a real eye opener, but it even throws in peripheral vision for free. As a direct result of following Louise's methods, I now trade competently and sleep soundly.

Matt Forster, bookkeeper, SA

Andrew is confident and successful now

Until I read *Trading Secrets* I was focused entirely on trade selection. I now realise that this is in fact only a minor part of being a successful trader. *Trading Secrets* opened my eyes to personal psychology, risk management and having a written trading plan. As a result, I am now a confident and successful trader.

Andrew Phillips, full-time trader, NSW

Get educated

Read this book and follow up on other education by Louise. Grab her free 5-part e-course from <www.tradinggame.com.au>. Your trading will be profitable and you will get endless support, plus you will not waste time reading a lot of rot by people without Louise's skills and heart.

Lewes Golden, self-employed, QLD

Louise is your ideal trading mentor

A must-read for those who want to take control of their financial future. Louise is one of Australia's leading trading mentors. There is no doubt in my mind that this book will help you develop the mindset and skills of a successful trader.

Peter Hunt, business manager, VIC

Retirement may be sooner than you think

Do not buy this book if you want to continue in the workforce until retirement age; you may leave sooner than you planned. If you have read all the fluff and hype that is out there and still continue to lose money, why not get serious and buy this book?

Craig Denny, trader, NSW

It's time to take control

Read *Trading Secrets* and take control of your finances. You will never have a better opportunity to really learn how to trade successfully than by immersing yourself in Louise Bedford's world. Think of this book as the golden key that opens the door to the wonderful world of successful trading.

Felicity Rolls, body corporate manager, VIC

'The gold standard...'

Trading Secrets sets the gold standard for trading education. Spare yourself the trauma of listening to the inane, ill-informed musings of the so-called financial experts who aren't traders. Louise Bedford's knowledge, integrity and logic, jumps out from every page. This book is a must read.

Naomi Wilkie, trader, NSW

A perfect foundation

An outstanding book that provides you with a perfect foundation for a successful trading career. Essential reading if you are serious about becoming a trader.

Kirsten Stoldt, primary producer, WA

Index

More from Louise...

Trading Secrets is the ideal book for you, whether it is the first book on trading that you've picked up, or you've read a few other books and you're looking to consolidate your knowledge. It is designed to work as a companion to Louise Bedford's *Charting Secrets,* which also provides practical exercises on technical analysis to give you an edge in recognising chart patterns and using indicators. These two books work well when read as a pair, providing enough information to safely get you started trading or investing. Once you've read these titles, move onto *The Secret of Candlestick Charting,* which will give you more detailed information on this fascinating charting technique. When you've worked out how to trade shares, you may feel ready to apply leverage and read *The Secret of Writing Options.*

In addition to these books, you can visit Louise's website at <www.tradingsecrets. com.au> and complete the *Candlestick Charting Home Study Course* or watch *The Secret of Candlestick Charting Video Program.* The *Trading Psychology Home Study Course* is also available at the website and you may find the reference posters valuable, too. Posters currently available are *The Secret of Candlestick Charting Poster* and *The Secret of Pattern Detection Poster.* The current range of CD products includes *Trading Secrets, Psychology Secrets, Relaxation for Traders, Power Trading — Trade CFDs like a Professional, Share Trading 101, and Leverage 101.*

The Mentor Program

Louise also runs a six-month Mentor Program. For over a decade this program has continuously booked out every time it opened for bookings. Mentorees love that they can repeat the course as many times as they like for free. Have a look at <www.tradingsecrets.com.au> and <www.tradinggame.com.au> for more information. If you're the type of trader who wants to learn how to trade every instrument over every time frame, safely and confidently, by using your own bulletproof trading plan, then the Mentor Program is just what you've been looking for.

Your free trading pack

Make the best decision of your life. Register now for your trading pack when you visit <www.tradingsecrets.com.au> ... and best of all it's FREE. Here's what you'll get:

- an incredibly valuable trading plan template
- a free monthly email newsletter
- a five-part e-course valued at $99
- a free month of access to the Trading Game Forum
- a the chance to win a home study course.

Why is Louise giving you this pack for free?

I'll tell you why. So she can begin a relationship with you. Louise says, 'I'm hoping that after you've used my free resources, one day you'll come to one of my advanced seminars. I love helping people who want to take control of their sharemarket returns. It's my goal to put money into share traders' pockets and make it stick, even if they only have 30 minutes a day available, and limited knowledge about trading.'

Excellent traders are action takers. Don't delay. Go to
<www.tradingsecrets.com.au> and grab your
FREE trading pack right now.

Register NOW for your FREE five-part e-course!

Also by Louise Bedford

Charting Secrets

Given enough opportunities to practise your skills, you can become a successful trader. All you need to do is master the basics. Charting is a cornerstone skill for any trader. It can help you visualise changes in the market so that specific trading rules can be developed.

Not just another trading book, *Charting Secrets* is a workbook that will have you practising what you have read and really learning the techniques, rather than just reading about them.

Learn the secrets of trend detection, set-ups and triggers, going long and short, trading psychology, and the importance of a systematic approach to analysing market direction.

Also by Louise Bedford

THE SECRET OF
Candlestick Charting

Most traders in the Australian stock and futures markets begin by using conventional bar charts to generate buy and sell signals—until they discover the analytical power of candlestick charting.

This Japanese technique dates back over 300 years. Candlestick charts pinpoint trend changes prior to many other methods. Whether you are a beginner or a sophisticated investor, you can learn how to use candlestick charting to trade the markets profitably, beginning with your next trade.

In this book you will discover a technique that has the potential to completely alter the way you view charting, yet is complementary to any of the knowledge you have accumulated so far about technical analysis. Written in easy-to-understand language, these techniques are highly recommended for any traders or investors who wish to develop their technical analysis abilities and enhance their profitability.

Also by Louise Bedford

THE SECRET OF
Writing Options

Once thought to be the domain of highly-skilled investors, today more and more private investors and traders are entering the options market. One of the big attractions of options trading is that, unlike a traditional investor, an options trader can still make money in a sideways-trending or falling market.

This book is highly recommended for newcomers to options trading in Australia, and those already trading in the options markets. It starts with the basics, and discusses the discipline and attitude necessary to trade successfully. There is also a cleverly constructed game to play to see if you are ready to enter the options market.

Louise Bedford has degrees in psychology and business from Monash University. She trades full-time from her home in Melbourne and is a regular speaker on trading. She also conducts workshops and seminars throughout Australia.

Charting Secrets, The Secret of Writing Options and *The Secret of Candlestick Charting* are published by and available from Wrightbooks, an imprint of John Wiley & Sons Australia, Ltd.